Entrepreneurial Marketing

Entrepreneurial Marketing

The Growth of Small Firms in the New Economic Era

Björn Bjerke
Professor of Entrepreneurship and Small Business,
Stockholm University, Sweden

Claes M. Hultman
Professor of Marketing, Faculty of Business,
Örebro University, Sweden

Edward Elgar
Cheltenham, UK • Northampton MA, USA

Published by
Edward Elgar Publishing Limited
Glensanda House
Montpellier Parade
Cheltenham
Glos GL50 1UA
UK

Edward Elgar Publishing, Inc.
136 West Street
Suite 202
Northampton
Massachusetts 01060
USA

Paperback edition 2004

A catalogue record for this book
is available from the British Library

Library of Congress Cataloguing in Publication Data

Bjerke, Björn, 1941–
    Entrepreneurial marketing : the growth of small firms in the new economic era /
    Björn Bjerke, Claes Hultman
        p. cm.
        Includes index.
        1. Marketing—Management. 2. Small business—Marketing. 3. Small
        business—Management. 4. Entrepreneurship. I. Hultman, Claes, 1947– II. Title.

    HF5415.13. B48 2002
    658.8—dc21

                                                                                    2002020228

ISBN 978 1 84064 912 3 (cased)
ISBN 978 1 84376 851 7 (paperback)
Printed on FSC approved paper
Printed and bound in Great Britain by Marston Book Services Ltd, Oxfordshire

Contents

Figures

Tables

Foreword

> ... to lay bare the questions which have
> been hidden by the answers.
>
> James Baldwin

Try to think of a successful business that has not undergone significant transformation over the past decade. Whether facing technological, social, governmental, economic or global changes, or customer or competitive paradigm shifts, few enterprises have escaped the revolution. And yet most still cling to traditional answers that hide the questions. This book not only lays bare critically important questions, but offers numerous new answers. Although the authors recognize the foundations from the past, they build to new heights. They modify and add new concepts, the building blocks of practical theories, to better repond to today's dynamic business milieu.

Both marketing and entrepreneurship may be defined as philosophies and fundamental orientations for firms to conduct business, *or* as concepts and methods for business leaders to use in carrying out entrepreneurship and marketing. Research regarding orientations has supported the relationship between marketing orientation and firm performance. And a positive relationship has also been confirmed between entrepreneurial orientation and performance. What is most striking, however, are the findings from *combining* a marketing and entrepreneurial orientation. Together an even stronger relationship to performance has been revealed.

Although marketing may be defined as an inherently entrepreneurial activity, attempts to professionalize and formalize marketing in recent decades have de-emphasized some of the more creative and entrepreneurial marketing dimensions. All business organizations, new, small, large or mature, benefit from some level of entrepreneurial marketing orientation, and this book superbly builds on this theme.

The second view of entrepreneurial marketing, that of management concepts and methods for newer, growing and/or smaller firms, is fully addressed in this book. It was naively assumed by many marketing thought leaders for decades that newer and smaller businesses only require a simplified version of marketing. Now, after 15 years of The University of Illinois at

Chicago (UIC) Research Symposia on Marketing and Entrepreneurship, with American Marketing Association co-sponsorship, it is increasingly documented that marketing in smaller and newer firms is fundamentally different rather than simpler. Entrepreneurial flexibility, rapid response times, customer/market immersion, intense target market focus, cash-flow sensitivity and an entirely rational mix of personal and business are but a sampling of the entrepreneur/firm characteristics underlying major differences in marketing within the most successful growing small and medium-sized enterprises (SMEs). This book addresses these differences, and more importantly, interprets their many implications for marketing practitioners. This is a more valuable book for students, entrepreneurs, SMEs and related scholars than any of the leading marketing textbooks worldwide. The existing textbooks, with at most one exception, are based on sets of assumptions from large mature firms.

Although some traditional marketing concepts only need modification or different importance weighting for growing SMEs, other existing concepts are dangerously misleading. Typical marketing research teaching, for example, assumes a chief executive officer who does not have frequent in-depth customer contact. This is compared to proactive, opportunistic and calculated risk-taking entrepreneurs who are typically immersed on a day-to-day basis with their customers' preferences and perceptions of the marketing offering. Is it any surprise that many, if not most, business owners place limited value on formal marketing research or even view such efforts with outright disdain? What is sometimes alluded to as 'gut feeling' or intuitive decision making is often, in fact, exceptionally well-founded market-oriented decision making. The authors of this volume go far beyond this simple example, addressing the implications for marketing and entrepreneurship across national cultures; outlining the importance of exploitative and explorative learning; presenting the concept of co-creation of customer value; and recommending an integration of transactional and relationship marketing.

This book goes to press based on full documentation that new firms and SMEs provide the economic engine for global economic progress. Every political system of any size in the world has explicitly or implicitly embraced the market system, entrepreneurship and marketing. Studies worldwide, again and again, report the disproportionate employment generation of new and smaller firms, highlighting what is even more true today than before – that large organizations and scale economies rarely provide for competitive advantage. As this book demonstrates, small is beautiful.

The authors of this volume are pioneers. This book will one day be cited by marketing thought historians as a definitive statement of a new School of Marketing Thought, entrepreneurial marketing. I applaud this writing, both for its practical merit as well as its scholarly richness. The reader will be rewarded by the cutting-edge, frontier contributions to new knowledge.

Professor Gerald E. Hills
Coleman Chairholder in Entrepreneurship and Marketing, University of Illinois at Chicago; former President of the American Marketing Association Academic Council; International Council for Small Business and the US Association for Small Business and Entrepreneurship.

Acknowledgements

This book is based on discussions over many years with entrepreneurs and scholars worldwide. To learn from entrepreneurs, who really accomplish the feat of challenging the world by generating new business ventures, has been a fantastic experience in our case. Like bumblebees, flying without knowing that they 'technically' should not be able to, many entrepreneurs take off with only the sky as a limit and with thinking and methods often very different from what can be read in standard marketing and entrepreneurship textbooks.

With growing fascination we have learned that there are many roads to success and that traditional perspectives need to be broadened and, sometimes, even need to be replaced. Further, the intellectual stimulation obtained from discussing phenomena which are the focus of our interest with fellow scholars has triggered us to dig deeper and deeper into our field from a theoretically point of view. As a result, we would like to express our profound thanks to everybody who has spent his or her valuable time to share with us the experience and knowledge gained from hard work.

In particular, we would like to mention the participants in the 'International Symposium on Marketing and Entrepreneurship', organized by Professor Gerald E. Hills at the University of Illinois at Chicago and involving an international group of researchers, where we have had the opportunity to be true partners of discussions for a number of years. The solid expertise of this group has been the foundation upon which we have built our results in researching the interface between marketing and entrepreneurship.

The contributions to the symposium are published annually by the University of Illinois in 'Research at the Marketing/Entrepreneurship Interface'. This series of books is a unique source of information about marketing in SMEs and entrepreneurial firms. Further, the Academy of Marketing in the UK runs similar seminars and publications. We highly recommend this literature.

In the final stage of our writing some colleagues in particular have made very insightful and important comments. In the US, we recognize especially Professor Gerald Hills at the University of Illinois at Chicago, Professor Morgan Miles at Southern Georgia State and Professor Richard Teach at Georgia Tech in Atlanta, GA; in Europe, Professor David Carson at the University of Ulster and Professor Evert Gummesson at Stockholm

University; and finally in Australia, Associate Professor Gus Geursen at Monash University. We thank them all for their invaluable comments.

Björn Bjerke and Claes M. Hultman

1. Small is beautiful?

INTRODUCTION

For centuries the logic of 'economies of scale' remained unchallenged as a general business law. The welfare of modern economies was built up during the twentieth century by firms, which grew big, which organized mass production, which generated the modern pattern of consumption and which provided jobs as well as status to those who worked there. The economic rule that 'big is better' was established and, seemingly, became irrefutable. However, a new business alternative is being established. Today, in a new millennium, there are new business ventures, sometimes based on revolutionary innovation, occasionally on a superior business vision but often on simply an ability to have a better feeling for what the consumer wants. These business ventures are often able to dominate their market while still remaining small, at least in terms of traditional measures of size such as the number of employees. Also, new constellations of cooperating small firms, linked together in more or less tight networks such as all kinds of strategic alliances and even 'virtual organizations',[1] manage to challenge the old business logic of economies of scale. Important assets from yesteryear, such as production capacity and financial strength, are to an ever increasing extent replaced by more intangible, but yet more relevant and adequate, skills of constructing and using information, knowledge and relations to other business vendors and to customers/consumers. These capabilities do not seem to improve with size; on the contrary, they often seem to be best understood as consisting of fast-moving small business units with leaders having both ears and noses close to the customer and with loose 'organizational structures' for highest flexibility and intimacy. Such units can be found as legally independent business firms as well as progressive fronts in bigger firms trying to act as if they were small. These are units of a 'new' society which are presenting an 'alternative business thinking', a thinking which is preached by updated management gurus and discussed in a growing number of business seminars. 'Small is beautiful' is the new business thinking and the new business paradigm.[2] Not following this thinking might even lead to 'diseconomies of scale'.

THE NEW ECONOMIC ERA

In the Bible (the Book of Ecclesiastes) it is written that nothing new will take place under the sun. From a religious point of view this may be so. However, from an economic point of view something new is going on in some frontline sectors and industries in our more advanced nations. Dozen of books, hundreds of articles in various journals and even more comments in the daily press contribute to the discussion of 'The New Economy'.[3]

But, the opinion that a *genuinely new* economy is emerging is not unchallenged. Some commentators claim that what is new is no more than new aspects of our old economy, perhaps in business thinking, in market orientation and in a need to cooperate across competitive borders, an economy, however, which is based on the same fundamentals as before.

In this book, we do not want to enter the discussion whether there is a radical shift in the economy or not. Nevertheless, as we see it, there are several phenomena of the economic scenes of today which have not been there before and successful business firms in industries directed to the future are often run very differently from what we have seen only 10–15 years ago. Each of these phenomena (and resulting business modes) may not, on their own, mean radicality, but taken together these phenomena are many enough to justify the name 'the new economic era' (without having to claim that the economic and business fundamentals have changed or that they have not). Some major phenomena of the new economic era are:

- Many *changes* take place. Much is in a state of flux. Some of these changes are even drastic and very difficult, if not impossible, to predict.
- It is increasingly difficult to plan the future, however *genuine uncertainty* is a part of the picture.
- The most important strategic resource of a firm is no longer financial capital. It is rather to have, among its staff and workforce, some *change agents*, who, at best insightful and visionary, take it upon themselves to introduce new models and procedures in the firm and on the market. If this leads to new business ventures, we refer to these people as 'entrepreneurs'.
- There is a *different view on business capital*. This capital is not only of a financial sort, but increasingly we can talk about capital invested in business processes, local databases, willingness to learn, vendor networks, contacts and so on.
- Successful firms at the edge of development seem to strike pre-emptively. They come to the future first. The race is often more like *survival of the fastest* than survival of the fittest (which are often fattest).

- The dominant means of competition is generally through *knowledge*. The only meaningful resource today is knowledge and the modern business challenge is to handle knowledge workers, says Peter Drucker.[4] Some commentators claim that we are gradually moving into a knowledge economy, if we are not there already.
- There is a revival of the prominence of markets and liberalization. *Corporatization and privatization* are in fashion. Even such revered old institutions as mailservice and telecommunications, which have traditionally been owned by the public sector, are becoming more market and business oriented as limited corporations, with shares bought and sold in open stock markets.
- As more players enter the business scene, market *competition* becomes *more intense*. This also takes place increasingly on a global scale. Global markets also make forecasts harder.
- Another factor leading to more competition as well as an interesting phenomenon in its own right is that *industrial borders* become *blurred*. Furthermore, traditional industries are often invading each other's markets or merging. One hot example is telecommunications, computers and entertainment.
- Finally, involved in all the other aspects is *technology*, which by almost every way we look at it (say, product lifetime, complexity, miniaturization) seems to be moving faster and faster and to become ever more advanced and complex. Also, technology plays a more strategic role than before.

It is true, of course, that no national or regional economy anywhere *in its totality* has entered a new economic era. There are traditional economies which have hardly been moved by this era at all. Also, in advanced economies, only specific sectors and industries are involved in this era and, even within these sectors and industries, it is normally possible to see only some of the phenomena mentioned above. So, for instance, the dairy industry does not contain many aspects of the new economic era. On the other hand, much of the information technology (IT) sector is in there.

WHY SMALL FIRMS?

The Dominance of Small Firms in the New Economic Era

There seems to be a general understanding among researchers, politicians and public commentators alike that in the new economic era we are increasingly moving in the direction of favouring small firms (or smaller units in bigger firms). A sign of this is that the contribution to employment by small businesses in an economy is growing almost uniformly across the industrialized world.[5] Furthermore, the average small firm is most often doing better than the average big firm in an economy – and the successful small firm doing much better than the successful big firm. There are many reasons for this development of smallness (some of these reasons were touched upon in the last section discussing the new economic era):

1. An increasing number of work tasks have to do with managing information in a wide sense in some form or another, a decreasing number with managing physical objects. The industrial engine, therefore, becomes more and more dependent on the carriers and processors of this information, that is individuals.[6] Small firms will probably play an even more important role in the future, now that more and more competition will be knowledge based.
2. Many industry entry barriers have been erased, and there are fewer natural economies of scale for most business activities. This is a simpler economy to enter but also an economy in which it is easier to fail.[7]
3. Advancing computer and telecommunication technology is 'demassifying' production and distribution. It is possible today to turn out, and to deliver, short runs of highly varied, even customized, products at costs approaching those of mass production and distribution.[8]
4. Flexibility is becoming increasingly important. Turbulence in the economy from factors like bouncing currencies can hurt any firm, big or small. Smaller firms, however, are inherently more flexible than bigger firms and often more resilient in riding the waves. Constant innovation and constant change has become part of the establishment.[9]
5. The move towards a service-based economy is a characteristic of all developed economies. Small firms are typically more prevalent in such economies.[10]
6. The removal of competition-crushing regulation has spawned shoals of minnows in industries like airlines and telecommunications. Those minnows are, on the other hand, often quickly eaten by bigger fish.[11]
7. Technological change and increasingly more open economies raise the level of international competition. Many business functions spill over national boundaries, sometimes integrating activities of small units in many nations into a network of a single productive effort.[12]
8. Consumer taste is changing. Mass markets are breaking up. Consumers are increasingly put off by the idea of buying the same products as their neighbours. They will pay for unique and upmarket products. The result is a flood of small companies in various niche markets.[13]
9. More women in the workforce have created an ample supply of the sorts

of people who create and staff small firms. Well-educated women with small children are today particularly likely to start their own businesses to balance home life with careers.[14]

In all nations, a majority of business firms are small and the profile of small business is remarkably similar among most free-market nations:[15]

> SMEs [small and medium-sized enterprises] play an important economic role both in static and dynamic terms. Although their contribution varies widely between economies, in static terms they typically make up around 98% of enterprises, contribute over 50% of employment, about 50% of GDP, and over 30% of exports. Their dynamic contribution to economic and social development is harder to assess, but most evidence points to SMEs playing an important role as an 'entrepreneurial engine' which generates 70% of new jobs, is a significant source of innovation, and is a major source of economic renewal and adaptation to changing economic and social conditions.[16]

It is safe to conclude that small firms are dynamically important in the new economic era.

What Is a 'Small' Firm?

Small enterprises are normally the most common form of enterprise or establishment in a nation regardless of industry, and most small businesses consist of a single establishment.[17] Small firms are often identified by their type of business, for instance, service (such as professional service or an import–export agency) or manufacturing (like subcontracting). More generally, there are several classifications of small firms suggested in the literature. A common classification is:[18]

- *'marginal' firms* – 'ordinary' new independent business ventures, often started as a means to substitute income, and commonly based on some kind of service orientation – the overwhelming majority of small firms;
- *'lifestyle' firms* – usually started based on the entrepreneur's profession and skills, not aimed at growing, but at providing a good salary, perquisites and flexibility in the lifestyle of the owner; and
- *'high-potential' firms* – companies started with the aim of increasing sales and profits and becoming a big corporation (the entrepreneur's big dream), and therefore receiving the greatest investment interest and publicity.

But what is meant by a 'small' firm? There are many answers to this question. First of all, the public definition of small and medium-sized enterprises (SMEs) differs from one country to another. For instance:

1. In the United States, a small business does not dominate its industry, has less than US$20 million in annual sales and fewer than 500 employees;[19]
2. In the United Kingdom, government statistics on SMEs are concentrated on those firms that employ fewer than 200 people;[20]
3. The official European Union (EU) definition of an SME is a firm which has no more than 250 employees, is not more than 25 per cent owned, either singly or jointly, by a bigger company and has an annual turnover of no more than € 40 million;[21]
4. In some Asian countries:[22]

   • Japan divides its SMEs into three groups, namely, mining, manufacturing, transportation and construction industries as one group; wholesalers as a second group; and retailers and service industries as a third. In the first group, an enterprise is counted as an SME if it has up to 300 employees, in wholesalers up to 100 employees, and in retailers up to 50. There are also (different) limits to the amount of capital that can be invested in the three groups to be counted as a 'small and medium-sized enterprise' in Japan;
   • Hong Kong limits the number of employees in its understanding of SMEs to 100 in manufacturing and to 50 in non-manufacturing industries;
   • Malaysia restricts its public interest in SMEs to manufacturing only and prefers to talk about 'small and medium-sized industrial firms', (SMIs) to stress this fact;
   • the Philippines divides enterprises with fewer than 200 employees into 'medium' (with 100–199 employees), 'small' (with 10–99 employees) and 'cottage enterprises' (1–9 employees). If cottage enterprises have assets not exceeding 100,000 pesos, they are called 'micro enterprises'.

Every definition of a small firm has a purpose, of course. It could also be said that *any definition of a small firm is a theory* (like most definitions are). Those definitions just presented are based on public ambitions to assist small firms in need,[23] and such ambitions differ between countries. What should be generally accepted as 'small' (or medium sized) obviously defies clear definition.

The aim of this book includes understanding the role marketing plays among entrepreneurial small firms as against big firms. There is no reason for us to set a specific limit on the size of a firm in terms of, for instance, number of employees, sales or assets, in order to count it as a small firm and not as a big (or medium-sized) one. This has to remain implicit in this book. Also, to set the exact borderline between small, medium-sized and big business firms will not alter the discussions and conclusions of this book. Generally, it is understood here that small firms have *limitations* in number of employees and in other physical resources. In this sense, they are the smallest in their genre. This does not, however, prevent some of them from growing and even being highly successful. In fact, such small growing firms are, as mentioned already, of particular interest in this book!

A general understanding of small firms can be summarized as follows[24] (some of the content in this list will be confirmed, and some of it will be modified and even altered, later in this book):

- in all economies, a majority of firms are small;
- as aggregates, small firms are important to the development of an economy; they may not feel themselves important individually;
- small firms are found more in retailing and service than in manufacturing; some small firms are in crafts-based manufacturing or subcontracting; a growing field is franchising;
- small firms are net providers of new jobs and an important source of innovation;
- small firms can open up new markets and expand the customers' choice;
- most training of workers in a country takes place on their jobs in a small firm;
- there are many kinds of small firms, classified by industry or otherwise; most of them are marginal firms, but some fit the lifestyle of the founders, and some may even have a high potential for growth;
- small firms are often started on the premises to supplement income for an individual, often with his or her spouse;
- benefits associated with owning and running a small firm include an opportunity to self-development, making money, contributing to society, and having a more enjoyable life;
- drawbacks associated with owning and running a small firm include uncertainty, economic risk, hard work, lower quality of life (at least in the beginning), and a greater burden of responsibility;
- small firms are intimately associated with the style of the founder/entrepreneur/owner, and this style is a common fault factor if small firms fail;
- when the small firm senior manager is good at spotting opportunities, action oriented and knowledgeable but willing to seek help when necessary, the chance of the survival of the firm is improved; small firm managers should generally acquire skills to spot new opportunities as well as running existing businesses;

- for the sake of the progress of a small firm, it is foolish to ignore the expertise, opinions and knowledge of its employees; most owners of small firms, however, are reluctant to delegate;
- small firms at their best are run in non-sophisticated, non-bureaucratic, flexible organizational structures, where all employees are working in a creative team and able to contribute;
- financial planning, in particular cash management, is important to a small firm; a creative approach to financial management is necessary;
- market-focused small firms, close to their customers, have a larger chance of survival; the primary function of a small firm (indeed, the major reason for success of any business) is to create and maintain customers;
- there are several possible marketing advantages of small firms, including close customer interface, flexibility, speed and ability to find a market niche;
- Understanding of marketing management is generally limited among small firms; this may differ with the size and age of the firm.

WHY ENTREPRENEURSHIP?

Entrepreneurship Is Changing Our Societies

If one word would characterize the new economic era, that word would be *change*. And entrepreneurship is the result of the *change agents* in this era, that is, the entrepreneurs. It is clear that entrepreneurship has become a force driving both the economy as well as the rest of the society.[25] It is fair to say that they 'are the seedcorn for industrial and commercial development in most capitalist societies'.[26] But the role of entrepreneurship in economic development involves more than just increasing per capita output and income; it involves initiating and constituting changes in business and society. This is principally done in two ways:

- entrepreneurs pursue opportunities. They do this by setting up new independent start-ups or by rejuvenating existing business establishments; and
- they force unsuccessful or unpromising business ventures to close down ('creative destruction').

Above all, entrepreneurs are gathering, directing and using resources in opportunities rather than allocating them to problems.[27] *Entrepreneurs generate innovations!* An innovation can, of course, be of varying degrees of uniqueness.[28] Most innovations introduced to the market are ordinary, that is, with little variation from what exists already and without any new technology. As expected, there are fewer technological and breakthrough innovations, with the number of the actual innovations decreasing as the technology involved increases.

Regardless of its level of uniqueness, innovativeness or technology, each innovation evolves and develops to commercialization through one of three mechanisms: the government, intracorporate entrepreneurship and independent entrepreneurship. Of these three, the last two, that is, entrepreneurship of different sorts, are generally recognized as the most effective method for bridging the gap between science and the marketplace. Furthermore, small firms (using independent entrepreneurship from the beginning or intracorporate entrepreneurship later) produce more innovations than do big outfits.[29]

There are many commentators of business who assert that the most important *strategic* resource in an increasing number of industries, and in all economies, is no longer financial capital, but people with drive, energy and willingness to start new business ventures either independently on their own or with their employers.[30] Entrepreneurs move a firm, an industry and a nation forward – the more of them, the better!

> From the rows of kiosks selling goods on nearly every block in Moscow to the cramped factories in Taiwan, Russian *biznezmen* and Chinese *changshang* are reshaping their nations' economies in much the same way as those ingenious Yankees created the basis for America's business culture just after independence was won.[31]

To conclude on the importance of entrepreneurs for an economy, we can say that they:[32]

1. contribute to employment;
2. play a role as the 'innovators' of technology, goods and services;
3. play a role as exporters to world markets; and
4. expand the band of consumers' choice by responding to the change in market trends and offer more diversified, sophisticated and specialized goods and services.

Every country needs to learn how to encourage and develop entrepreneurs today. Every advanced country needs:[33]

1. new independent entrepreneurs;
2. entrepreneurship within existing companies; and
3. to organize for entrepreneurship and innovation.

The Entrepreneurial Engine

There is a lot of research and many research findings related to the importance of small firms and entrepreneurship to an economy.[34] One clear, revealing and thorough picture of this importance is provided by Hall.[35] He refers to this as 'the entrepreneurial engine'. The discussion in this section follows his presentation.

- For every million people in developed economies there will be about 50,000 non-agricultural small firms.

The approximate number of firms per million people in some economies is provided in Table 1.1. Care should be taken when interpreting these figures. As mentioned earlier, the statistical definition of a small firm varies widely as to the purpose of the statistic and to the degree of formality of the firm. For example, the US figure in the table includes all firms registered for tax purposes only, while the Indonesian one is a rough estimate including all informal and unregistered (non-farming) small firms.

- For every 50,000 firms in an economy, about 5,000 new small firms will start up every year.

Start-up rates in some economies (according to different studies) are (in very rough figures) listed in Table 1.2. In any given year about 4 per cent of the adult population are thinking seriously about starting a firm, but less than 2 per cent actually do something about it. Evidence on exit rates varies widely, but to be consistent with observed growth and start-up rates of the population of small firms, about 75 per cent of small firms exit within 8 years of start-up.

Table 1.1   Population of people and small firms, in selected countries

Economy	Population (in millions)	Small firms ('000s)	Small firms ('000s) per million people
USA	260	15,000	58
Japan	125	7,000	56
Australia	17	900	53
Hong Kong	6	290	48
Indonesia	205	13,000	63

Table 1.2   Start-up rate of new firms in selected countries

Economy	Start-up rate (%)	Economy	Start-up rate (%)
USA	12–15	Sweden	11
Japan	4–7	Germany	17
Australia	9–16	UK	7

Note that *exit* rates are referred to here, not *failure* rates. A firm can exit an economy for all sorts of statistical reasons without actually failing. For instance, a firm that changes its name or is acquired by another firm is normally counted as one 'exit'; a firm that changes its legal status from a proprietorship to a limited company is counted as one 'exit' and one 'start-up' and so on.

Exit rates are the converse of survival rates. Estimates of exit rates and survival rates vary widely, but indicate roughly that (compare Table 1.3):

- 20 per cent to 30 per cent will survive more than 8 years;
- 50 per cent will survive about 5 years;
- 70 per cent will survive 3 years;
- 85 per cent will survive the first year.

- The bulk of job creation is from expansions, not from start-ups.

Most job gains are from expansions, not start-ups. Similarly most job losses are from contractions, not closures. This suggests that, in terms of jobs, it is more important what happens *after* a firm is established rather than its start-up *per se*; put differently, intracorporate entrepreneurship is more important than independent entrepreneurship in terms of job creation.

- Evidence suggests that small firms contribute more than proportionally to net job growth and that about 70 per cent of net jobs are attributable to a small group of only about 5 per cent of fast-growing small firms.

Some firms are growth oriented – and successful in growing. As a proportion of all firms this is not much. Most small firms do not grow much; they are better envisaged as small stores and 'lifestyle' businesses – they may grow from one to two or four employees, but they stop there. Perhaps about 25 per cent of all small firms are serious about seeking growth, but only 5 per cent are successful in actually achieving it. These firms seem to contribute around 70 per cent of all net job growth.

*Table 1.3   Survival rates among small firms after five years, in selected
            countries*

Economy	Survival rate (%)	Economy	Survival rate (%)
USA	38	France	48
Australia	17	Germany	63

In a developed economy, the rough pattern among small firms in terms of
growth is:

- 5 per cent are high-growth firms;
- 20 per cent are growth-oriented survivors;
- 75 per cent are low/no-growth small firms.

- High-growth small firms are more likely to be more innovative than
  other small firms, but only a small proportion will be in emerging
  leading-edge industries. Most will be in niches in industries in growth
  or restructuring stages.

Although high-growth firms are more likely to be leading-edge firms in their
industry, the industry itself does not have to be an emerging, leading-edge,
fast-growth industry in order for a successful firm to achieve rapid growth.
Industries tend to go through a life cycle,[36] starting with a few innovative firms
in an emerging stage, moving to a growth stage where there are many firms,
and then to a rationalization and shake-out stage where the number of firms
declines and the industry moves to a core of a few bigger firms surrounded by
a periphery of smaller firms. Finally the industry may move to a declining
stage. Most of the jobs created by small (or medium-sized) firms seem to
occur at the growth and shake-out stages.

As mentioned earlier, the statistics presented in this section are from Hall's
extensive research in the field.[37] Of course one may question the exact figures
as in all cases of comparative international statistics. There can be no doubt,
however, that entrepreneurship and small firms are very important to the
structure, growth and development of any economy!

The Entrepreneurship – Small Firm Interface

It is a common thought that entrepreneurship and a small firm are not the
same. We share this thought. Entrepreneurship can take place in a firm of any

size and many small firms are not entrepreneurial. New business ventures are established all the time. Sometimes this is done as a legally independent small firm, sometimes this is done as a new product, possibly in a separate department or division, next to those already existing in a (small or big) established firm. Also, after a new business venture is established in a firm of any size, the firm may live (partly or wholly) on this venture without any further changes, that is, the firm may stop behaving entrepreneurially.

Nevertheless, entrepreneurship in small firms (as first business ventures or as new ventures later in the life of small firms) is of special interest. We do not deny the importance of big firms, we do not deny that big firms sometimes come up with important innovations, we do not deny that big firms are sometimes run as a group of small business units, each behaving as if it was a very small independent firm, but the new economic era seems to grow ever stronger and small firms seem to have something to show us about proper business behaviour in this new economic era – at least from a marketing point of view. This marketing behaviour among successful small firms is what we want to bring forward in this book.

WHY MARKETING?

Marketing is commonly seen as a business function of a firm along with others such as manufacturing and financing. For a small firm such a strict separation between various business functions is problematic, if for no other reason because a small firm consists of a few persons, maybe only one single owner-manager. In a small firm, therefore, every member must often be something of a jack-of-all-trades, knowing a bit of every business function, including marketing.

Nevertheless, marketing is of special interest to small firms. Managers of small firms and business scholars (the last category not until recently and still not including everybody) have come to realize that marketing of small firms is not (and should not be) a mini-version of marketing of bigger established enterprises.

Maybe more importantly, marketing plays a special role in the success of small firms. The saying goes that an entrepreneurial small firm succeeds due to good marketing and fails due to bad management. There is some truth in this. For a new business venture to establish itself and to survive, it must sooner or later attract a number of customers (as first-time and/or as repeat buyers) to keep on doing business. This is, in principle, done through marketing. In other words, marketing is closely related to *growing* small firms.

WHY GROWTH?

Some business scholars[38] claim that it is reasonable to refer only to growing small firms as entrepreneurial small firms. We agree – with some modifications. We look at growth from the point of view of the *individual* firm (not from the point of view of the total market or from the point of view of the society at large) and growth can take place *qualitatively* and/or *quantitatively.*[39] So, starting a new independent firm is always growth (and an entrepreneurial act) to us. When, later, a firm generates new business ventures, that is, intrapreneurially, this also always means qualitative growth. It may also mean quantitative growth, that is, more sales, more income (in the firm at large), more employees and so on. It is almost a tautology to say that (successful) entrepreneurship means change for the better – and growth.

So, can a firm grow without doing it entrepreneurially? Yes, a firm can, *in principle*, sell to more customers (or more to the same customers) with an existing product by repeating an existing success pattern. We may refer to this as 'managerial growth' to separate it from 'entrepreneurial growth', which includes more of change.[40]

ENTREPRENEURIAL MARKETING AS A SUBJECT OF ITS OWN

Given the change of the idea of business in the new economic era from 'big is better' to 'small is beautiful', one may ask: 'What is known of the success pattern of growing small firms?'. Unfortunately, this knowledge, even if growing, is still shallow and fragmented. This is due to a number of circumstances, which will be clarified as we move on in this book and which is one major reason why this book was written in the first place:

- As we see it, *success equals growth*. Theories of growth have been around for a long time. However, one may ask how many of these theories are of interest to, or even concern, the individual small firm. In fact, the insight that highly successful small and growing firms – the 'gazelles' of the business world[41] – are extremely important to an economy is not much more than ten years old.
- There are many modes of growth. One such mode, on everybody's lips today, is *growing through entrepreneurship*, that is, growing by doing something different and not simply by doing 'more of the same' (managerial growth). The term 'entrepreneurship' was coined several hundred years ago,[42] research in this area (originally in the academic field of economics) has been going on ever since, highly intensified

(now in the academic field of business) during the past couple of decades, and few topics in business, in theory as well as in practice, are as 'hot' as entrepreneurship is today.[43] However (and this will be shown later in this book), several lines of research on entrepreneurship have turned out to be dead ends and still other lines are not much more than extracts from research on management and/or business leadership in general. We would like to claim that entrepreneurship is not simply an aspect of management or an aspect of business leadership, nor is it a combination of the best from both of these areas (even though it may apply much from both). Rather, *management is basically a task, business leadership a role, but entrepreneurship more of a lifestyle.* This is particularly so for growing small firms in the new economic era.

- There is one aspect of entrepreneurship which seems to be accepted by most theorists as well as practitioners of it. Some successful entrepreneurs are performing better in the market than others. This leads naturally to the area of *marketing*. However, a fact which is still not accepted by everybody and which will be explored as well, marketing in small firms is not the same as marketing in big firms, nor is the former simply a mini-version of the latter. Marketing in small firms is, at least partly, an area of its own.

So, there is an abundance of theories of growth, research on entrepreneurship has been going on for at least two centuries, and marketing has been an established, as well as highly successful, line of business for many years. Nevertheless, the combination of the three, that is, marketing of small firms growing through entrepreneurship, is still a virgin today. Furthermore, this combination seems to be of utmost importance to that part of the business world and to those economic sectors, which have entered the new economic era. This fact justifies the label 'entrepreneurial marketing' and the title of this book.

If entrepreneurs and their endeavours, that is, new firms and renewed old firms, are leading others in the new economic era, it is essential to understand more about these people and what it is they do. Also, one decisive aspect of being better as an entrepreneur in this era is to excel in marketing. The economic future may well be to understand and develop abilities in entrepreneurial efforts – and marketing of such efforts is a critical skill.

Let us, towards the end of this introductory chapter, summarize different small business modes along our three dimensions:

- entrepreneurship;
- marketing; and
- growth.

First of all, the start of a new business entity standing on its own (from a legal point of view), that is, independent entrepreneurship, always means growth (which, to repeat, we always look at from the individual firm's point of view). We believe that marketing plays a crucial role at such establishments. Many, if not most, of such small business entities stop growing after having established themselves and stop behaving entrepreneurially. Others may, on some later occasion(s), generate one (or several) more business venture(s) – often related to the first one, if they enter intrapreneurial phases (where, again, marketing skills may be decisive for success). This gives us Figure 1.1.

Most small firms stay small and do not grow (deliberately or not), relying on the original business venture on which they started. Other small firms may grow *managerially* by expanding market coverage with their original venture. Still other small firms may try to grow *intrapreneurially* by adding new business ventures to the one they started (or replacing it). The typical high-growth firm is growing by implementing marketing successfully.

THE STRUCTURE OF THIS BOOK

In this book, marketing of growing small firms will be discussed. The focus will be on marketing in firms, which grow entrepreneurially, that is, by

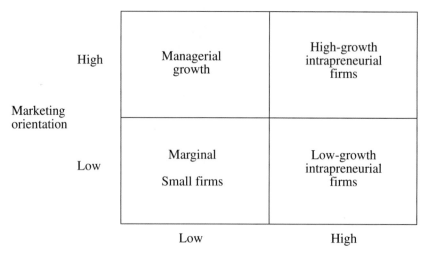

Figure 1.1   Small business growth modes

generating new business ventures. This could be called 'entrepreneurial marketing'. The theoretical foundations of entrepreneurial marketing are in marketing theory as well as in entrepreneurship theory. It can be put such that the central interest in this book is marketing in small firms when they behave entrepreneurially.

There are several reasons why we decided to write this book and why we feel there is a need for it:

- There is no generally accepted conceptual structure, especially adapted to entrepreneurial marketing, even if there is one for entrepreneurship and another one for marketing and even, to some extent, one for innovative marketing of big firms.
- Entrepreneurship, growth and development is highly topical today and marketing is a key to entrepreneurial success. This has been accepted in practice for about two decades, but not yet adequately reflected in the literature.
- The two authors of this book found a valuable and productive combination and synergy in the fact that one of us is a specialist in entrepreneurship and the other in marketing.

This book will follow the structure as given in Figure 1.2. This chapter provides an introduction to the book. It also contains an analysis of the importance of entrepreneurship and small firms for an economy. A brief discussion of how a small firm is 'defined', of our three key words 'entrepreneurship', 'marketing' and 'growth', of the ambitions and the structure of the rest of the book, is also held. One conclusion from this chapter is that 'entrepreneurial marketing' is very important in the new economic era and that this topic has been inadequately covered in the literature.

Chapter 2 provides a picture of how the subject of marketing has evolved in the old economic era. It states the position of mainstream marketing today. One conclusion from this chapter is that marketing as an academic field (and much of its application in practice) has not, to any large extent, incorporated the consequences of doing business in the new economic era. Much of marketing, as it stands today, is based on a rational planning and control perspective where marketing is seen as a formal administrative function and process only, which is, as we see it, of less relevance to growing small firms in general and to small firms in the new economic era in particular. Furthermore, we also find the recent concept of relationship marketing, the way it has been applied to date, is not complex enough to cover what we find necessary for promoting entrepreneurial growth in this era.

Chapter 3 does for entrepreneurship what Chapter 2 does for marketing. It takes a broad look at entrepreneurship. It is based on the idea that the result of

Entrepreneurial marketing

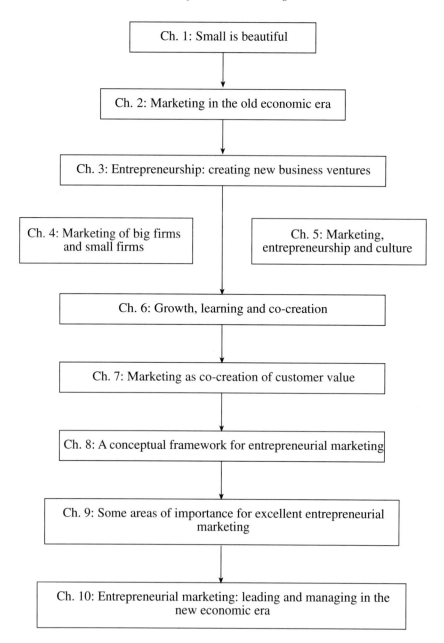

Figure 1.2   Structure of this book

entrepreneurship is new business ventures, that is, to start a new independent business venture or, at a later stage of the existence of a firm, to modify its business enough to call it 'new' or even to add a new business venture to the existing line of a firm (the last two modes of entrepreneurship are commonly called 'intrapreneurship'), as long as the result is still a small firm. This chapter includes a discussion about the differences between 'management', 'leadership' and 'entrepreneurship' and what it means to 'explain' versus to 'understand' entrepreneurship. One conclusion from this chapter is that entrepreneurship, in the new economic era, should best be seen as a lifestyle, driving processes, into which small firms may enter during various phases of their existence.

In Chapters 4 and 5, 'detours' are made in the sense that answers to two questions are looked at in further detail:

- Chapter 4: Which similarities and differences exist in marketing by small firms and by big firms? One conclusion from this chapter is that differences between marketing of small firms and big firms are wide enough to separate the two.
- Chapter 5: What are the similarities and differences in marketing and entrepreneurship in different national cultures? One conclusion from this chapter is that the cultural context can contribute much to obtaining a better picture of marketing as well as entrepreneurship in the new economic era.

The result of these 'detours' is to place the discussions in the rest of the book in perspective.

Chapter 6 starts by discussing the process of growth of a firm, separating managerial growth from entrepreneurial growth. Closely related to business growth is learning. There are two kinds of learning, that is, exploitative and explorative learning. Explorative learning takes place, to a large extent, in networks and so-called virtual organizations. Finally, we introduce our concept of 'co-creation'. One conclusion from this chapter is that there are different types of growth and organization and different modes of learning. Not to separate these types and modes may lead to wrong, even dangerous, conclusions about how business is and should be conducted among small firms.

Chapter 7 discusses marketing as co-creation of customer value. Such co-creation takes place for a growing firm in the new economic era in some kind of networking, where even the customer may be a party. To understand such co-creation we look at the value-creation process as an interaction on three levels, that is, the individual entrepreneur, the focal growing firm and the network itself. One conclusion from this chapter is that the process of creating offerings to customers is more complex than what is normally understood.

Chapter 8 presents a new framework for the marketing of growing entrepreneurial firms, that is, entrepreneurial marketing, and examines the consequences of such a framework. The framework involves creating a capability within the firm of a new, more adequate, offer, but also a more complex view of such an offer and of the value of this offer to the customers' own value-creating process. It presents *an integrated model of transactional and relationship marketing*. This chapter contains a discussion of different growth patterns and what could be behind such patterns. The chapter ends with a discussion of the firm's internal structure to facilitate co-creation, to improve its flexibility to learn and to raise its entrepreneurial spirit. One conclusion is that the concept of 'entrepreneurial marketing' offers an adequate picture of how to acquire high growth for small firms in the new economic era.

Chapter 9 provides a further discussion of some important aspects of entrepreneurial marketing, including some possible future developments. One conclusion is that we have only come to the beginning of understanding growth of firms in the new economic era.

Chapter 10 summarizes the book. From this summary we derive and present some advice on how to grow successfully in the new economic era.

What this book wants to demonstrate can also be presented as follows:

- marketing means many different things; there are no generally valid marketing answers; however, there are general marketing questions – and even specific answers if the context is made explicit (Chapter 2);
- a contextual process view on entrepreneurship is of value when studying and trying to understand small firms in their growth phases (Chapter 3);
- there is a difference in kind between marketing of big firms and marketing of small firms and either one of these two ways of marketing does not have to be inferior to the other one (Chapter 4);
- culture is a commonly neglected variable in discussing marketing and entrepreneurship and is needed to get a better understanding of entrepreneurial marketing in the new economic era (Chapter 5);
- there are reasons to separate business venturing into different types and modes of growth, organizing and learning (Chapter 6);
- co-creation of customer value is an interesting concept (Chapter 7);
- it is useful to look at entrepreneurial marketing for growth as a mix of transactional and relationship actions (Chapter 8);
- there is still much to do in order to understand entrepreneurial marketing (Chapter 9);
- what is good or bad entrepreneurial marketing of small firms is mostly

a contextual matter, however a few general principles can be derived (Chapter 10).

This study is not an attempt to criticize what other researchers have done and what they have published. On the contrary, it summarizes what is already understood as entrepreneurial marketing and it provides a development, a supplement and, to some extent, an alternative to this understanding, specifically geared to growing small firms in the new economic era.

NOTES

1. Hedberg, B., G. Dahlgren, J. Hansson and N. Olve (1997), *Virtual Organizations and Beyond: Discover Imaginary Systems*, London: Wiley.
2. The concept of 'small is beautiful' in fact dates back to 1973, when the German economist E.F. Schumacher published a book by that name (Schumacher, E.F. (1973), *Small is Beautiful*, New York: Harper). The concept stood for sustainable, ecologically sound development of societies, struggling to come up to the standard of the industrialized world. Small-scale economies, intermediate technology, structures of manageable size, small communities and gradual changes are the core themes of Schumacher's philosophy. It has also been coined 'development as if people matter'.
3. These contributions are too numerous to mention. Some of the more prominent ones, however, are Eisenhardt, Kathleen M. (1989), 'Making fast strategic decisions in high-velocity environments', *Academy of Management Journal*, **32**, (3), pp. 543–76; Drucker, Peter (1993), *Post-Capitalist Society*, New York: Free Press; Bernstein, P.L. (1998), 'Are networks driving the new economy?', *Harvard Business Review*, November/December, **76** (6), pp. 150–159; Kelly, Kevin (1999), *New Rules for the New Economy: 10 Radical Strategies for a Connected World*, Penguin USA. The discussion in this section of the book is based on these publications, among others.
4. Drucker, Peter (1995), *Managing in a Time of Great Change*, Oxford, UK: Butterworth-Heinemann, pp. 226–7.
5. 'Munchkin management' (1989), *The Economist*, 14 October, p. 91; Howard, Robert (1990), 'Can Small Business Help Countries Compete', in 'Entrepreneurship. Creativity at Work', *Harvard Business Review* paperback No. 90076, pp. 118–19.
6. Bjerke, Björn (1989), *Att skapa nya affärer* [Creating new business ventures], Lund, Sweden: Studentlitteratur, p. 71; Toffler, Alvyn (1991), *Power Shift*, London: Bantam Books, p. 238.
7. Bjerke (1989), p. 49; 'Enterprise' (1993), *Business Week*, 6 December, p. 52.
8. 'Munchkin management' (1989), p. 91; Toffler (1991), p. 238.
9. Bjerke (1989), p. 71; 'Munchkin management' (1989), p. 91; Toffler (1991), p. 239; Hall, Chris (1995), 'Investing in Intangibles: Improving the Effectiveness of Government SME Advisory Services in the APEC region', keynote speech at 1995 APEC Symposium on Human Resources Development for SMEs, Taipei, 8–10 November, p. 2–5.
10. Hall (1995), pp. 2–5.
11. 'Munchkin management' (1989), p. 91.
12. Bjerke (1989), p. 71; Toffler (1991), pp. 239–40; Hall (1995), pp. 2–5.
13. 'Munchkin management' (1989), p. 91.
14. Ibid.; Naisbitt, John (1995), *Megatrends Asia*, London: Nicholas Brealey, pp. 188ff.
15. Holt, David H. (1992), *Entrepreneurship: New Venture Creation*, Englewood Cliffs, NJ: Prentice-Hall, p. 67.
16. Hall (1995), pp. 2–5.
17. Kuratko, Donald F. and Richard M. Hodgetts (1995), *Entrepreneurship. A Contemporary*

Approach (3rd edn), Orlando, FL: Dryden Press, p. 13.

18. Compare Bjerke (1989), pp. 652–3, or Hisrich, Robert D. and Michael P. Peters (1992), *Entrepreneurship. Starting, Developing, and Managing a New Enterprise* (2nd edn), Homewood, IL: Irwin, pp. 13-14.

19. Wheelen, Thomas J. and J. David Hunger (1995), *Strategic Management and Business Policy* (5th edn), Reading, MA: Addison-Wesley, p. 362.

20. Carson, D., S. Cromie, P. McGowan and J. Hill (1995), *Marketing and Entrepreneurship in SMEs. An Innovative Approach*, Hemel Hempstead, UK: Prentice-Hall International (UK) Limited, p. 61.

21. From EU home pages on Internet.

22. 'The APEC Survey on Small and Medium Enterprises' (1994), APEC Committee on Trade and Investment, APEC Secretariat.

23. This means, for instance, that small firms which are owned by bigger firms are normally not included in the statistics.

24. Bjerke, Björn (2000), 'A typified, culture-based, interpretation of management of SMEs in Southeast Asia', *Asia Pacific Journal of Management*, **17**, pp. 103–32:107.

25. Zimmerer, Thomas W. and Norman M. Scarborough (1996), *Entrepreneurship and New Venture Formation*, Englewood Cliffs, NJ: Prentice-Hall, p. 2.

26. Carson et al. (1995), p. 3.

27. Holt (1992), p. 7.

28. Hisrich and Peters (1992), p.150

29. 'Enterprise' (1993), p. 51.

30. Bjerke (1989), p. 49; Toffler (1991), p. 239.

31. 'Enterprise' (1993), p. 50.

32. Ushido, Yoshio (1995), 'Small and Medium Enterprises and Government Policy', paper presented at 1995 APEC Symposium on Human Resources Development for SMEs, Taipei, 8–10 November, pp. 1–2.

33. Drucker, Peter and Isao Nakauchi (1997), *Drucker on Asia*, Oxford, MA: Butterworth-Heinemann, pp. 77-9.

34. No textbook on small business and/or entrepreneurship can avoid stating this fact.

35. See Hall (1995) and Hall, Chris (1998), 'Squeezing the Asian Entrepreneurial Engine; the impact of the credit squeeze on sustainable entrepreneurial job creation in Asia', paper presented at ICSB 43rd World Conference, Singapore, 8–10 June.

36. Jovanovic, B. and G.M. MacDonald (1994), 'The Life Cycle of a Competitive Industry', *Journal of Political Economy*, **102** (2), pp. 322–47.

37. Hall (1995) and (1998).

38. For instance, Stevenson, H. and W. Sahlman (1986), 'Importance of entrepreneurship in economic development', in Hisrich, R. (ed.), *Entrepreneurship, Intrapreneurship, and Venture Capital*, Lexington, MA: D.C. Heath, pp. 3–26; Sexton, D.L. And N.B. Bowman-Upton (1991), *Entrepreneurship: Creativity and Growth*, New York: Macmillan.

39. A more detailed discussion of growth will take place in Chapter 6.

40. We do not have, of course, two clear situations where, on one hand, nothing changes (except for the fact that changes takes place quantitatively), that is, managerial growth and where, on the other hand, everything changes (internally as well as externally to the firm), that is, entrepreneurial growth. We shall later separate partial entrepreneurship (where change may include only, say, design of the product or a firm goes international with existing products) from complete entrepreneurship, where all major aspects of a new business venture differs from before (still seen from the individual firm's point of view, as mentioned in the text).

41. David Birch (Birch, David (1987), *Job Creation in America: How Our Small Companies Put the Most People to Work*, New York: Macmillan) classifies companies into elephants, mice and gazelles in terms of their contribution to the development and growth of the US economy. The new ventures that grow rapidly, tend to locate in select 'feeding places' and are based on significant innovations are termed 'gazelles'.

42. Richard Cantillon, a French economist of Irish descent, is often credited with giving the concept of entrepreneurship a start as a subject of its own. In his *Essai sur la nature du commerce en général*, published posthumously in 1755, Cantillon described an entrepreneur

as a person who pays a certain price for a product to resell it at an uncertain price, thereby making decisions about obtaining and using resources while consequently assuming the risk of enterprise.

43. For the explosion of entrepreneurial education in the US, for instance, see Vesper, Karl H. (1993), *Entrepreneurship Education*, Los Angeles: Entrepreneurial Studies Center, University of California, Los Angeles.

2. Marketing in the old economic era

NEW AND OLD ECONOMIC ERAS

Chapter 1, among other topics, provided a list of some of the characteristics of the 'new economic era'. These characteristics are:

- Many changes occur; many of these changes are drastic and difficult, if not impossible, to predict.
- Genuine uncertainty undermines much of the basis for planning.
- The most important strategic resource for a firm is not financial capital but to have some insightful and visionary change agents among its owners/managers/employees, at best oriented towards generating new business ventures.
- Capital is not only of a hard financial kind, but also of a softer type such as adequate processes, local data bases, willingness to learn and a relevant net of contacts and business vendors.
- Survival of the fastest is often more important than survival of the fittest.
- The most important business resource (some say, the only meaningful business resource) is knowledge.
- Corporatization and privatization take place in all economic sectors, even in ones traditionally protected by the government.
- Competition is more intense than ever, often on a global scale.
- There is no longer such a thing as a set of clearly defined industries with established ways of doing business.
- The impact of technology can never be neglected; and technology is changing fast.
- Small firms show the way to a new business order.

This contrasts with an 'old economic era', whose, characteristics are as follows:

- Changes are few and, if they take place, follow trends and other predictable patterns.
- Relatively clear circumstances and relations between various contextual factors – plus the fact that predictions can be made – make planning possible and meaningful.

- It is more important to success to have access to a proper amount of financial capital in order to grow in relatively predictable patterns than to have fast-acting people willing to experiment in unprecedented directions.
- Willingness to learn and relevant contacts are not to be neglected but such factors are of a more tactical than strategic importance. Of more strategic importance are things like adequate structures, solid experience and central databases.
- To fit a given set of contingent circumstances is better than trying to be too innovative. To be second, and learn from the mistakes made by the one who was first, might be the most profitable position.[1]
- Knowledge is not so much invested in subjective individuals as in common traditions, business success patterns, superior products and well-established distribution lines.
- There is a clear separation in the economy between activities which are better run by the private business sector and activities which are better taken care of by public institutions.
- Competition is less intense and mainly domestic. Competitors are relatively easy to specify.
- Business is done within structurable industries and the way business is done in one industry is often different from the way business is done in another industry.[2]
- Technology is taken for granted and is rarely a business success factor on its own.
- Big businesses dominate and show the way.

Note that both the above descriptions are in the present tense. Even the most advanced economy is a mix of the old and the new economic eras and, furthermore, most economic sectors are a mix of both (which was mentioned earlier).

What is important here is that the field of marketing, as an academic discipline and as a praxis (at least in big firms), was developed in the spirit of the old economic era and is still dominated by the same thinking. Let us, in this chapter, look at the development of this marketing field and, at the end of it, take a preliminary critical look at the adequacy of mainstream marketing in the new economic era.

THE EARLY SCHOOLS

A Twentieth-century Phenomenon

Marketing is indeed influenced by US business practice, research and writing.

It is therefore natural to take the development in the US as the starting-point for an overview of the progress in marketing as an academic discipline – later supplemented with contributions from some other countries.

Marketing is generally regarded as a twentieth-century phenomenon. Although Adam Smith[3] pointed out the importance of matching the sellers' and the buyers' needs in a free and competitive exchange, more systematic research activities about marketing started only in the first part of the last century.

Much of practical modern marketing originated from big companies in the US, like International Harvester, Curtis Publishing, and US Rubber around the time of the first world war. However, by 1905 academic courses in marketing were already being offered at the University of Pennsylvania in the US.

Early research in 'marketing' in the US mainly followed *three different streams*:

1. *The commodity stream* focusing on market mechanisms for certain commodities, for instance such as, agricultural goods.
2. *The institutional stream* focusing on different marketing organizations.
3. *The functional stream* focusing on exploration and identification of marketing functions.

Sheth et al. state that:

> The commodity school proposed that marketing could best be understood by analyzing the types of goods being exchanged, while the functional school asserted that the focus of analysis should be on the activities conducted in the course of the exchange. While institutional theorists appreciated the arguments advanced by their colleagues in these other two schools, they nonetheless believed that the marketing discipline could benefit by paying greater scholarly attention to the organizations that actually perform the functions required to move the goods from the producer to the consumer.[4]

For later development of marketing, the functional stream was probably the most important one of the above three.

The Commodity Stream

The commodity school came from research on agricultural goods and some of its knowledge is still with us. One example is the conclusion that marketing practice very much depends on the characteristics of the product or of the type of product being marketed. Several systems for classification of goods were developed within the commodity school, most often based on buyer habits, like convenience goods, emergency goods and shopping goods;[5] convenience goods, shopping goods and speciality goods[6]; red, orange and yellow goods[7]; shopping and nonshopping goods (convenience goods and speciality goods).[8] Later classifications were suggested on the basis of other customer aspects as well, for instance, behavioural sciences aspects, perceived risk and expected effort from buyers.

The Institutional Stream

The role of middlemen was not obvious in the early days of marketing, that is, did they just add costs or did they contribute to the process of transforming and transporting goods from the producer to the consumer? The functions, efficiency and profits by middlemen and other actors in marketing channels were highlighted within the institutional school of marketing.

Butler[9] created the famous concept of 'utilities' that have to be created for producers and consumers, that is, *elementary utility* (what the goods fundamentally perform); *form utility* (to develop the goods and make them palatable to the consumers); *place utility* (the buyers normally need the goods in places other than where they are produced – transportation); and *time utility* (storage between the time for production and the time for consumption). It was suggested that middlemen were able to produce time and place utility more efficiently than the producers.

A direct link from the research within the institutional stream can be traced to modern studies of channel relations in marketing (and relations in general between actors in marketing systems).

The Functional Stream

In early research in marketing, distinctions between its more specific activities were not originally made. The idea within the functional school was to identify different activities that the marketing process consisted of and find out what structure was needed to carry out those activities.

One author[10] found four types of activities:

- selling;
- assembling, assorting, reshipping or delivering;
- risk sharing; and
- financing.

In principle, all organizations were assumed to perform these activities, and all of them were to operate in their own separate geographical area. However, as we know, in practice it was not that simple. There are economies of scale in many of the above activities. Therefore, risk sharing and development of specialized channel structures could be seen functionally (for example, transporting and insuring) as well as geographically (for example, assembling, assorting and delivering).

From the 1950s, different marketing activities were understood as being related to one another. Exchange of goods and services with associated payments and change of ownership would take place only if time, place as well as assortment were appropriate. Marketing as a whole was expected to make sure that this was the case!

The functional stream was probably the earliest predecessor to the concept of the '*value chain*', later popularized by Porter.[11]

MAINSTREAM MARKETING

Foundations

The basic structure of modern marketing theory developed from the three streams presented in the last section.[12] From about the 1960s until today some major thoughts in the field can jointly be labelled 'mainstream marketing'. Its theoretical foundations are economics with influences from behavioural sciences, systems theory, political science and organizational theory, especially interorganizational theory. In turn, mainstream marketing can be looked at as a *structure of subschools*. In the following sections of this chapter, some mainstream marketing subschools will be discussed briefly:

- macromarketing;
- consumer behaviour;
- managerial marketing;
- marketing channels and distribution;
- international marketing; and
- industrial marketing.

Marketing and the Environment: Macromarketing, Megamarketing

As in other research influenced by systems theory, the wider links between marketing and the environment are focused in *macromarketing* research.[13] The area is defined by Hunt:[14] 'Macromarketing refers to the study of (1) marketing systems (2) the impact and consequences of marketing systems on society and (3) the impact and consequences of society on marketing systems'.

Kotler[15] suggests that marketers must engage in *megamarketing* where power and public relations are important. For instance, in blocked or protected markets, marketing should be more of a political nature:

In addition to the four Ps of marketing strategy – product, price, place and promotion – executives must add two more – power and public relations. I call such strategic thinking megamarketing. … Megamarketing thus takes an enlarged view of the skills and resources needed to enter and operate in certain markets. In addition to preparing attractive offers for customers, megamarketing may use inducements and sanctions to gain the desired responses from gatekeepers.[16]

In situations where relations between sellers and buyers act in any form of administrated system or as Arndt[17] calls it, 'domesticated markets', marketing changes character and becomes more of a political issue.

Consumer and Buyer Behaviour

Buyer behaviour theory has given important contributions to marketing knowledge.[18] Sheth et al.[19] mention important concepts such as perceived risk;[20] information processing;[21] reference group influence;[22] social class;[23] involvement;[24] psychographics;[25] attitudes;[26] and situational influences.[27]

The focus of buyers and their needs is one of the most fundamental aspects of modern marketing. In the expanding economy of the 1950s and 1960s, the consumers' behaviour was of utmost importance, and marketing was the business function to deal with this:

Growing acceptance of this consumer concept has had, and will have, far-reaching implications for business, achieving a virtual revolution in economic thinking. As the concept gains ever greater acceptance, marketing is emerging as the most important single function in business.[28]

Other important concepts from behavioural sciences included in marketing were reference group, cognitive dissonance, attitudes and motivation.

The Managerial Paradigm Became the Dominant View

During the 1950s and 1960s, a managerial-oriented perspective of marketing emerged and became its dominating view. Early contributors were, for example, Howard[29] and McCarty.[30] With its origin in the well-established theory of microeconomics, based on the assumption of an open market with pure transactions and influenced by recent findings in behavioural sciences, the managerial view was soon accepted and became *the* paradigm of marketing. One of its benefits was that the managerial paradigm offered a distinct guide to managers in their actions, and a framework that was very easy to understand.

One of the most widespread definitions of marketing, the present official definition from the American Marketing Association (AMA), has a distinct character of the managerial paradigm: 'Marketing is the process of planning and executing the conception of ideas, goods and services to create exchanges that satisfy individual and organizational objectives'.[31] This definition has not been changed by the AMA since 1981; it establishes the managerial perspective almost as *the* mainstream. This perspective still dominates marketing and marketing education in most of the world. In the UK, Ireland, the Nordic countries and Australia, however, more inductively based research has led to a modified view of marketing. This will be discussed later in this chapter.

Well-known marketing terms are *marketing concept*;[32] *market myopia*;[33] *marketing mix*;[34] *marketing planning*; *segmentation*;[35] *product life cycle*;[36] *market positioning*;[37] *market orientation*[38] – the list of contributions from the managerial school to marketing is very long. Some of these terms will be discussed briefly below.

Marketing mix is popularly referred to as the '4-7 Ps'. Originally, the concept of the 4 Ps[39] included product, price, place and promotion only. Today, in the latest edition of Kotler's *Marketing Management*, the concept is still as valid as before: To transform marketing strategy into marketing programs, marketing managers must make basic decisions on marketing expenditures, marketing mix and marketing allocation ... Second, the company has to decide how to divide the total marketing budget among the various tools in the marketing-mix: product, price, place, and promotion.[40]

All marketing students and marketing managers are familiar with the *marketing planning* model as presented in various forms in almost all textbooks all over the world. In Figure 2.1 the main structure of the managerial planning model is outlined.

In general, the perspective of decision making and planning within the managerial school is very rational with assumptions of behaviour in accordance with the *economic man* in microeconomics.

Many marketing planning models were developed in the 1950s and 1960s. At that time the big corporations were often bureaucratic and hierarchical in their structure[41] and large planning systems were natural both from a corporate perspective and from the messages in management seminars.

An example of the view of benefits from marketing planning was Oxenfeldt's.[42] He cited six benefits that a firm derives from setting up a plan:

- the coordination of the activities of many individuals whose actions are interrelated over time;
- identification of expected developments;
- preparedness to meet changes when they occur;
- minimization of non-rational responses to the unexpected;

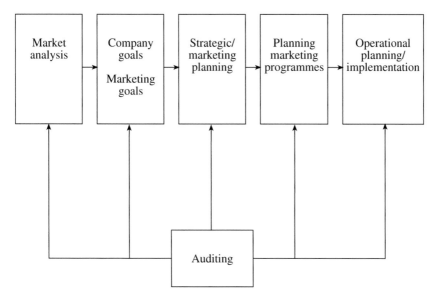

| Market analysis | Company goals

Marketing goals | Strategic/ marketing planning | Planning marketing programmes | Operational planning/ implementation |

Auditing

Figure 2.1   Standard model of marketing planning within the managerial school

- better communication among executives; and
- minimization of conflicts among individuals which, if individuals are on their own, would result in a suboptimization of the goals of the company.

A modern textbook from that time presents the advantages of planning as follows:

> The trend toward increased acceptance of marketing planning is a fundamental premise of business adjustment to present and future market patterns. As planning becomes a basic management technique and the cornerstone of management philosophy in designing market systems, practical methods of linking many market-related decisions and programs will be developed. The firm will be better able to capitalize on areas of market opportunity and profit, thereby achieving corporate goals in the market.[43]

Criticism of the managerial paradigm comes from many directions; it has also been criticized from a more general perspective by many authors.[44] The question of where it is applicable – if the theories really are relevant for other situations than standardized consumer goods – is probably the most fundamental of all critical opinions.

Distribution and Marketing Channels

The literature on marketing channels is extensive. Its origins are to be found not only in disciplines such as economics, political science and the behavioural sciences, but also in areas such as organization theory and operations research.

The developments in 'channel theory' could be described as evolutionary. In earlier work, economic factors were believed to determine channel behaviour. Starting from the late 1960s and early 1970s, behavioural processes were introduced and later dominated research in parallel with research done within the discipline of *logistics*. In the latter case the dominant perspective is still based on economic considerations.

Bucklin[45] deals with the structure of marketing channels. He tried to find the key factors explaining channel structure. Because of the distance in time and space between production and consumption certain activities or functions must be performed to bridge that gap. Performing these functions leads to distribution costs.

The interaction between the demand of the buyers and the decisions made in the channel will determine the channel structure. During normal competition and with reasonable barriers against entry, the channel will be structured such that no other arrangements will give lower production costs for the service outputs, so the thinking goes. Also, buyers are expected to request high service but to be willing to pay only a low price, and the middlemen will get low production costs through economies of scale. Further, since both price and effects of scale are negatively correlated with higher service outputs, the optimal structure will minimize the total costs at the balance between the buyers' demand for as high a level of service as possible and the middlemen's wish for as low a level of service as possible.

The channel structure will also be affected by the external environment. Environmental changes and their underlying forces interact with marketing channels and can have profound effects on these channels in both the short and the long runs.[46] A common categorization of the channel environment in the literature is:

- economic environment;
- technical environment;
- competitive environment;
- sociocultural environment; and
- legal environment.

So far, in our discussion, only economic considerations were expected to guide the different actors in marketing channels. But since the actors are human beings, factors other than economic ones could also be expected to affect their behaviour. First to set the stage was Ridgeway[47] who pointed out the need for coordination in channels and the need for power to deliver rewards and punishments to reinforce the manufacturer's wishes. He was followed by Mallen[48] who focused on interplay conflict, control and cooperation, and argued for the need of a 'leader' to take actions to force or 'help' channel members to cooperate. From the late 1960s, Louis Stern had a great influence on this type of research, and aspects such as roles,[49] conflicts in social systems[50] and power[51] were then considered.

In later research, attempts have been made to investigate interrelations between different subsystems of marketing channels instead of a partial analysis. The idea was to build models where political, social and economic factors were taken into consideration at the same time.[52] Such studies were made within frameworks based on interorganization theory.

Linkages between organizations and the environment exist because organizations interact with one another. In the literature there are several names for these linkages, such as 'connections', 'bindings' and so on. The term 'relation', however, is often used for many different aspects of such linkages.

The theoretical developments within modern distribution research have had much bearing on progress in network cooperation such as strategic alliances and virtual/imaginary organizations. Marketing implications of these phenomena, however, are rarely discussed within the marketing discipline.

International, Industrial and Service Marketing

Some important special areas of marketing grew into prominence during the 1960s, 1970s and 1980s. Noteworthy among these special areas are international, industrial (or business-to-business, B2B, as it is often referred to today) and service marketing.

The Industrial Marketing Committee Review Board defined the field of *industrial marketing*.[53] Early works in this area were done for example by Robinson et al.;[54] Webster and Wind;[55] Sheth;[56] and in Europe among others by Håkansson and other members of the IMP (Industrial Marketing and Purchasing) group.[57]

In *service marketing*, foundations were laid by scholars such as Richard Normann, Evert Gummesson and Christian Grönroos[58] in the Nordic countries as well as for example Robert Judd, Lynn Shostack and Leonard Berry in the US.[59] Much of the work done in this area can be contained in the managerial paradigm or in relationship marketing (which will be discussed later in this chapter). However, service marketing and the special conditions related to marketing of services are commonly regarded as a special area of marketing much related to the differences between goods and services. These differences, however, can be questioned in the context of marketing today. In most marketing situations what is offered to the market is a product combination which has tangible as well as intangible components which are inseparable and where differences between these components are very blurred. Activities associated with marketing goods and marketing services are no longer useful to separate, at least not from a practical point of view, as no goods can be sold without services being involved one way or another. Every product is more or less service dominated.

Models for firms' internationalization and international marketing behaviour are developed within *international marketing*. Neoclassical trade theory has been used to explain the pattern of movements of products across borders. Burenstam Linder[60] claimed that home market demand was the driving force in development of potential export products. Exports could be expected to be directed to similar foreign markets, and the more similar demand structures in two markets was, the higher the trade potential between the two countries. Vernon[61] later developed this thinking into the *product cycle theory*.

Following the traditions of Simon[62] as well as Cyert and March[63] many studies have followed a behaviouristic approach towards internationalization; the so-called 'Uppsala School' suggested, for instance, a sequential pattern of internationalization.[64]

International business research was mainly interested in big multinational corporations and their investments. Local market characteristics as well as internal firm characteristics were used to explain the selection of foreign markets and the establishment of foreign subsidiaries.[65]

THE CONTEMPORARY SITUATION

In General

Let us discuss the contemporary position of the marketing discipline under four headings:

- marketing as a general management responsibility;
- market orientation;
- the 'controversy' of transactional marketing versus relationship marketing; and
- complex perspectives.

Marketing as a General Management Responsibility: The Domain of Marketing

The discussion whether marketing is a specialist function (among others) within the company or if marketing is a general philosophy involving all of the firm's actors is relevant to pinpoint in this context.

Marketing as an important function within the company was stressed by consumer behaviour research: in the expanding economy of the 1950s and 1960s, consumers' behaviour was of utmost importance, and *marketing* was regarded as a company function to deal with this:

> Growing acceptance of this consumer concept has had, and will have, far-reaching implications for business, achieving a virtual revolution in economic thinking. As the concept gains ever greater acceptance, marketing is emerging as the most important single function in business.[66]

Hence, marketing was regarded as a function among others in a functionally divided firm even if very essential for business survival.

The discussion of a broader concept of marketing started in an Ohio State University position paper from 1965.[67] A few years later, Kotler and Levy[68] brought the discussion of marketing's domain out into the open.

Brown[69] refers to this discussion of marketing as something broad and general, valid not only in the business world:

> Marketing was an all-pervasive activity which applied as much to the selling of politicians, universities and charities as it did to toothpaste, soap and steel. As a consequence of dramatic, post-war social changes and the emergence of large complex professionally managed non-business organizations, such as museums, police departments and trade-unions, it has become necessary to broaden the concept of marketing. Traditional notions of the 'product', the 'consumer' and the marketing 'tool-kit' had to be re-defined in non-business terms and attempts made to transfer the principle of effective marketing management – generic product definition, target groups identification, customer behavior analysis, integrated marketing planning, continuous feedback and so on – to the marketing of services, persons and ideas.

Kotler and Levy[70] stated that organizations could not function efficiently without a marketing perspective and the choice was simply stated as 'whether to do it well or poorly'.

Brown continues:[71]

> Developing this theme Kotler (1972)[72] went on to argue that it was necessary to extend the concept even further. There were, he maintained, three stages of marketing consciousness. The first represented the traditional view of marketing

that it was essentially a business-oriented philosophy involving market transactions, the economic exchange of goods and services. Consciousness two held that marketing was applicable to all organizations that had customers or clients, even though payment in the normal sense may not take place. However, the third level of consciousness, deemed the 'generic' concept, contended that marketing was not only relevant to *all* organizations, be they churches, political parties or government departments, but to the relations between the organization and *all* of its publics, not only the consuming public. ... he [Kotler] concluded that 'marketing can be viewed as a *category of human action*, distinguishable from other categories of human action such as voting, loving, consuming and fighting'. ... Needless to say, not everybody shared Kotler's marketing megalomania.

Gummesson as well as Grönroos[73] claimed early that marketing is more of an overall management responsibility than a specialist function: different forms of contacts with the market were spread all over the firm and there were a large number of part-time marketers[74] in all organizations. This means that a number of individuals in different specialist functions also contribute to the firm's marketing efforts, both directly and indirectly.

Market Orientation: A General Remedy

One much discussed phenomenon in modern marketing is the marketing concept (versus the product concept). This is related to the need for market orientation in a company. The *marketing concept*, as for a long time interpreted by Kotler:[75] 'holds the key to achieving its organizational goals consists of determining the needs and wants of the target markets and delivering the desired satisfactions more effectively and efficient than competitors'. The marketing concept can be seen as a threefold conceptualization concerned with:

1. orientation on customers and their needs;
2. long-run profitability as an objective rather than sales volume; and
3. integration and coordination of marketing and other corporate functions.

On the other hand, the *product concept*: 'holds that consumers favor those products that offer the most quality, performance, or innovative features. Managers in these organizations focus on making superior products and improving them over time assuming that buyers can appraise quality and performance.'[76]

Market orientation, which can be understood as conceptualizing and operationalizing the marketing concept, is commonly regarded as critical for long-term success and superior performance at the marketplace[77] and is seen, if it exists, as part of a firm's culture, affecting both its learning capability and its strategic resources position. In the marketing literature we can read that market orientation comprises three components (compare the marketing concept above):

1. customer orientation;
2. competition focus; and
3. cross-functional coordination.

Kohli and Jaworski[78] conclude: '[Market orientation provides] a unifying focus for the effects and projects of individuals, thereby leading to superior performance'.

The Narver and Slater[79] components of market orientation (being customer driven, competition focused, and internally coordinated) as discussed above are regarded as directly related to business performance. The components of market orientation influence a firm's 'core capabilities' such as customer service, quality, and innovation. These core capabilities may in turn affect aspects of the firms' 'competitive advantage' (customer loyalty; new product success; market share) leading overall to positive business performance such as profitability and sales growth.[79]

Langerak[80] extends the constructs made by Narver and Slater and looks at market orientation as the business philosophy that commits the organization to the continuous creation of customer value, doing this by encouraging four key skills:

- customer orientation;
- competitor orientation;
- supplier orientation; and
- interfunctional coordination.[81]

Transactional Marketing Versus Relationship Marketing

One fundamental theoretical argumentation in marketing today is whether the concepts of transactions or relations are the core of what marketing is all about. The traditional US perspective (which is ruling today) is that research in marketing ultimately studies transactions driven by exchanges of value. On the other hand, contemporary schools among some researchers, especially in the Nordic countries and in the UK, claim that relationships to customers and others are the essence of the marketing discipline. No representative from the two perspectives, however, excludes the importance of the other, but supports the prominence of the own focus.

One leading advocate of the US research on *transactional marketing*[82] writes that:

> The core concept of marketing is the transaction. A transaction is the exchange of values between two parties. The things-of-values need not be limited to goods, services, and money; they include other resources such as time, energy, and feelings.

Another leading US researcher[83] states: 'that the basic subject matter of marketing is the exchange relationship or transaction. ... marketing is the behavioral science that seeks to explain exchange relationships'.

Transactions are explained by exchanges of value. Oliver, in a textbook with the challenging title *Marketing Today*, says:[84]

> Despite the difficulty in defining the edge of marketing, the central focus is on exchange. An exchange is precipitated when a person recognizes that another person has something he would like to have. They both assign values to that which they currently have, and to that which they would like to have. If they both value what the other has, more than they value what they have themselves, then the exchange will be mutually beneficial. Fundamental marketing activities therefore include the need to understand what it is that buyers value, to design an offering so that it has those values, and to ensure that the values are communicated effectively.

Bagozzi[85] goes so far as to claim that marketing can be regarded as the 'science of exchanges'; he asserts that marketing is a general business function of universal applicability and marketing is the discipline of exchange behaviour.

Especially in the Nordic countries and in the UK, research in the marketing discipline has for a long time focused on different *relational aspects*. This does not necessarily mean that other aspects have been neglected but a growing interest in relationships started early in that part of the world, for example within research[86] in industrial marketing as well as in service marketing. In half a decade or so the number of relationship papers presented at US marketing conferences has been increasing rapidly.

One could say that *customer relationships* are part of the marketing core; promises are mutually exchanged and kept between buyers and sellers. As a result customer relationships are established, strengthened and developed for commercial purposes. As an advocate for 'relationship marketing', Grönroos defines marketing:[87]

> Marketing is to establish, maintain and enhance long-term customer relationships (often but not necessarily always long-term customer relations) so that the objectives of the parties invoved are met. This is done by mutual exchange and fulfilment of promises.
>   Furthermore, this definition can be accompanied by the following supplement: The resources of the seller – personnel, technology and systems – have to be used in such a manner that the customer's trust in the resources involved and, thus, in the firm itself is maintained and strengthened. The various resources the customer encounters in the relation may be of any kind and part of any business function.

However, these resources and activities cannot be totally predetermined and explicitly categorized in a general definition.

Several approaches to research where relationships are important exist in parallel, for example, the network approach,[88] interactive marketing,[89] direct marketing[90] as well as the concept of relationship marketing as introduced by Berry[91] in 1983. These approaches to marketing are often presented as alternatives to the managerial paradigm; it is even sometimes stated that the relationship perspective is more relevant in the modern business world of today. What these approaches have in common is the prominence of relationships as an important concept in marketing.

The idea of transactional marketing versus relationship marketing is sometimes seen as two ends of the same dimension of intended time of involvement with individual customers.[92] This view can be further illustrated by a view from Gummesson:[93]

> In order to conceptually incorporate transaction marketing in RM [relationship marketing], it can be seen as a zero point on the *RM scale*. The scope of the relationships can then be enhanced until a customer and a supplier are practically the same organization. ... No doubt we were misled by the authoritarian neo-classical economics in which markets are made up of standardized goods and anonymous masses who behave according to simplistic and distinct laws. Only the *price relationship* exists, and I call that the *zero relationship* on the RM scale.

In our opinion, this is too much of a simplification of how the two perspectives relate to each other. Since the two perspectives focus upon different aspects of marketing, we can claim that both are needed if we want to understand marketing behaviour. The problem is, however, that while the conceptual framework for transactional marketing is more elaborated – especially as perceived by most people through the well-known managerial perspective – the conceptual status of relationship marketing is still scattered, although integrative progress has been made in recent years, for example by Gummesson. So, in order to get a more specific conceptual orientation of relationship marketing to the new economic era, we shall often stress the 'co-creational' aspects of it.

Business relations operate in general at many different levels and relationship marketing can follow this pattern as well. Within the area of marketing, relationship marketing is, as we have seen, often referred to as focusing upon long-lasting relations with customers. However a more extensive perspective can be taken as three different levels for relationship marketing are identified:[94]

1. *Integration of the development of long-term customer relationships with*

the traditional marketing activities Relationship selling is then 'marketing oriented toward a strong, lasting relationship with individual accounts',[95] or, described differently, 'the goal of relationship selling is to earn the position of preferred supplier by developing trust in key accounts over a period of time'.[96]

2. *Relations as a change in the firm's strategic orientation* Here the conceptual aspects of customer relationships and its strategic consequences are in focus for marketing, supported by a well-known statement by Berry: 'Relationship marketing is attracting, maintaining and – in multi-service organizations – enhancing customer relationships'.[97]

3. *General relationship management* is the third category. *Broadened relationship marketing* can be described as follows: 'Relationship marketing refers to all marketing activities directed towards establishing, developing and maintaining, successful relational exchanges' in supplier, lateral, buyer and internal partnership.[98] This can be defined as a type of relationship management/marketing as an orientation to establish close interactions with selected customers, suppliers and competitors. This creation of value is developed through cooperative and collaborative efforts.[99] To manage all types of business relations in the network is the key to success.

Complex Perspectives

So far the focus has been on either transactional marketing or relationship marketing. Recently, attempts have been made to present marketing such that firms perform different types of marketing in parallel, that is, *complex perspectives*. Coviello et al.[100] investigated whether organizations practised a low, medium or high level of each of what they called '4 types of marketing':

- *Transaction-based marketing*: the marketing mix.
- *Database marketing*: a tool or a technique used by marketers to develop and manage long-term relationships between the firm and its identified customers by the use of information technology.
- *Interaction-based marketing*: interactions within relationships, mostly a personal, one-to-one interaction level, both formal and informal, and within the context of organizations operating within industry value systems.
- *Network marketing*: basically a set of connected relationships, often strategic in nature, and at both formal interfirm levels and informal interpersonal levels. It may also involve strategic alliances and partnerships between organizations operating within a single industry value system.

Brodie et al. found that a majority of organizations practised more than one type of marketing approach, if not all of them to a varying degree, and they found that some combinations were more common than others: 'There appears to be a movement towards increased customer orientation (at the very least), if not full efforts to improve customer understanding, and develop synergistic relationship and partnership'.[101]

THE DOMINANT VIEW OF MARKETING FITS THE OLD ECONOMIC ERA

The story of the development of marketing as an academic discipline could have been made longer. We could also have included a flurry of different approaches to 'how to become successful' in the marketplace, which were suggested during the 1990's (some no doubt are attempts to adapt marketing to new times) like *micromarketing*,[102] *maximarketing*,[103] *database marketing*,[104] *new marketing*,[105] *value-added marketing*,[106] *neo-marketing*,[107] *guerilla marketing*,[108] *chaos marketing*,[109] and influences from *postmodernism*.[110] However, our ambition has been to give a picture of how marketing is seen in major academic camps in the industrialized world today, in order to prove our point: *the dominant view of marketing fits the old economic era*! It is not difficult to support this argument. Below are some ideas on which mainstream marketing is based:

Changes, trends and predictability:

- Extensive research has been done to construct models of consumers and how they react to various steps taken by the firm, in order to follow trends in the market and to make the marketing planning context more predictable. Customers are not expected to make drastic moves.
- The focus on buyers/consumers and their needs is one of the cornerstones of mainstream marketing.
- To capitalize on market opportunities in order to achieve long-term profitability is often the objective par excellence.

Contextual factor relations and conditions for planning:

- There are relatively clear relations between contextual factors, predictions can be made and planning is possible and meaningful.
- The planning context, by and large, consists of individuals and organizations which actually perform the functions required to move the goods from the producer to the customer. A customer is a customer,

a supplier is a supplier, a competitor is a competitor and so on.
- The stepwise constructed managerial marketing planning model is strictly adhered to.

Financial capital, patterned growth and 'odd' people:

- Financial strength is an important foundation of successful marketing; good finance may support such activities as marketing research, effective distribution and breaking into new markets.
- Conflicts among participants in the marketing planning process are to be minimized.

Adequate structures, solid experience and central databases:

- Various functions of marketing are clear and distinct, for example, there is planning, there is research and there is control. Furthermore, structure follows function.
- Products are clearly defined by industry, and type of product and, consequently, industry determines the marketing mode.
- Various marketing activities are seen as related to one another and the formula for success is to build up 'complete' marketing systems.

Fitness and innovativeness:

- The managerial paradigm is the dominant view among many marketing scholars; terms, such as marketing mix, segmentation and marketing positioning are important.
- The environment is often divided into separate aspects, such as economic, technical, competitional, sociocultural and so on. In this separation it is functional to identify expected developments, to be prepared and to minimize non-rational responses.

Success pattern and knowledge:

- The chain of distribution is clear, at its fullest it consists of wholesalers, retailers and various other middlemen. This chain is where pattern and knowledge is based.

Public duties and private business:

- The American way is very much to separate business from politics. If the public sector attempts to do marketing, it is still political. If the private

sector is marketing itself to the public sector, it is public relations.
- Marketing influences society more than society influences marketing.

Competition:

- Many marketing theories are based on microeconomics, assuming open markets, fair competition and few, if any, monopolists.
- Coordinated marketing provides a definite competitive advantage.
- International marketing is a relatively recent development.

Industry structure and its consequences:

- To structure the environment is not only desirable but also possible. Much of marketing knowledge is based on various classifications, say, in terms of types of commodities, business vendors, industries and so on.

The role of technology:

- Technology takes part only functionally and is not to play any leading role.

Small and big business:

- In America, 'big is (was?) better' and much of practical modern marketing originates from big business.
- A wide, holistic, structured approach (modelled from mass consumption) is the way to go. Service marketing and international marketing were late inventions. Furthermore, international marketing is almost exclusively devoted to understanding multinationals (that is, big business).

All this questions the applicability of mainstream marketing in the new economic era. This will be elaborated several times in this book, next time in Chapter 4, where we compare marketing of big firms with marketing of small firms. First, however, after having clarified one part of the main title of this book, that is, 'marketing', we should clarify the second part of it as well, that is, 'entrepreneurial'. This will be done in the next chapter.

NOTES

1. *In Search of Excellence*, a best-selling business book of the 1980s by Tom Peters and

Robert Waterman (1984, New York: Harper & Row) stated that even the most profitable and successful companies often were those that were 'second to the market and proud of it'.

2. Michel Porter's famous model for how to succeed strategically was based on the idea that one should gain a sustainable competitive advantage in the industry to which one belongs (Porter, Michel (1980), *Competitive Strategy*, New York: Free Press and Porter, Michel (1985), *Competitive Advantage*, New York: Free Press).

3. Smith, A. (1776), *The Wealth of Nations*, Reprinted 1991, London: Everyman's Library.

4. Sheth, J., D. Gardner and D.E. Garrett (1988), *Marketing Theory, Evolution and Evaluation*, New York: Wiley, pp. 73-4.

5. Ibid., p. 37, here Charles Parlin is given credit for generating the initial classification system in 1912 published in *Department Store Report*, Volume B (October).

6. Copeland, M. (1923), 'The Relations of Consumer Buying Habits to Marketing Methods', *Harvard Business Review*, **1** (April), pp. 282-9.

7. Aspinwall, L. (1958), 'The Characteristics of Goods and Parallel Systems Theories', in Eugene J. Kelly and Willam Lazer (eds), *Managerial Marketing*, Homewood, IL: Richard D. Irwin.

8. Bucklin, L. (1962), 'Retail Strategy and the Classification of Consumer Goods', *Journal of Marketing*, **27** (October), pp. 50-55.

9. Butler, R.S. (1923), *Marketing and Merchandising*, New York: Alexander Hamilton Institute, pp. 20-21.

10. Shaw, A. (1912), 'Some Problems in Market Distribution', *Quarterly Journal of Economics*, **12** (99), pp. 1, 703-65.

11. See, in particular, Porter (1985).

12. There were other influences involved as well, of course, for example, from geography (by, for instance, the law of gravity; Reilly, W.J. (1931), *The Law of Retail Gravitation*, Austin, TX: University of Texas), from Alderson's functionalist approach to marketing (Alderson, W. (1954), 'Factors Governing the Development of Marketing Channels', in Clewitt, R.W. (ed.), *Channels for Manufactured Products*, Homewood, IL: Richard D. Irwin, pp. 5-34; see also Alderson, W. (1957), *Marketing Behavior and Executive Action: A Functionalist Approach to Marketing Theory*, Homewood, IL: Richard D. Irwin) and from systems thinking as applied to marketing, see, for example, Fisk, G. (1967), *Marketing Systems: An Introductory Analysis*, New York: Harper & Row; Dowling, G.R. (1983), 'The Application of General Systems Theory to an Analysis of Marketing Systems', *Journal of Macromarketing*, **3** (Fall), pp. 22-32; Howard, J.A. (1983), 'Marketing Theory of the Firm', *Journal of Marketing*, **47** (Fall), pp. 90-100.

13. See, for example, Holloway R.J. and Hancock, R.S. (1964), *The Environment of Marketing Behavior: Selections from the Literature*, New York: John Wiley & Sons; Fisk (1967).

14. Hunt, S. (1977), 'The Three Dichotomies Models of Marketing: An Elaboration of Issues', in Slater, Charles C. (ed.), *Macro-Marketing: Distributive Processes from a Societal Perspective*, Boulder, CO: Business Research Division, Graduate School of Business Administration, University of Colorado, p. 56.

15. Kotler, P. (1986), 'Megamarketing', *Harvard Business Review*, **64** (March–April), pp. 117-24.

16. Ibid., p. 119.

17. Arndt, J. (1979), 'Toward a Concept of Domesticated Markets', *Journal of Marketing*, **43** (Fall), pp. 69-75.

18. See, for example, Katona, G. (1953), 'Rational Behavior and Economic Behavior', *Psychological Review*, **60** (September), pp. 307-18; Howard, J. and Sheth, J. (1969), *The Theory of Buyer Behavior*, New York: Wiley; Howard, (1963), *Marketing; Executive and Buyer Behavior*, New York: Columbia University Press.

19. Sheth, et al. (1988)

20. Bauer, R. (1960), 'Consumer Behavior as Risk Taking', in Robert S. Hancock (ed.), *Dynamic Marketing for a Changing World*, Chicago: AMA, pp. 389-98.

21. Bettman, J.R. (1979), *An Information Processing Theory of Consumer Choice*, Reading,

MA: Addison-Wesley.

22. Bourne, F.S. (1965), 'Group Influences in Marketing and Public Relations', in J.V. McNeal (ed.), *Dimensions of Consumer Behavior*, New York: Appleton-Century-Crofts, pp. 137-46.

23. Martineau, P. (1958), 'Social Classes and Spending Behavior', *Journal of Marketing*, **23** (October), pp. 121-9.

24. Krugman, H. (1965), 'The Impact on Television Advertising: Learning Without Involvement', *Public Opinion Quarterly*, **29** (Fall), pp. 349-59.

25. Wells, W.D. (1975) 'Psychographics: A Critical Review', *Journal of Marketing Research*, **12** (May), pp. 196-213.

26. Hansen, F. (1972), *Consumer Choice Behavior: A Cognitive Theory*, New York: Free Press.

27. Belk, Russel W. (1974), 'An Exploratory Assessment of Situational Effects in Buyer Behavior', *Journal of Marketing*, **38**, pp. 156-63.

28. Keith, R. (1960), 'The Marketing Revolution', *Journal of Marketing*, **24** (January), p. 35.

29. Howard, J.A. (1957), *Marketing Management: Analysis and Decisions*, Homewood, IL: Richard D. Irwin.

30. McCarty, E.J. (1960), *Basic Marketing: A Managerial Approach*, Homewood, IL: Richard D. Irwin.

31. Bennett, P.D. (ed.) (1995), *Dictionary of Marketing Terms* (2nd edn), Chicago: AMA.

32. McKitterick, B. (1957), 'What is the Marketing Management Concept', in Frank Bass (ed.), *The Frontiers of Marketing Thought and Action*, Chicago: AMA, pp. 71-2; Keith, R.J. (1960), 'The Marketing Revolution', *Journal of Marketing*, **24** (January), pp. 35-8.

33. Levitt, T. (1960), 'Marketing Myopia', *Harvard Business Review*, **38** (November/December), pp. 45-6.

34. McCarty, (1960); Borden, N.H. (1964), 'The Concept of the Marketing Mix', *Journal of Advertising Research*, Advertising Research Foundation, Inc. (June), pp. 2-7.

35. Smith, Wendell R. (1956), 'Product Differentiation and Market Segmentation as Alternative Marketing Strategies', *Journal of Marketing*, **21** (July), pp. 3-8.

36. Levitt, T. (1965), 'Exploit the Product Life Cycle', *Harvard Business Review*, **43** (November/December), pp. 81-94.

37. Ries, A. and J. Trout (1981), *Positioning: The Battle For Your Mind*, New York: McGraw-Hill.

38. Narver J. and S.F. Slater (1990), 'The Effects of Market Orientation on Business Profitability', *Journal of Marketing*, **54** (October), pp. 20-35.

39. McCarty (1960).

40. Kotler, P. (2000), *Marketing Management, The Millennium Edition*, Upper Saddle River, NJ: Prentice-Hall, p. 87.

41. Webster, F.E. Jr. (1992), 'The Changing Role of Marketing in the Corporation', *Journal of Marketing*, **56** (October), 1-17.

42. Oxenfeldt, A.R. (1966), *Executive Action in Marketing*, Belmont, CA: Wadsworth, pp. 36-9.

43. Kelley, E. (1972), *Marketing Planning and Competitive Strategy*, Englewood Cliffs, NJ: Prentice-Hall, p. 54.

44. See, for example: Håkansson, H. (ed.) 1982), *International Marketing and Purchasing of Industrial Goods - An Interactive Approach*, Chichester: John Wiley & Sons; Webster (1992); Grönroos, C. (1990), *Service Management and Marketing Managing the Moments of Truth in Service Competition*, Lexington, MA: Free Press/Lexington Books; Grönroos, C. (1994), 'Quo Vadis, Marketing? Toward a Relationship Marketing Paradigm', *Journal of Marketing Management*, **10**, pp. 347-60; Gummesson, E. (1999), *Total Relationship Marketing: From the 4Ps - Product, Price, Promotion, Place - of Traditional Marketing Management to the 30Rs - The Thirty Relations,* Oxford: Butterworth-Heinemann; Brown, S. (1995), *Postmodern Marketing*, London: Routledge.

45. Bucklin, L. (1966), *A Theory of Distribution Channel Structure*, Berkeley, CA: Institute of Business and Economic Research, University of California.

46. Dwyer, F. Robert and M. Ann Welsh (1985), 'Environmental Relationships of the Internal Political Economy of Marketing Channels', *Journal of Marketing Research*, **22** (November), pp. 397–414.

47. Ridgeway, V. (1957), 'Administration of Manufacturer–Dealer Systems', *Administrative Science Quarterly*, **1** (March), pp. 464–83.

48. Mallen, B. (1963), 'A Theory of Retailer–Supplier Conflict, Control and Cooperation', *Journal of Retailing*, **39** (Summer), pp. 24–32, 51.

49. Gill, L. and L.W. Stern (1969), 'Role and Role Theory in Distribution Channels Systems', in Lou Stern (ed.), *Distribution Channels: Behavioral Dimensions*, Boston, MA: Houghton Mifflin, pp. 22–47.

50. Stern L. and R.H. Gorman (1969), 'Conflicts in Distribution Channels: An Exploration', in Stern (ed.), pp.156–175.

51. El-Ansary, A. and L. Stern (1972), 'Power Measurement in the Distribution Channel', *Journal of Marketing Research*, **9** (February), pp. 47–52.

52. Stern, L. and Torger Reve (1980), 'Distribution Channels as Political Economies: A Framework for Comparative Analysis', *Journal of Marketing*, **44** (3), Summer, pp. 52–64.

53. Industrial Marketing Committee Review Board (1954), 'Fundamental Differences Between Industrial and Consumer Marketing', *Journal of Marketing*, **19** (October), pp. 152–8.

54. Robinson, P.J., C.W. Faris and Yoram Wind (1967*), Industrial Buying and Creative Marketing*, Boston, MA: Allyn & Bacon.

55. Webster, F.E. Jr. and Y. Wind (1972), 'A General Model for Understanding Organizational Buying Behavior', *Journal of Marketing*, **36** (April), pp. 12–19.

56. Sheth, J.N. (1973), 'A Model of Industrial Buyer Behavior', *Journal of Marketing*, **37** (October), pp. 50–56.

57. See for example Håkansson (ed.) (1982).

58. Gummesson, E. (1977), *Marknadsföring och inköp av konsulttjänster* [Marketing and Purchase of Consultancy Services], Stockholm: Stockholm University; Normann, R. (1978), 'Kritiska faktorer vid ledning av serviceföretag' [Critical factors for management in service firms], in *Utvecklingsstrategier för svenskt servicekunnande*, Stockholm: SIAR; Gummesson, E. (1979), *Models of Professional Service Marketing*, Stockholm: LIBER/MTC; Grönroos, C. (1979), 'Marknadsföring av tjänster. En studie av marknadsfunktionen i tjänsteföretag' [Marketing of services. A study of the marketing function of service firms], dissertation from Swedish School of Economics and Business Administration, Helsinki, Finland, in Swedish with English summary, Stockholm: Akademilitteratur/MTC; Grönroos, C. (1983), *Strategic Management and Marketing in the Service Sector*, Cambridge, MA: Marketing Science Institute; Normann, R. (1984), *Service Management*, Chichester: Wiley. For an overview of the evolution of the Nordic schools service marketing, see: Grönroos, C and E. Gummesson (eds) (1985), *Service Marketing – Nordic Schools Perspective*, Stockholm: Stockholm University, Series R:2.

59. See, for example, Judd, R.C. (1964), 'The Case for Redefining Services', *Journal of Marketing*, **28** (January), pp. 58–9; Shostack, G. Lynn (1977), 'Breaking Free from Product Marketing', *Journal of Marketing*, April, pp. 73–80; Berry, L.L. (1980), 'Services Marketing Is Different', *Business*, May–June, pp. 24–30.

60. Burenstam Linder, S. (1961), *An Essay on Trade and Transformation*, New York, NY: John Wiley.

61. Vernon, R. (1966), 'International Investment and International Trade in Product Life Cycle', *Quarterly Journal of Economics*, **80**, May, pp. 190–207.

62. Simon, H. (1947), *Administrative Behavior*, New York: Macmillan.

63. Cyert R.M. and J.G. March (1963), *A Behavioral Theory of the Firm*, Englewood Cliffs, NJ: Prentice-Hall.

64. See, for example, Johansson, J. and J.-E. Vahlne (1977), 'The Internationalization Process of the Firm – A Model of Knowledge Development and Increasing Foreign Market Commitments', *Journal of International Business Studies*, Spring/Summer, pp. 23–32.

65. Calvert, A.L. (1981), 'A Synthesis of Foreign Direct Investment Theories and Theories of the Multinational Firm', *Journal of International Business Studies*, Spring/Summer, pp. 43-59.

66. Keith, R. (1960), 'The Marketing Revolution', *Journal of Marketing*, **24** (January), p. 35.

67. Hunt, S.D. (1976), 'The Nature and Scope of Marketing', *Journal of Marketing*, **40**, July, pp. 17-28.

68. Kotler, P. and S.J. Levy (1969), 'Broadening the concept of marketing', *Journal of Marketing*, **33**, January, pp. 10-15.

69. Brown (1995), p. 35.

70. Kotler and Levy (1969), p. 15.

71. Brown (1995), p. 35-36.

72. Kotler, P. (1972), 'A Generic Concept of Marketing', *Journal of Marketing*, **36**, April, pp. 46-54.

73. Gummesson, E. (1975), *Marknadsfunktionen i företaget* [The marketing function in the firm], Stockholm: Norstedts, in Swedish; Grönroos (1990).

74. Gummesson, E. (1990), *The Part-Time Marketer*, Karlstad: CTF Research Report 90:3; Gummesson, E. (1991), 'Marketing Revisited: The Crucial Role of the Part-time Marketers', *European Journal of Marketing*, **25** (2), pp. 60-67.

75. Kotler (2000), p. 29. On page 19 a slightly modernized version of the marketing concept is used: 'The marketing concept holds the key to achieving its organizational goals consists of the company being more effective than competitors in creating, delivering, and communicating customer value to its chosen target markets'. This change in the interpretation of the marketing concept is made without any other alterations in the previous and following texts compared to previous editions. This definition is also used in Kotler, P. (2001), *A Framework for Marketing Management*, Upper Saddle River, NJ: Prentice-Hall, pp. 12 and 17.

76. Kotler, (2001), p. 11.

77. See Kohli, A.K. and B.J. Jaworski (1990), 'Market Orientation. The Construct, Research Propositions, and Management Implications', *Journal of Marketing* (April), pp. 1-18; Narver and Slater (1990), pp. 20-35; Jaworski, B.J. and A.K Kohli (1993), 'Market Orientation: Antecedents and Consequences', *Journal of Marketing*, **57** (July), pp. 53-70.

78. Kohli and Jaworski (1990), p.13.

79. See, for example, Narver and Slater (1990), pp. 20-35; Slater, S. and J. Narver (1994), 'Market Orientation, Customer Value, and Superior Performance', *Business Horizons*, March–April, pp. 22-28; Slater, S.F. and J.C. Narver (1995), 'Market Orientation and the Learning Organisation', *Journal of Marketing*, **59** (July), pp. 63-74; Slater, S and J. Narver (1994), 'Competitive Strategy in the Market Focused Business', *Journal of Market Focused Management*, **II**, pp. 59-74.

80. Langerak, F. (1997), 'The Effects of Market Orientation on Business Performance in Industrial Markets' (in Dutch), unpublished PhD thesis, Erasmus University, Rotterdam.

81. Langerak, F., H. Commandeur, R. Frambach, and M. Napel (1997), 'The Moderating Influence of Strategy on the Market Orientation–Performance Relationship', in William M. Pride and G. Tomas M. Hult (eds), *Enhancing Knowledge Development in Marketing*, 1997 AMA Educators' Proceedings, Volume 8, Chicago, IL: American Marketing Association, pp. 147-8.

82. Kotler (1972), p. 48.

83. Hunt, S. (1983), 'General Theories and the Fundamental Explanada of Marketing', *Journal of Marketing*, **47** (Fall), pp. 12-13.

84. Oliver, G. (1990), *Marketing Today*, Hemel Hempstead: Prentice-Hall, p. 114.

85. Bagozzi, R.P. (1974), 'Marketing as an Organized Behavioral Systems of Exchange', *Journal of Marketing*, **38** (4), (October), pp. 77-81; Bagozzi, R.P. (1975), 'Marketing as Exchange', *Journal of Marketing*, **39** (4), (October), pp. 32-9.

86. See work in industrial marketing by the IMP group, for example, Ford, D. (ed.) (1990), *Understanding Business Markets: Interactions, Relationships and Networks*, London: Academic Press; Ford, D. (ed.) (1998), *Managing Business Relationships*, Chichester, UK:

John Wiley & Sons; in service marketing, for example: Gummesson (1999).

87. This definition is from Grönroos, C. (1990), 'Relationships Approach to Marketing in Service Contexts: The Marketing and Organizational Behavior Interface', *Journal of Business Research*, **20**, pp. 3-11:5. Very similar definitions are found, for example, in Grönroos, C. (1989), 'Defining Marketing: A Market-Oriented Approach', *European Journal of Marketing*, **23** (1), pp. 53-60: 57-58; Grönroos, C. (1990), *Service Management and Marketing: Managing the Moments of Truth in Service Competition*, Lexington, MA: D.C. Heath/Lexington Books, p. 138.

88. See, for example, Johanson J. and L.G. Mattsson (1993), '*The Markets-as-Networks Tradition in Sweden*', manuscript to be published in G. Laurent (ed.), *Research Traditions in Marketing*, Dordrecht: Kluwer.

89. Håkansson, (ed.) (1982).

90. Davies, J.M. (1992), *The Essential Guide to Database Marketing*, Maidenhead: McGraw-Hill.

91. Berry, L.L. (1983), 'Relationship Marketing', in L.L. Berry, G.L. Shostack and G.D. Upah (eds), *Emerging Perspectives of Service Marketing*, Chicago, IL: American Marketing Association, pp. 25-28.

92. See, for example, Grönroos, C. (1991), 'The Marketing Strategy Continuum: A Marketing Concept for the 1990s', *Management Decision*, **79** (1), pp. 7-23; Gummesson (1999).

93. Gummesson, E. (1995), *Relationsmarknadsföring: Från 4P till 30 R*, Malmö, Sweden: Liber Hermods, in English translation: *Total Relationship Marketing: From the 4Ps - Product, Price, Promotion, Place - of Traditional Marketing Management to the 30Rs - The Thirty Relations,* Oxford: Butterworth-Heinemann.

94. Li, F., B.A. Greenberg and T. Li (1997), 'Toward a General Definition of Relationship Marketing', in William M. Pride and G. Tomas M. Hult (eds), *Enhancing Knowledge Development in Marketing,* 1997 AMA Educators' Proceedings, Volume 8, Chicago, IL: American Marketing Association, pp. 238-44.

95. For example, Jackson, Barbara Bund (1985), *Winning and Keeping Industrial Customers*, Lexington, KY: Lexington Books.

96. Doyle, S.X. and G.T. Roth (1992), 'Selling and Sales Management in Action: The Use of Insight Coaching to Improve Relationship Selling', *Journal of Personal Selling and Sales Management*, **12** (Winter), pp. 59-64.

97. Berry (1983), p. 25.

98. Hunt, S.D. and R.M. Morgan (1994), 'Relationship Marketing in the Era of Network Competition', *Marketing Management*, **3** (1), pp. 19-28: 23. See also Morgan R.M. and S.D. Hunt (1994), 'The Commitment-Trust Theory of Relationship Marketing', *Journal of Marketing*, **58**, pp. 20-38: 22.

99. Parvatiyar, A. and Jagdish Sheth (1994), 'Paradigm Shift in Marketing Theory and Approach: The Emergence of Relationship Marketing', in J. Sheth and A. Parvatiyar (eds), *Relationship Marketing: Theory Methods and Applications*, Atlanta, GA: Centre for Relationship Marketing, Emory University.

100. Coviello, Nicole, R.J. Brodie and H. Munro (1997), 'Understanding Contemporary Marketing: Development of a Classification Scheme', *Journal of Marketing Management* **13** (6), pp. 501-22.

101. Brodie, R.J., N. Coviello, R.W. Brookes and Victoria Little (1997), 'Towards a Paradigm Shift in Marketing? An Examination of Current Marketing Practices', *Journal of Marketing Management*, **13**, pp. 383-406: 402.

102. Schlossberg, H. (1992), 'Packaged-goods Experts: Micro-marketing the Only Way to Go', *Marketing News*, **26** (14), p. 8.

103. Rapp, S. and T.L. Collins (1990), *The Great Marketing Turnaround: The Age of the Individual and How to Profit from It*, Englewood Cliffs, NJ: Prentice-Hall.

104. Davies (1992).

105. McKenna, R. (1991), 'Marketing Is Everything', *Harvard Business Review*, **69** (1), pp. 65-79.

106. Nilson, T.H. (1992), *Value-added Marketing: Marketing Management for Superior Results*, Maidenhead: McGraw-Hill.

107. Cova, B. and C. Svanfeldt (1992), 'Marketing beyond Marketing in a Post-modern Europe: The Creation of Societal Innovations, in K.G. Grunert and D. Fuglede (eds), *Marketing for Europe - Marketing for the Future*, Aarhus: EMAC, pp. 155-71.
108. Levinson, J.C. (1993), *Guerilla Marketing - How to Make Big Profits from a Small Business*, London: Judy Piatkus, GB printing in 1994.
109. Nilson, T.H. (1995), *Chaos Marketing*, Maidenhead: McGraw-Hill.
110. Brown (1995).

3. Entrepreneurship: creating new business ventures

INTRODUCTION

'Marketing' was the theme of the last chapter. The theme of this chapter is the other half of the main title of this book, that is, 'entrepreneurial'. The word 'entrepreneurship' is on many lips and contained in many agendas today. This will be discussed first in this chapter.

The next step is to provide a brief summary of the long history of entrepreneurship research. In spite of this long history, we shall see that the opinion of what entrepreneurship means today is far from settled or generally accepted. When we have presented a few examples of attempts to classify research on entrepreneurship today, we shall suggest our own classification system, that is:

- the role of entrepreneurship in society;
- entrepreneurial traits and psychology;
- entrepreneurial environments/intrapreneurship; and
- entrepreneurial processes.

One approach to society and life, is to try to 'explain' it. Another approach is try to 'understand' it. We shall draw a distinction between 'explaining' and 'understanding' and discuss what it means for researching entrepreneurship. Most research on entrepreneurship (and until recently the only one) is of an explanatory type.

The present popularity of entrepreneurship has led to a plethora of contexts, where it is accepted and welcome – sometimes imposed. This, in turn, has led to an extreme variety of opinions of what entrepreneurship and related concepts are all about, but, occasionally, to confusion and to a long line of myths. To bring some order to the area and a focus to this book, one fundamental trio of concepts will be discussed next in this chapter, that is, 'management', 'leadership' and 'entrepreneurship'.

We shall finish this chapter by presenting our own view of 'entrepreneurship', a view which we think is adequate in the new economic era.

ENTREPRENEURSHIP: A PART OF MODERN LIFE

Exactly how the present entrepreneurial movement came into being and is still going strong is not clear, but may well be due to a number of interacting factors.[1]

One factor was the revival of small businesses in Europe as well as in the United States. This was supported by the change in the ruling economic – political ideology – from Keynesianism to a radical pro-market ideology. That change came about with the coming to power in 1979–80 of Margaret Thatcher (in the UK) and Ronald Reagan in the United States. Practically all business schools have by now at least one course in entrepreneurship, and it is increasingly being realized that business people of today need more entrepreneurship and leadership and less management.[2]

Another factor behind the present popularity of entrepreneurship is the widespread deep concern with unemployment and the general belief that only the creation of new businesses can provide jobs on a sufficient scale in a society with a shrinking industrial labour force:

> It is widely recognized that entrepreneurs – people who formulate new ideas, recognize opportunities and translate these into added value to society by assuming the risk of starting a business – are a major source of economic growth for many economies.[3]

For any business to survive in a global economy, it is increasingly realized that constant change and innovation are simply a necessity. Change is experienced as a foe, if it takes place beyond a person's control and it is even a threat if he or she does not understand it. A person may, however, experience change as a friend if a person has the feeling that he or she can control it. It may even be seen as an opportunity if the person knows a way to use it to his or her advantage.

If there is one word to characterize our modern situation as social human beings, that word could be 'change'. Almost no matter how entrepreneurship is presented and discussed today, it is about change. It is commonly about seizing opportunity, about living in change, even providing change. That is probably the single most important reason why entrepreneurship is such a hot topic today.

One question, which is difficult to answer, is to what extent the new economic era makes us identify more entrepreneurs or to what extent the total number of entrepreneurs actually is higher!

ENTREPRENEURSHIP: A BRIEF HISTORY

Writing the history of how entrepreneurship has been understood over the years was not a purpose in itself. Like the description of the history of marketing in the last chapter its aim was to find out how history has influenced our current understanding of the subject.

Richard Cantillon, a French economist of Irish descent, is credited with giving the concept of entrepreneurship a role in economics by recognizing persons involved in such activity in eighteenth-century France.[4] He associated entrepreneurs with the 'risk-bearing' activity in the economy. This risk meant to pay a certain price for a product to resell it at an uncertain price, thereby *consciously* making decisions about obtaining and using resources.[5] In England during the same period, the Industrial Revolution was evolving, with the entrepreneur playing a visible role in risk taking and the transformation of resources.[6] The originally French term 'entrepreneur' was incorporated into the English language.[7]

Cantillon was followed by other economists.[8] Adam Smith spoke of the 'enterpriser' as an individual who undertook the formation of an organization for commercial purposes. Entrepreneurship is the force that is driving his 'invisible hand', at least on the supply side. In Smith's view, entrepreneurs reacted to economic change, thereby becoming the economic agents who transformed demand into supply. Adam Smith, however, did not put much stress on entrepreneurship in economic development. Jean-Baptiste Say broadened the definition of entrepreneurship to include the concept of combining factors of production. The entrepreneur was a coordinator of those factors and was also a risk taker in this role. An entrepreneur, according to Say, had exceptional insights into society's needs and was able to fulfil them.

By the end of the nineteenth century, economics turned from a macro-economic interest to a stronger focus on micro-economic issues. The interest in entrepreneurship moved from Europe to the United States.

The modern concept of entrepreneurship was introduced by Joseph Schumpeter, an Austrian–American economist. He defined entrepreneurs and entrepreneurship as follows:[9]

> The carrying out of new combinations we call 'enterprise'; the individuals whose function it is to carry them out we call 'entrepreneurs'. These concepts are at once broader and narrower than usual. Broader, because in the first place we call entrepreneurs not only those 'independent' businessmen in an exchange economy who are usually so designated, but all who actually fulfill the function by which we define the concept, even if they are, as is becoming the rule, 'dependent' employees of a company, like managers, members of boards of directors, and so forth, or even if their actual power to perform the entrepreneurial function has any other foundations, such as the control of a majority of shares. As it is the carrying out of new combinations that constitutes the entrepreneur, it is not necessary that he should be permanently connected with an individual firm; many 'financiers', 'promoters', and so forth are not, and still may be entrepreneurs in our sense. On the other hand, our concept is narrower than the traditional one in that it does not

include all heads of firms or managers of industrialists, who merely may operate established business, but only those who actually perform that function. ... But whatever the type, everyone is an entrepreneur only when he actually 'carries out new combinations', and loses that character as soon as he has built up his business, when he settles down to running it as other people run their businesses.

Schumpeter introduced the entrepreneur as an *innovator*:[10]

The function of entrepreneurs is to reform or revolutionize the pattern of production by exploiting an invention or, more generally, an untried technological possibility for producing a new commodity or producing an old one in a new way, opening a new source of supply of materials or a new outlet for products, by reorganizing a new industry.

Schumpeter was perhaps the first economist to see the entrepreneur as a person creatively destructing that equilibrium and optimization which had been the focus of the majority of economists for more than 100 years.

One common opinion is that entrepreneurs are looking for and exploiting opportunities. One initiator of this thought in the area of economics was Israel Kirzner,[11] who saw entrepreneurs as those who look for disequilibria on the market, who coordinate resources more effectively than before and, as a consequence, create a new equilibrium.

We can summarize the contribution of economists to theories of entrepreneurs and entrepreneurship as follows:[12]

- Entrepreneurs are risk takers (Richard Cantillon).
- Entrepreneurs are coordinators and planners of the productive process, principal agents of production, mediators (Jean-Baptiste Say).
- Entrepreneurship = Management (Alfred Marshall).
- Entrepreneurs provide capital (Adam Smith and David Ricardo).
- Entrepreneurs are innovators (Joseph Schumpeter).
- Entrepreneurs exploit opportunities (Israel Kirzner).
- Entrepreneurs are industrial leaders.
- Entrepreneurs are speculators.
- Entrepreneurs are negotiators.
- Entrepreneurs are sources of information.

What still seems to be with us as business scholars in many definitions of entrepreneurship from the economic era of researching the topic is its association with:

- risk-taking;
- management;

- innovation; and
- exploiting opportunities.

Some examples of these are:

> Entrepreneurship is the dynamic process of creating incremental wealth. The wealth is created by individuals who assume the major risks in terms of equity, time, and/or career commitment or provide value for some product or service. The product or service may or may not be new or unique but value must somehow be infused by the entrepreneur by receiving and allocating the necessary skills and resources.[13]

> Entrepreneurship is the ability to create and build a vision from practically nothing: fundamentally it is a human, creative act. It is the application of energy to initiating and building an enterprise or organization, rather than just watching and analyzing. This vision requires a willingness to take calculated risks – both personal and financial – and then to do everything possible to reduce the chances of failure. Entrepreneurship also includes the ability to build an entrepreneurial or venture team to complement your own skills and talents. It is the knack of sensing an opportunity where others see chaos, contradiction, and confusion. It is possessing the know-how to find, marshal, and control resources (often owned by others).[14]

> Entrepreneurship has been defined as the process of identifying opportunities in the marketplace, marshaling the resources to pursue those opportunities, and committing the actions and resources necessary to exploit the opportunities for long-term personal gain.[15]

> Entrepreneurship is the process of creating something different with value by devoting the necessary time and effort, assuming the accompanying financial, psychic, and social risks, and receiving rewards of monetary and personal satisfaction.[16]

> Today, an entrepreneur is an innovator or developer who recognizes and seizes opportunities; converts those opportunities into workable/marketable ideas; adds value through time, effort, money, or skills; assumes the risks of the competitive marketplace to implement these ideas; and realizes the rewards from these efforts.[17]

Out of the four qualities just mentioned in this book we shall stress mainly *innovation* and *exploiting opportunities*. We find the concept of risk to be overused when talking about entrepreneurs today. Not only is risk a very multifaceted concept. Objectively, entrepreneurs are facing financial as well as career, family/social and psychic risks.[18] But life is full of risks – for everybody! Also, subjectively, entrepreneurs often neglect risk and are more optimistic than other people.[19] Apparently the perceived context (knowledge and situational characteristics) is a more important determinant of entrepreneurial risk taking than personality.[20] Entrepreneurs may give more weight to the likelihood of missing out on a strategic opportunity than to the likelihood of a new venture failing.[21] Finally, in the new economic era it seems more of a risk *not* doing anything than doing at least something!

ENTREPRENEURSHIP: A GENERALLY ACCEPTED CONCEPT TODAY?

In spite of centuries of research on entrepreneurship, until the middle of the twentieth century practically exclusively within economics, many scholars claim today that the area can be seen as a young field of research (at least from a business point of view) and critics claim that the field is very wide without clear limits and without clear definitions of central concepts:[22]

> Along with the increase in entrepreneurship has come growth in the number of endowed chairs in business schools; positions in research institutions, foundations, professional organizations; and journals in the field of entrepreneurship. Yet in spite of those developments, entrepreneurship researchers complain that the field lacks a distinct professional identity, one defined by a unified body of knowledge based on generally accepted social science theories. Surveys describe the field as organized by camps, where the lack of cross-level and cross-disciplinary interaction tends to obscure the overall picture of what gives rise to entrepreneurship. Many commentators on the field have called for an increase in the quality, interdisciplinary nature, and development of unifying schemes to integrate pieces of research on entrepreneurship.[23]

One problem is that entrepreneurs are found in all professions – education, medicine, research, law, architecture, engineering, social work and distribution, just to give a few examples. It is, therefore, hard to include all types of entrepreneurship in a general definition.[24]

Some feel that the search for a definition of an entrepreneur has not progressed much since 1971, when Peter Kilby related the search for a definition of an entrepreneur to that for the Heffalump in *Winnie the Pooh*:

> The search for the course of dynamic entrepreneurial performance has much in common with hunting the Heffalump. The Heffalump is a large and rather important animal. He has been hunted by many individuals using various ingenious trapping devices, but no one so far has succeeded in capturing him. All who claim to have caught sight of him report that he is enormous, but they disagree on his particularities. Not having explored his current habitat with sufficient care, some hunters have used as bait their own favorite dishes and have then tried to persuade people that what they caught was a Heffalump. However, very few are convinced, and the search goes on.[25]

Let us, in spite of this lack of clarity, try to summarize the standing of entrepreneurship research today.

EXISTING ENTREPRENEURIAL KNOWLEDGE

Introduction

Until the 1950s, the majority of definitions and references to entrepreneurship came from economists. From then on, other academic disciplines also recognized entrepreneurship. During the past half a century, entrepreneurship has been growing as a recognized phenomenon in society. We have mentioned two possible reasons for this growth, new political–economic orientation in some leading countries and the need for new jobs to be created. Other reasons could be as follows:[26]

- Sagging productivity growths in the industrial economies redirected interest to the role of business management and of entrepreneurs. Growth of 5 per cent or more of an economy was no longer taken for granted.
- High levels of marginal taxes and other social contributions were, in the eyes of some economic actors, factors limiting the interest to venture into new business projects; they restricted the willingness to take on high financial risks associated with such projects.
- Slowing growth in the economy of many countries underlined the importance of new sectors like electronics, robotics, telecommunications, microprocessing and so on.
- Too many regulations of industry were seen as a negative factor among people interested in organizing new businesses. Many countries, therefore, reduced the number of such regulations and started to support the introduction of new business ventures.

Economists always tried, with few exceptions, to place entrepreneurs in their macroeconomic models, while business scholars attempt to find out who are the entrepreneurs and what they actually do.

One sociologist[27] classifies entrepreneurship literature into two schools: one taking the *supply-side* perspective and the other, the *demand-side* perspective: 'The supply-side school focuses on the availability of suitable individuals to occupy entrepreneurial roles; the demand-side, on the number and nature of the entrepreneurial roles that need to be filled.'[28]

Stevenson and Jarillo[29] categorize entrepreneurial research on what question the researcher was interested in. The three groups were:

- *What* happens when entrepreneurs are acting?
- *Why* do entrepreneurs act the way they do?
- *How* do they act?

Another way to classify entrepreneurship research could be to look at entrepreneurs from the level of study employed,[30] that is, to look at entrepreneurs from a social, business or individual level.

Views on entrepreneurship over the years could also be presented as consecutive eras, as in Table 3.1.[31]

Over the years, the development has been such that present understanding of entrepreneurship (and entrepreneurs) covers more ground. Originally intended to mean only privately owned, new, independent upstarts in the business sector of an economy, entrepreneurship has come to include new businesses within existing already established corporations, so-called 'intrapreneurship',[32] and even non-profit organizations may be counted as entrepreneurial today. At the same time, attempts have been made to be more specific in terms of required behaviour for a person to be called entrepreneurial.

So, there are many ways to classify our present understanding of entrepreneurship. The fourfold classification used in this book is:

- the role of entrepreneurship in society;
- entrepreneurial traits and psychology;
- entrepreneurial environments/intrapreneurship; and
- entrepreneurial processes.

The above classification provides a natural background to the entrepreneurial focus in this book. It will be clear that some special aspects of entrepreneurship are excluded, for instance, entrepreneurial heroes, female entrepreneurship, ethnic entrepreneurship and entrepreneurship outside the business area. However, any attempt to classify must be limited and should be focused. Ours is a focus on entrepreneurship in the new economic era, towards which the above four categories, covering the mainstream of entrepreneurship research going on today, will lead us.

The Role of Entrepreneurship in Society

Looking at entrepreneurship in the growth and development of a society at large, there are three kinds of causal arguments.[33] Many researchers see entrepreneurship as a significant factor, maybe the most significant causal factor, in the process of economic growth and development of societies. Differences in entrepreneurship are consequently assumed to cause their different rates of growth and development. According to this opinion, societies, which contain individuals willing and eager to fulfil the entrepreneurial function or role, can accelerate the growth and development process; those societies, which lack this necessary component, will fall behind.

The advocates of this opinion are probably attributing the amount of

Table 3.1   Economic eras and the idea of entrepreneurship

Era	Idea of the human being	Idea of entrepreneurship
Traditional • Consumption and production in the same entity • Social order created by feudalism and the crafts system	God's unique creation, whose place in society was based on his class at birth	Entrepreneurship started its journey in semantics • Adventurer, risk taker • Project-based assignments from the Crown
Transition from traditional to modern: early 1700s to late 1800s Towards industrialization • Feudalism and crafts system broken • Liberalism and democracy as ideals • Demand and supply start to diverge	God's unique creation or an animal among other animals	Entrepreneurship as individual and entrepreneurship as creator of economic success • Entrepreneurship breaks old models of behaviour and old systems, crafts and feudalism • Creates new forms of work and ownership • Innovator, coordinator • Takes responsibility and risks his/her life • Applies new knowledge
Modern: early 1900s Industrialization • Continuous, implied growth • Expanding market • Growing prosperity and the public sector • Full employment • Supply oriented, unhistorical, rationality • Efficiency • Standardization • Bureaucracy, hierarchy, control • Unified culture • The domination of the Western world	From animal to a machine or a part of a system	Entrepreneurship, small business management and ownership • Fighting for its existence in small firms
Postmodern transition: 1970– Postindustrial phase Information society • More complicated environment and systems • Saturation of consumer demand • Demand-oriented fragmented market • Polarization, diversity, discontinuity, unemployment and insecurity • Public sector gets a more complicated role in society	Uniqueness as a universal feature in human being Human being as a feeling entity and social actor Woman as a human being among other human beings	Three forms of entrepreneurship 1. The small enterprise, meaning the individual entrepreneur and his/her firm 2. Intrapreneurship, meaning an organization's collective behaviour 3. Individual, self-oriented entrepreneurship, meaning an individual's self-oriented behaviour Entrepreneurship An instrument for changing the culture

entrepreneurship within a society to a constellation of factors, which in a general sense are non-economic by nature. According to them, entrepreneurship will probably emerge either as a consequence of a specific combination of (social) circumstances, or when a society has a big enough supply of individuals with specific psychological characteristics. In other words, we have here a combination of two groups of factors, causing growth and development (Figure 3.1).

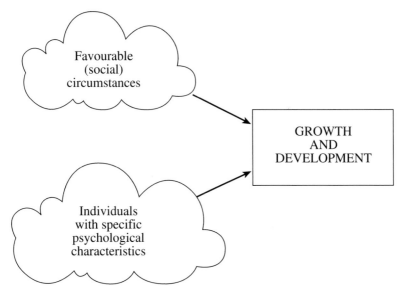

Figure 3.1   Entrepreneurship as a cause of economic growth and development

Others offer an almost opposite argument as far as the importance of entrepreneurship and its causes are concerned. From this point of view, entrepreneurship is not a significant causal factor in economic growth and development; nor are social or psychological factors decisive supporting factors. Entrepreneurship is rather looked upon as fulfilling the function of a leader or a mediator of more basic causes, and these causes are held to be economic in nature. This argument means that economic growth and development (and entrepreneurship) are more likely to emerge in situations where specific economic conditions are most favourable. If they are more favourable, entrepreneurship will, given the basic human motivation to maximize their return, emerge and economic growth and development will be the result. If the economic conditions are not favourable, entrepreneurship will not emerge and the economy of the society will stagnate (Figure 3.2).

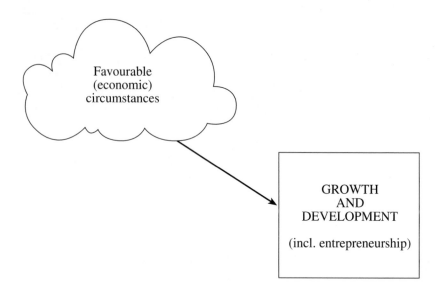

*Figure 3.2   Entrepreneurship as an effect of favourable economic circum-
stances*

Two rather different opinions about the significance of entrepreneurship in
the process of economic growth and development have been presented so far.
The first, where entrepreneurship is seen as a *transformer* or *generator*, that is,
as a significant independent variable causing growth and development, is
usually held by sociologists and psychologists. The second, where
entrepreneurship is seen as a *conductor*, that is, as a dependent variable in
growth and development, is commonly held by economists.

In business (as an academic discipline), entrepreneurship is usually
conceptualized not as a dependent variable, which economists have a tendency
to do, or as an independent variable, which behavioural scientists have done,
but as an intervening variable between prior conditions on one hand and
creation of new business ventures (which in turn causes economic growth and
development) on the other (Figure 3.3).

This third view is favoured in this book, but that is not all. Developments in
the social, technological and economic circumstances have an impact on
entrepreneurship. However, there is also a need to consider and to get a picture
of what type of person might be involved in entrepreneurship.

Entrepreneurial Traits and Psychology

As mentioned earlier, since around the mid-twentieth century,

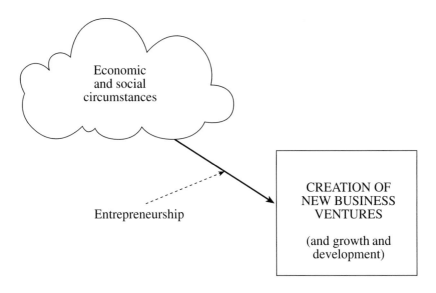

Figure 3.3   Entrepreneurship as an intervening variable

entrepreneurship has, with a few exceptions, disappeared in the economists' models. Behavioural science researchers saw an open field here. One pioneer was David McClelland, who was the first to present empirical studies within the area of entrepreneurship from the point of view of the behavioural sciences. In his famous study *The Achieving Society*,[34] he attempts to explain why countries differ in economic growth and development. McClelland's answer is that the need for achievement of the people living in a country is central to explain such differences.

McClelland's work meant that the personal characteristics of the entrepreneur achieved a prominent position within behavioural science entrepreneurial research during the 1960s and 1970s, that is, to try to answer the question: 'Who are the entrepreneurs?' The idea was that entrepreneurship is done better by people with certain qualities (more specifically, characterized by certain personality traits). Four lists of such qualities (traits) are presented below:

McClelland[35]
- desire for responsibility;
- preference for moderate risk;
- confidence in the ability to succeed;
- desire for immediate feedback;
- high level of energy;
- future orientation;

- skill at organizing;
- value of achievement over money.

Pleitner[36]
- self-confidence;
- perseverance, domination;
- energy, diligence;
- resourcefulness;
- ability to take calculated risks;
- need to achieve;
- creativity;
- initiative;
- flexibility;
- independence;
- foresight;
- dynamism, leadership;
- ability to get along with people and accept criticism;
- profit orientation;
- perceptiveness;
- optimism.

Gibb[37]
- creativity;
- initiative;
- high achievement;
- risk taking (moderate);
- leadership;
- autonomy and independence;
- analytical ability;
- hard work;
- good communication skills.

Kuratko and Hodgetts[38]
- commitment, determination and perseverance;
- drive to achieve;
- opportunity orientation;
- initiative and responsibility;
- persistent problem solving;
- seeking feedback;
- internal locus of control;
- tolerance of ambiguity;
- calculated risk taking;

- integrity and reliability;
- tolerance for failure;
- high energy level;
- creativity and innovativeness;
- vision;
- self-confidence and optimism;
- independence;
- team building.

More generally, a summary of what the literature says about the personality of entrepreneurs could be:[39]

- they have a strong need to achieve and they like challenges;
- they ask much of themselves and they have a high energy level;
- they want to do something out of the ordinary;
- they accept uncertainty, willing to take risks, but they are realistic and are not gamblers;
- they are not set back by various obstacles and they commit themselves long term;
- they are very willing to learn from mistakes and to use feedback;
- they are self-confident and independent, but they network and are able to manage other people, if necessary;
- they have an internal locus of control and a willingness to create their own future;
- they see possibilities, are decisive, take initiatives and act;
- they do not waste time or resources; and
- they show their entrepreneurial talents early in life and they often create more than one venture.

Surprisingly to some, perhaps, efforts to uncover differences between entrepreneurs and others with respect to aspects of personality met with only modest success. Researchers could not pin down clear-cut differences between entrepreneurs and other people with respect to what seemed to be the most relevant dimensions of personality.[40] Thus, as noted by Hatten:[41] 'The conclusions of 30 years of research indicate that there are no personality characteristics that predict who will be a successful entrepreneur. ... Successful small business owners and entrepreneurs come in every shape, size, color, and from all backgrounds.'

Carson et al.[42] offer several limitations of trait approaches to understanding entrepreneurship:

1. They have been unable to differentiate clearly between entrepreneurial

small business owners and equally successful professional executives in more established organizations. This latter group has demonstrated comparable levels of achievement motivation or risk-taking propensity, for instance.

2. Using the trait approach only may fail to identify and prioritize the aspects of a person's personality that are deemed to be particularly entrepreneurial.[43]
3. Trait theories need to recognize that entrepreneurship is a dynamic, constantly changing process. Not only is a person never always and for ever an entrepreneur, different entrepreneurial qualities may be needed in different phases of an entrepreneurial venture.
4. Trait approaches may easily lead to the conclusion that the entrepreneur springs from the cradle with all faculties, drives and qualities preformed, needing only the opportunity to exploit them later in some suitable business environment. If that would be the case, it would be a blow to many entrepreneurial training centres, science parks and, for that matter, large sections of modern business schools.

> Part of the problem with trait approaches arises from how the entrepreneur and entrepreneurship are defined. In the first instance a focus only on the individual who establishes a new venture is arguably too narrow. It fails to recognise sufficiently the entrepreneurial potential of people who work to develop and grow established enterprises. In addition, there is the difficulty raised by the fact that entrepreneurs are not an easily identifiable, homogeneous group. Entrepreneurs, it appears, come in all shapes and sizes, from different backgrounds, with varying motivations and aspirations. They are variously represented and addressed in the literature as opportunists or craftworkers, technical entrepreneurs or so-called intrapreneurs.[44]

However, this is not to say that entrepreneurs are not different from other people. We think we know, for instance:

- There is consistent empirical support suggesting that there is a relationship between entrepreneurship and achievement motivation.[45]
- Women are underrepresented among entrepreneurs.[46]
- A large proportion of self-employed people have parents who themselves were self-employed.[47]
- Entrepreneurship can sometimes be explained by ethnicity.[48] For instance, self-employment is often suggested as a way of establishing a new immigrant group in the economy when other career options are closed for various reasons.[49] Also, ethnic or racial groups differ in their propensity to become self-employed.[50]
- Education and work experience influence entrepreneurs-to-be.[51]

Other circumstantial factors include that there must be a reason for an entrepreneur to start a business. There are basically three reasons why people make the vocational choice of starting a new business venture according to one author:[52]

1. the desire for achievement combined with a sense of independence and autonomy;
2. the desire for a change due to dissatisfaction with present working conditions; and
3. the desire to follow traditional family role models.

There are also potential drawbacks to becoming an entrepreneur which might scare some people off:[53]

*   uncertainty of income;
*   risk of losing one's entire invested capital;
*   long hours and hard work;
*   lower quality of life until the business gets established; and
*   complete responsibility.

Some roles are not seen as entrepreneurship:[54]

1. A person who owns an enterprise or gives the orders is not necessarily an entrepreneur.
2. A person who assumes the risk of his or her capital is not necessarily an entrepreneur.
3. A creative person is not necessarily an entrepreneur.

Also, a team may act as an entrepreneur and it can be misleading if it is taken to refer only to the activity of a sole individual.[55]

Faced with disappointing results in trying to find entrepreneurial traits, many behavioural science researchers turned to a distinctly different approach, which emphasized the potential role of cognitive factors and processes in entrepreneurship, that is, instead of trying to find out who are the entrepreneurs the question became: 'How do entrepreneurs think?'.[56]

According to Delmar and Davidsson,[57] two popular theories in this context are: the theory of planned behaviour;[58] and the theory of self-efficacy.[59]

As a conclusion of this section, we may say that even if behavioural sciences associate entrepreneurs with specific personal characteristics and thinking, these sciences have not come as far (if they ever will) as to say with any greater certainty that persons with specific characteristics and thinking will become entrepreneurs.

However, there are three major outcomes of the discussion in this section, which we shall bring along as we move on in this book:

- A cognitive approach points at a more process-oriented attitude to entrepreneurship, an attitude which we favour.
- Some cognitive research on entrepreneurship[60] provides a ground for understanding entrepreneurship as creating success through intensive social interaction (related to what we later in this book shall refer to as 'co-creation').
- Maybe it is time to move beyond individual personal skills, thinking and behaviour among entrepreneurs and instead talk about general entrepreneurial 'capacities'. This is a term we shall use in this book.

Entrepreneurial Environments/Intrapreneurship

Much of entrepreneurship research has tried to identify those contextual factors which favour entrepreneurship. This group of knowledge of entrepreneurs and entrepreneurship places these phenomena within a wider social and economic context. It acknowledges the influence of numerous background factors on the propensity of an individual to behave entrepreneurially and to continue to do so.[61] Examples of such factors, of which some were illustrated in the previous section, are family and social background, education, religion, culture, work and general life experiences. These will either facilitate or hinder the potential of an individual to launch new business ventures or further develop existing ones.

Various kinds of *opportunities* to do business and to create a new business may exist, appear or be created. Such opportunities can often be characterized as 'incongruous situations'. An incongruity will fall into one of several generic groups:[62]

1. a mismatch between the way something is currently done and how it could be done more effectively using a different approach;
2. a poorly satisfied user demand that can be better met by new goods or services;
3. an opportunity for a new venture arising out of some change in the economic, legal or business climate; and
4. a recognition of an incipient user demand resulting from the creative application of some new technology.

For such opportunities to be exploited, *timing* may be a crucial element.[63] Opportunities must be assessed versus venture needs on one hand and personal capabilities and preferences of the potential entrepreneur on the other.[64]

So, many factors may influence a person's decision to behave entrepreneurially (Figure 3.4).

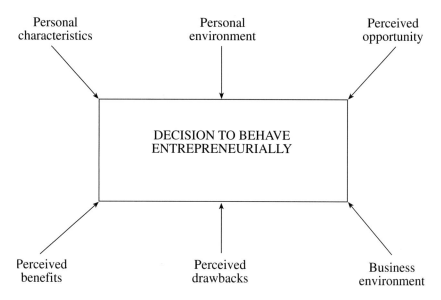

Figure 3.4   Factors influencing decision to behave entrepreneurially

As mentioned earlier, it must not be forgotten that entrepreneurs might also include those who generate new ventures within existing organizations, a kind of continued entrepreneurship, so-called 'intrapreneurs'. Therefore, part of the picture of entrepreneurship as a result of circumstances should recognize the fact that some corporations are better than others in generating intrapreneurship. According to Pinchot III, a climate for promoting such entrepreneurship honours the following factors:[65]

1. *Self-selection*   To become an intrapreneur is a voluntary thing; intrapreneurs appoint themselves and receive the corporation's blessing for their self-appointed task.
2. *No handovers*   People involved in an innovative idea are not switched; intrapreneurs stay with their own projects as long as they find it suitable to do so.
3. *The doer decides*   Decisions are made on the spot where action is taken, not by somebody having to wait for approval; some organizations push decisions up through a multilevel approval process so the doers and the deciders never even meet.
4. *Corporate 'slack'*   There is room to manoeuvre and to do things

differently, not according to tight rules and a fixed schedule; intrapreneurs need discretionary resources to explore and develop new ideas.

5. *Ending the home-run philosophy*   Money is invested in people and in many projects, which run in parallel and might even compete with each other, not in one Grand Project only; no project is perfect, and it is better to try more times with less careful and expensive preparation for each.

6. *Tolerance of risk, failure and mistakes*   Innovation cannot be achieved without risk; to do something new always means some mistakes and failures; this is accepted in intrapreneurial cultures, even seen as chances to learn to become better.

7. *Patient money*   Innovation takes time, even decades, but the rhythm of corporations is annual planning; it may take a long time to get return on money invested in new business ventures, and such return does not follow the calendar.

8. *Freedom from turfiness*   People are not afraid to enter into someone else's area, and they are not afraid of being entered by others; new ideas almost always cross the boundaries of existing patterns of organizations.

9. *Cross-functional teams*   People cooperate with and supplement one another in the name of progress; small teams with full responsibility for developing an intraprise solve many of the basic problems of innovation.

10. *Multiple options*   Entrepreneurs live in a multioption universe; there is no single best way to do anything in the world of new business ventures, and intrapreneurs should not be forced to follow granted options only.

To study entrepreneurship as a 'natural' outcome of circumstances and/or of entrepreneurial personalities[66] is not enough for a business researcher with our orientation. First of all, many such discussions may sound rather trivial (for instance, a statement like 'in order for a new business venture to be started, an opportunity for doing so must exist' does not seem to add much to existing knowledge of the entrepreneurial process). They also often seem to be culturally biased (for instance, personal qualities such as 'need to achieve something as an individual', 'independence' and 'profit orientation' sound very American and such qualities may not characterize entrepreneurs in other cultural settings; more about this in Chapter 5). Conclusions from entrepreneurial research following the circumstantial and/or the personality approach may therefore not be much more than rational prescriptions, given specific cultural assumptions (for instance, a statement like 'entrepreneurs are willing to learn from mistakes and be open to feedback from the environment' may be a good piece of advice in societies where mistakes do not lead to social disgrace and where people trust each another – this is not so in all societies).

Therefore, even if later on we shall incorporate some of the ideas (and even results) from this category of knowledge of entrepreneurship, we shall, by and large, favour the fourth and last group of knowledge, that is, entrepreneurial processes.

Entrepreneurial Processes

Partly as a reaction against some narrow individual-based definitions of entrepreneurship which have developed within the behavioural sciences and partly as a consequence of the strongly growing interest in entrepreneurship in business science, several authors have suggested alternative definitions of entrepreneurship.[67] Many modern definitions of entrepreneurship are based on the idea of entrepreneurship as a process. According to Bygrave and Hofer,[68] the entrepreneurial process has several special characteristics:

- it is discontinuous;
- it is dynamic;
- it is unique;
- it involves lots of different variables; and
- the outcome of the process is extremely sensitive to the input value of those variables.

These are characteristics (or 'entrepreneurial capacities', as we prefer to call them) which we shall meet several times in this book.

However, entrepreneurship is not just a result of specific circumstances (including the personality of the entrepreneur). It is not even a series of isolated activities and events. At a minimum, it is a process, where individuals sometimes plan their activities and sometimes act without planning, where they acquire resources, manage people, market their enterprises, manufacture goods, provide services, control expenses and much more. Entrepreneurship is about *action* and *change*:

> Entrepreneurship is about change and the roles people play to bring it about. It is about innovation and doing new things to improve the circumstances of the enterprise. It is best understood as a process, the constituents of which are entrepreneurs, their persistent search for opportunities and their efforts to marshall the resources needed to exploit them. It can occur in either a new venture start-up or within an established enterprise.[69]

Without denying that the entrepreneur is still central, to look at entrepreneurship as a process is to shift from the focus on the characteristics of the entrepreneur as a person to the characteristics of the entrepreneurial process,[70] and entrepreneurs are identified by their participation in this process.[71] The following question is asked: 'What do entrepreneurs do?'. The focus is on understanding how attitudes, behaviours, skills and know-how, past experience, and so on, all combine in determining entrepreneurial success.[72] This is fruitful even though we know that each entrepreneurial situation is, at least partly, unique and the future always differs from the past, because some tricks repeat well. Knowledge of precedents can expand virtuosity in a would-be entrepreneur for creating effective approaches in new situations.[73]

One very powerful and popular orientation along this line has been provided by William Gartner, who simply defines entrepreneurship as the creation of new organizations,[74] possibly as a context-dependent, social and economic process.[75]

During the past decade, the number of entrepreneurial studies applying the network metaphor has been increasing. The reason behind such studies has been to find out how business opportunities are created and organized. Networks are in such a context an emerging framework for the entrepreneurial process where necessary resources and contacts are identified. Networks will be very important to us later.

Network researchers within entrepreneurship have mainly concentrated on resources being accessed through those networks. Both *social*[76] as well as *personal*[77] networks have been the focus.

Intrapreneurship can also be described in stages and can be placed in a more general growth model of a type which we have just seen. One suggestion is:[78]

Stage 1.   Project definition
Stage 2.   Coalition building
Stage 3.   Action

- handling interferences
- maintaining momentum
- secondary redesign
- external communication.

However, it is important to note, that every business may have existed in phases which could be called entrepreneurial or not, and it may exist at the moment in a phase which is entrepreneurial or not.

One outcome of looking at entrepreneurship as a process is trying to identify roles played by different people in this process or to identify different kinds of entrepreneurs.

It seems as though several 'persons' (or 'roles') may be necessary for an innovative project to be successful. These are:

- *a person with an idea* – an 'inventor' in a wide sense;
- *an entrepreneur* – a source of energy, a go-getter;
- *a guardian angel* – a person in a senior position (sometimes called a 'godfather' or a 'godmother');
- *a technical gatekeeper* – a person who (often informally) has all necessary 'technical' information.

There are three important comments to make about such a classification:

1. *The roles may differ in prominence and importance*, depending on what type of entrepreneurial venture is at hand. A well-positioned guardian angel may be crucial in an intrapreneurial venture, for instance. In high-tech ventures, the technical gatekeeper may be of high strategic importance.
2. *Several roles may be played by one and the same person* A person with an idea may, for instance, also be the technical gatekeeper. An entrepreneur may be his or her own guardian angel.
3. *Several persons may play the same role at the same time* Some examples may be that it could be important to identify several guardian angels in a politically complicated situation, or that a team may constitute the entrepreneurial role (even if one person may be the 'lead entrepreneur').

Such role discussions like the above is one way to avoid a common concentration on technical skills in entrepreneurial discussions:

> Existing entrepreneurship courses have tended to focus on technical skills: writing business plans; analyzing financial data; exploring legal issues. Yet entrepreneurship is fundamentally less about technical skills than about people and their passion.[79]

Several attempts have been made to classify entrepreneurs in different groups. First of all, there is the accepted distinction today between independent entrepreneurs and intracorporate entrepreneurs (intrapreneurs):

- *independent entrepreneurs* (may work in teams) create new business ventures which they come to own themselves (at least in the beginning);
- *intracorporate entrepreneurs* or *intrapreneurs* (may also work in teams, of course) create new business ventures which come to be owned by their employers (at least in the beginning).

It is time to present the way entrepreneurship is used in this book. Before we do that, however, we need to clarify two matters: the differences between explaining and understanding entrepreneurship; and the relationship between management, leadership and entrepreneurship.

EXPLAINING AND UNDERSTANDING ENTREPRENEURSHIP

To claim a difference between 'explaining' and 'understanding' may seem irrelevant to some. However, it has become customary, though by no means among everybody, to distinguish between trying to get a picture of how events relate to each other and trying to penetrate human efforts as acts. It is suggested that the term 'understanding', in contrast to 'explaining', ought to be reserved for the latter.[80]

When *explaining*:

- this is done as models (deliberately simplified pictures of a supposedly complicated world) in structures or processes or a combination;
- it is possible, in principle, to explain all aspects of the world by objective, causal laws, manifested in effects/events (whether the explanation is good or not is another matter).

When *understanding*:

- this is done as interpretations (deliberately problematized pictures of a world which is simplified by human beings), where culture and language play an important role;
- our world (the social one) is believed to be constructed inter-subjectively and constantly being partly confirmed, modified and/or forgotten.

Table 3.2 illustrates this from the world of entrepreneurship. Why not combine the two, that is, to take the best from explaining entrepreneurship and understanding entrepreneurship in one picture? It is not that easy. A straightforward combination is not possible, because strict explaining and strict understanding are based on different, incompatible ontological and epistemological premises.[81] This also means that there is no objective way to say which of the two is best research (there is no neutral corner to choose from!).

We have an *explanatory approach* in this book. However, we apply aspects such as use of language and culture as variables (differently from the way language and culture is applied by strict 'understanders') along with other variables as in Figure 3.5.

Table 3.2   Explaining and understanding entrepreneurship

	As structure	As process	As culture	As language
What is entrepreneurship?	A person who reacts rationally to external conditions promoting new business ventures	A person who generates new business ventures, exploiting opportunities appearing in the economic system	A person who looks at creating new business ventures as a dominant part of his or her cultural world	A person who looks at creating new business ventures as a dominant part of his or her language world
How to improve on entrepreneurship?	By providing more and better external conditions, explaining the creation of new business ventures	By adapting entrepreneurs and/or suitable new business venture systems better to each other	By visualizing entrepreneurial aspects of culture	By talking about it incessantly
	EXPLAINING		UNDERSTANDING	

73

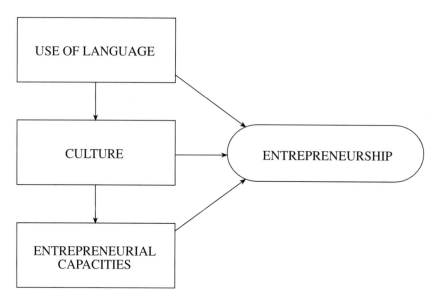

Figure 3.5   Explaining entrepreneurship: our base model

MANAGEMENT, LEADERSHIP AND ENTREPRENEURSHIP

We should like to make some distinctions between management, leadership and entrepreneurship. In real life, these three always exist in combinations, but, importantly, we only know the meaning, consequences and purposefulness of these combinations, if we know what they are combinations of!

Management is, basically, an occupation. Managers need technical skills in a wide sense, skills to be able to run a business or one part of it. They relate to their firm and its environment. Whether they do a good job or not is judged by the firm (and its owners). This is also true in the new economic era.

Leadership is founded on expectations – it is a role. Leaders need social skills in order to make other people work. They relate to other people, and their behaviour and results are judged by their followers. The new economic era may ask for a different kind of leadership, but it is basically still role based.

Entrepreneurship means to drive change. In order to do so, entrepreneurs need mental skills. Even if they relate to themselves, the market judges their results. Even if we can (as has been done over the years) discuss entrepreneurship in technical (management) and/or social (leadership) terms, there seems to be several new aspects added to it in the new economic era. As this situation is relatively new, we do not yet have much specific knowledge of what entrepreneurship means in the new economic era. However, it seems that entrepreneurship, on many occasions, has turned into a *lifestyle* ('a meaningful lifestyle ... for many'[82]), something you do from time to time in life. Also, when you do it, it is important to have fun. This seems to be particularly the case for small entrepreneurial firms.

Why do we make a notable distinction between management, leadership and entrepreneurship? There are at least two reasons for this: First, Carson et al.[83] have shown that entrepreneurship by tradition is intimately connected with 'good management' (Sexton and Bowman-Upton refer to the entrepreneur as 'a special kind of manager';[84] Peter Drucker believes in something he calls 'entrepreneurial management'[85]). We believe this is appropriate and adequate in the old economic era. However, in the new one, at least in the beginning of a new business venture being created, a combination of leadership and entrepreneurship is more appropriate and adequate. This is not to say that a firm does not need good management to survive, but in the initial creative (entrepreneurial) phase of it, it needs more of informal driving than formal planning, organizing and controlling (management)!

Second, following from the previous point: in different periods, a firm needs different combinations of management, leadership and entrepreneurship.

The relationship between management, leadership and entrepreneurship in one firm over time can be described as in Figure 3.6. This figure should be seen more as a conceptual, nominal model than a model describing the course of a typical firm or any other real firm over time.

Figure 3.6 is a picture of a hypothetical firm over a period of two phases of entrepreneurship (the initial start and, later, an intrapreneurial period) with a downturn in between. It is to be read like a seismograph – entrepreneurship is needed (extensively as well as intensively) more when new businesses are to be developed. Management is needed more when a business venture seems to be 'settled' and growing on its own. Leadership is needed more when the business venture is being built up the very first time (then leadership in the sense of playing an active role in building up networks and virtual organizations *around* the venture). Leadership is also needed if and when the existing venture seems to be going the wrong way (then leadership as playing a role model and a *generator of new energy* to turn the venture around). We will use this figure as an important ingredient of our framework for entrepreneurial marketing in Chapter 7.

ENTREPRENEURSHIP IN THIS BOOK

We want to define entrepreneurship by its result, that is:

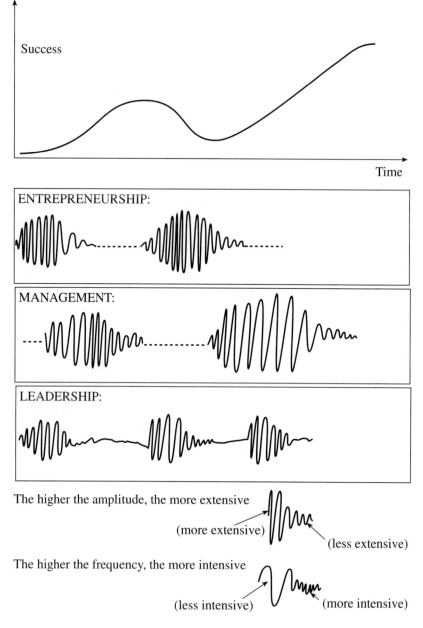

Figure 3.6   Extent and intensity of various activities in a hypothetical firm over time

Entrepreneurship = Creating new business ventures and renewing old ones.

'New' and 'renewing' does not need to mean radicality to the world. Most new businesses are rather more or less creative imitations of what exists already. Entrepreneurship always takes place in a context. Culture is one such important context.

In order for entrepreneurship to start, certain entrepreneurial prerequisites (such as certain mentality, attitude and so on) are necessary. How these come about is of no interest in this book. However, in order for an entrepreneurial process to take place, certain entrepreneurial capacities are required. Which they are, and what the entrepreneurial process looks like, is of specific interest in this book. We are looking for marketing capacities among entrepreneurs in the new economic era. We are also interested in the shape (and content) of various successful entrepreneurial growth patterns. When successful, entrepreneurship leads to new business ventures being created.

NOTES

1. Swedberg, Richard (1998), 'Entrepreneurship – The Social Science View', Working Paper No. 64, Department of Sociology, Stockholm University, pp. 2-3.
2. We shall return to the trio of management, leadership and entrepreneurship later in this chapter.
3. Baron, Robert A. (1998), 'Cognitive mechanisms in entrepreneurship: why and when entrepreneurs think differently than other people', *Journal of Business Venturing*, **13**, pp. 275-94: 276. The same conclusion can be read in most textbooks on entrepreneurship, for instance, Hatten, T.S. (1997), *Small Business: Entrepreneurship and Beyond*, Upper Saddle River, NJ: Prentice-Hall or Holt, D.H. (1992), *Entrepreneurship: New Venture Creation*, Englewood Cliffs, NJ: Prentice-Hall.
4. Cantillon, Richard (1931), *Essai sur la nature du commerce en général*, translated by H. Higgs, London: Macmillan.
5. Ibid., pp. 47-9, 53 and 151-3.
6. Kirzner, Israel M. (1979), *Perception, Opportunity, and Profit: Studies in the Theory of Entrepreneurship*, Chicago: University of Chicago Press, pp. 38-9.
7. In the history of economics, the English term 'undertaker' was used for a while to mean entrepreneur, but nobody really knows why this term came to mean the specific trade of managing funerals. So, the use of 'entrepreneur' in English is not meant to be a tribute to Richard Cantillon.
8. There are many publications presenting the development of our understanding of entrepreneurs and entrepreneurship until the present time. Some of them are Bjerke, Björn (1989), *Att skapa nya affärer* [Creating new business ventures], Lund, Sweden: Studentlitteratur, pp. 489-93; Holt (1992), pp. 3-6; Hisrich, R.D. and M.P. Peters (1992), *Entrepreneurship. Starting, Developing, and Managing a New Enterprise* (2nd edn), Homewood, IL: Irwin, pp. 6-9; Kao, Raymond (1995), *Entrepreneurship*, Singapore: Prentice-Hall, p. 71; Kuratko, D.F. and R.M. Hodgetts (1995), *Entrepreneurship. A Contemporary Approach* (3rd edn), Orlando, FL: Dryden Press, pp. 6-7; Zimmerer, T.W. and N.M. Scarborough (1996), *Entrepreneurship and New Venture Formation*, Upper Saddle River, NJ: Prentice Hall, pp. 2-3.
9. Schumpeter, J.A. (1934), *The Theory of Economic Development*, New York: Oxford University Press, p. 74.

10. Schumpeter, J.A. (1952), *Can Capitalism Survive?*, New York: Harper & Row, p. 72.
11. See Kirzner, Israel (1973), *Competition and Entrepreneurship*, Chicago: University of Chicago Press.
12. Contributions to this list come from Bjerke (1989), pp. 489–90, Haahti, Antti Juhani (1989), *Entrepreneurs' Strategic Orientation: Modeling Strategic Behavior in Small Industrial Owner-managed Firms*, Helsinki School of Economics: Helsinki, p. 199, and Hisrich and Peters (1992), p. 6.
13. Ronstadt, Robert C. (1984), *Entrepreneurship*, Dover, MA: Lord, p. 28.
14. Timmons, Jeffry (1990), *New Venture Creation* (3rd edn), Homewood, IL: Irwin, pp. 5–6.
15. Sexton, D.L. and N.B. Bowman-Upton (1991), *Entrepreneurship: Creativity and Growth*, New York: Macmillan, p. 4.
16. Hisrich and Peters (1992), p. 10.
17. Kuratko and Hodgetts (1995), p. 10.
18. Siles, Patrick R. (1974), *New Business Ventures and the Entrepreneur*, Homewood, IL: Irwin, pp. 14-15.
19. Baron (1998), pp. 285–7.
20. Delmar, Frédéric (2000), 'The psychology of the entrepreneur', in Carter, S. and J.-E. Dylan (eds), *Enterprise and Small Business*, London, Pearson Education, pp. 132–53: 141.
21. Ibid., p. 142.
22. Bull, I., H. Thomas and G. Willard (eds) (1995), *Entrepreneurship - Perspectives on Theory Building*, Oxford: Pergamon.
23. Thornton, Patricia H. (1999), 'The sociology of entrepreneurship', *Annual Review of Sociology*, **25**, pp. 19–46: 20.
24. Hisrich and Peters (1992), p. 9.
25. Kilby, P. (1971), *Entrepreneurship and Economic Development*, New York: Free Press, p. 1.
26. Bjerke (1989), pp. 492–3.
27. Thornton (1999).
28. Ibid., p. 20.
29. Stevenson, H.H. and J.C. Jarillo (1990), 'A paradigm of entrepreneurship: Entrepreneurial Management', *Strategic Management Journal*, **11**, pp. 17–27.
30. Sanner, Leif (1997), *Trust Between Entrepreneurs and External Actors. Sensemaking in Organising New Business Ventures*, Department of Business Studies: Uppsala University.
31. Kyrö, P. (1998), 'The Identity and Role of Entrepreneurship in the Postmodern Society', paper presented at 43rd *ICSB World Conference*, Singapore, 8–10 June, p. 7.
32. The term 'intrapreneur' (intracorporate entrepreneur) was coined by Gifford Pinchot III; see Pinchot III, Gifford (1985), *Intrapreneuring*, New York; Harper & Row.
33. Bjerke (1989), pp. 75–8; compare Wilken, Paul H. (1979), *Entrepreneurship - A Comparative and Historical Study*, Norwood, NJ: Ablex, Chapter 1.
34. McClelland, David (1961), *The Achieving Society*, Princeton, NJ: Van Nostrand.
35. McClelland (1961), p. 16.
36. Pleitner, Hans J. (1986), 'Entrepreneurs and New Venture Creation: Some Reflections of a Conceptual Nature', *Journal of Small Business and Entrepreneurship*, **4** (1), pp. 34–43.
37. Gibb, A.A. (1986/87), 'Education for Enterprise: Training for Small Business Initiation – Some Contrasts', *Journal of Small Business and Entrepreneurship*, **4** (3), pp. 42–8.
38. Kuratko and Hodgetts (1995), pp. 42–7.
39. Bjerke (1989), pp. 516–17.
40. Shaver, K.G. and L.R. Scott (1991), 'Person, process, choice: The psychology of new venture creation', *Entrepreneurship Theory and Practice*, Winter, pp. 23–42.
41. Hatten, T. S. (1997), *Small Business: Entrepreneurship and Beyond*, Upper Saddle River, NJ: Prentice-Hall, p. 40.
42. Carson, D., S. Cromie, P. McGowan and J. Hill (1995), *Marketing and Entrepreneurship in SMEs*, Hemel Hempstead: Prentice-Hall International (UK) Limited, pp. 51-2.
43. There are even studies reporting no significant differences in personality between entrepreneurs and others in a society. In a large and very thorough study of a cohort of 11,400 people in Britain (including 1,300 entrepreneurs) born in the first week of March,

1958, reported in *The Economist*, 14 March 1998 ('Entrepreneurs in order', pp. 63–5), those who became entrepreneurs were not more persistent, self-motivated or risk taking than the others. Almost the only common factor noted among entrepreneurs was that those who had received a monetary inheritance or gift had a higher tendency to start their own business, which does not sound very surprising.

44. Carson et al. (1995), pp. 51–2.
45. Delmar (2000), p. 142.
46. Delmar, Frédéric and Per Davidsson (2000), 'Where do they come from? Prevalence and characteristics of nascent entrepreneurs', *Entrepreneurship and Regional Development*, **12**, pp. 1–23: 4.
47. Shapero, A. and L. Sokol (1982), 'The social dimension of entrepreneurship', in Kent, C.A., D.L. Sexton and K.H. Vesper (eds), *Encyclopedia of Entrepreneurship*, Englewood Cliffs, NJ: Prentice-Hall, pp. 72–90.
48. Delmar and Davidsson (2000), p. 4.
49. Hage, E.E. (1962), *On the Theory of Social Change: How Economic Growth Begins*, Homewood, IL: Dorsey.
50. Shapero and Sokol (1982).
51. Delmar and Davidsson (2000), pp. 4-5.
52. Dubini, P. (1989), 'The Influence of Motivators and Environment on Business Start-Up: Some Hints for Public Policies', *Journal of Business Venturing*, **4** (1) (January), pp. 11–26.
53. Zimmerer and Scarborough (1996), pp. 3–4.
54. Bjerke (1989), p. 472.
55. Vesper, Karl H. (1990), *The Venture Strategies* (rev edn), Englewood Cliffs, NJ: Prentice-Hall, p. 8.
56. Baron (1998), p. 277; Delmar (2000), p. 133.
57. Delmar and Davidsson (2000), p. 5.
58. Ajzen, I. (1991), 'The theory of planned behavior', *Organizational Behavior and Human Decision Processes*, **50**, pp. 179–211.
59. Bandura, A. (1986), *Social Foundations of Thought and Action: A Social Cognitive Theory*, Englewood Cliffs, NJ: Prentice-Hall.
60. As summarized in Baron (1998), pp. 278–9.
61. Carson et al. (1995), p. 53. See also Hisrich and Peters (1992), pp. 56–62.
62. Robinson, David (1990), *Who Is an Entrepreneur?*, Holbrook, MA: Bob Adams, p. 19.
63. Vesper, Karl H. (1993), *New Venture Mechanics*, Englewood Cliffs, NJ: Prentice-Hall, p. 4.
64. Ibid., pp. 9–11.
65. Pinchot III (1985), pp. 198–9.
66. This does not deny the fact that we find some of the research done on entrepreneurship based on psychological models quite interesting and even useful for our purpose.
67. Landström, Hans (2000), *Entreprenörskapets rötter* [the roots of entrepreneurship'] (2nd edn), Lund, Sweden: Studentlitteratur, p. 96ff.
68. Bygrave, W.D. and C.W. Hofer (1991), 'Theorizing about Entrepreneurship', *Entrepreneurship Theory and Practice*, Winter, pp. 13–22.
69. Carson et al. (1995), p. 49.
70. Bygrave and Hofer (1991).
71. Carton, R., C. Hofer and M. Meeks (1998), 'The Entrepreneur and Entrepreneurship: Operational Definitions of their Role in Society', Paper presented at 43rd ICSB World Conference, Singapore, 8–10 June, p. 2.
72. Carson et al. (1995), p. 54.
73. Vesper (1990), p. 2.
74. Gartner, William B. (1985), 'A Conceptual Framework for Describing the Phenomenon of New Venture Creation', *Academy of Management Review*, **10** (4), pp. 696–706; Gartner, (1988), 'Who Is an Entrepreneur? Is the Wrong Question', *American Journal of Small Business*, Spring, pp. 11–32; Gartner (1990), 'What are we talking about when we talk about entrepreneurship?', *Journal of Business Venturing*, **5** (1), pp. 15–29; Gartner (1993), 'Words Dead to Deeds: Towards an Organizational Emergence Vocabulary', *Journal of Business Venturing*, **8**, pp. 231–9.

75. Reynolds, P.D. (1991), 'Sociology and entrepreneurship: concepts and contributions', *Entrepreneurship Theory and Practice*, **16** (2), pp. 47–70; Low, M.R. and E. Abrahamson (1997), 'Movements, bandwagons, and clones: industry evolution and the entrepreneurial process', *Journal of Business Ventures*, **12**, pp. 435–57.
76. Granovetter, M. (1973), 'The strength of weak ties', *American Journal of Sociology*, **78** (6), pp. 1360–80.
77. Johannisson, Bengt (1996), 'Personliga nätverk som kraftkälla i företagandet' [Personal networks as a source of power when venturing out], in Johannisson, B. and L. Lundmark (eds), *Företag, Företagare, Företagsamhet* [Ventures, Venturers, Venturing], Lund, Studentlitteratur, pp. 122–50.
78. Kanter, Rosabeth Moss (1983), *The Change Masters*, London: Unwin Paperbacks, pp. 217ff.
79. Kao, John J. (1989), *Entrepreneurship, Creativity and Organization*, Englewood Cliffs, NJ: Prentice Hall, p. 2.
80. For a more thorough discussion of differences between and consequences of using 'explaining' or 'understanding' in researching entrepreneurship, see Bjerke, B. (1996), 'Explaining or understanding entrepreneurship', paper presented at UIC/AMA Research Symposium on Marketing and Entrepreneurship, Stockholm, 14–15 June; Bjerke (2000), 'Understanding entrepreneurship – a new direction in research?', paper presented at ICSB World Conference 2000, Brisbane, 7–10 June.
81. Von Wright, G.H. (1971), *Explaining and Understanding*, London: Routledge & Kegan Paul.
82. Thornton (1999), p. 19.
83. Carson et al. (1995).
84. Sexton and Bowman-Upton (1991), p. 5.
85. Drucker, Peter F. (1985), *Innovation and Entrepreneurship*, New York: Harper & Row, p. 143. See also Stevenson and Jarillo (1990), pp. 17–27.

4. Marketing of big firms and small firms

INTRODUCTION

In the two previous chapters, we dealt with marketing and entrepreneurship. In both cases much of the discussion was about how knowledge has developed in each field over time. In this chapter, the focus is again on marketing – but now the discussion will be less on marketing in the general sense of it, but on some of its contextual aspects. Examples of contextual aspects of marketing could include:

- Is marketing understood differently for standardized goods in comparison with customized services?
- Is consumer marketing different from marketing to industrial and organizational buyers?
- What implications do new phenomena such as electronic commerce and strategic alliances have on marketing?

One contextual aspect of special interest to marketing of entrepreneurial efforts is the *size* of the firm. We can expect entrepreneurial firms to normally start small. To be able to discuss marketing of entrepreneurial efforts we need to know the influences of size of the firm on how marketing is conducted. Are there size-related differences in marketing or to be more specific, is size a contextual variable related to how marketing is organized and pursued in business firms? This is a crucial question to answer and is closely related to the suitability of mainstream marketing to the new economic era, a discussion held at the end of Chapter 2.

First, there will be a focus on marketing of big firms in different markets and organizational settings, such as for standardized consumer goods, in business-to-business situations and for service ventures. Then two recent business phenomena, that is, strategic alliances and electronic commerce, will be discussed in terms of their implications for the size of the firm. The content in the last part of the chapter will be more directly about the implications of firm size on marketing.

MARKETING AND BIG FIRMS

Generally

In the academic discipline of marketing most attention has been paid to research on big firms. Two outcomes of such research have been the managerial approach and the network approach.

The managerial approach[1] was discussed in Chapter 2. This perspective is relevant for the big corporations offering standardized products, which is often the case for big firms dealing with consumer products. But also a lot of industrial products are standardized and, therefore, managerially marketed as well as distributed in standardized channels to customers (other firms).

Another perspective is more relevant for the business-to-business-oriented firms, which offer specialized and customized goods or services. Here, the interaction and the network approaches[2] are better suited to illustrate how marketing is performed in big business-to-business firms. In the interaction approach, different forms of relationships between a seller and a specific buyer are focused upon. In the network approach, the formal organization of a firm is understood to be together with other organizations in a network.

In general, big corporations are often found to be functionally specialized and their decision making to be formalized in hierarchies and in planning procedures. Big corporations are commonly structured divisionally and divided geographically into suborganizations or subsidiaries having large marketing departments both at the corporate level and in the divisions. In charge of each is generally a vice-president of marketing, who is a member of the corporation's top-management team.

Marketing planning is an important activity in most big firms and marketing is required to be coordinated with other functional plans and planning activities in the organization. A corporation like Pharmacia Upjohn, for instance, has in total over 250 different marketing plans in its organization.

Standardized Offerings to the Market

Much of what is sold to consumers from big firms is standardized and what is offered is a balance between the need for economies of scale in production and the consumer's wish for customized products. This is the type of marketing situation reported in textbooks.

What is offered to the market, then, is based on what a majority of the market would be expected to buy. However, the total market is often divided into submarkets, segments, which are expected to be as homogeneous as possible within a segment and as heterogeneous as possible between segments.

Products, most of the time goods – not services – as well as most of the marketing actions are then designed and adapted to fit the majority of buyers in each submarket.

The product may be supported with different forms of service activities such as financing, after-sales services and so on. Distribution is mainly done through middlemen because the standardized offer benefits from economies of scale in the distributive operations.

Contacts with the consumers are also often one way. The seller is the sender of information and the buyers are the receivers. The seller makes the decisions in advance, often based on formalized marketing research and/or expert knowledge from consultants and sales people. Big firms generally have in-house marketing research departments but still often use additional external consultants.

In principle we find that in big firms marketing decisions are made in committees or teams – based on formalized information. The decisions are then further formalized into strategic plans as well as business and marketing plans at the division or business-unit levels. Although the recent phenomena of downsizing and re-engineering often have substantially reduced the number of hierarchical layers, decisions in big firms are often made far from the daily contact with users.[3]

To benefit from economies of scale there is often a need for a functional coordination among procurement, production, logistics and marketing. The complex planning processes in big firms make change expensive and less beneficial. An important marketing goal in the big firm is to target the planned quotas. After decisions are made about what features the (standardized) offer to the market is supposed to have, the 'marketing task' is generally to balance demand and the planned production quantity.[4] This often means creating sales. However, other goals may be to reduce, and if possible postpone, overdemand, *demarketing*, or reduce fluctuations over time – *synchromarketing*.

Examples of marketing tools in these situations are price reductions (or increases) and marketing communication. What is important is that buyers buy at the time that fits the planned production, otherwise an overstock may reduce the profit. Features such as quality, design and other product characteristics, distribution and image as well as price are to be as desirable as possible, of course. But when those features are set, the prime focus in marketing is to sell the manufactured quantities.

There is a focus on *transactions* in this type of marketing – but efforts are also made to tie customers to the company in the long run. It is generally regarded as cheaper to create a second and third buy from an old customer han to find new customers. This can occur in many different ways. Today there are different schemes available to give accumulated benefits to loyal customers, such as award programmes, frequent-flyer points, customer clubs and so on.

One primary task for the marketing function in big firms within the managerial perspective is to make other business functions consider customers' demands as early as possible in the process of developing business for the firm at large, to integrate the different business functional areas to maximize customer value and satisfaction (including the post-purchase period) in the long run, thereby creating maximum demand *and* profit, and, in the short run, to balance demand and the planned production level. Finally, 'the marketing department has to monitor and control marketing activities' continuously in an auditing process.[5] Altogether, not a small task!

Mass Customization, Flexible Manufacturing Systems

The picture presented above represents marketing in the traditional post-war big corporation. Today, new trends shake the bureaucratic dinosaurs from the past. One example is the phenomenon of 'mass customization'.

The idea is to combine requirements from production and demand from customers better – economies of scale in production at the same time as each customer is allowed to buy something as close as possible to his or her needs. Every sale is to be standardized but every purchase is to be customized is the motto in mass customization. *Flexible manufacturing* allows customization to be an important tool for marketers. An illustrative example is the automotive industry where at least in the upper segments of the market almost every produced car is adapted to the specification of an individual customer. Still, the production is standardized but flexible within certain limits.

We find that many of the big corporations take actions to improve their competitive edge – even in consumer marketing. The big corporations may need features that are traditionally the domain of smaller organizations, that is, quick response to market demands, customization and flexible manufacturing. In turbulent markets, the lead time between spotting a new opportunity and the actual launch of new products has been reduced drastically. Six months may be a very long time in some industries; shorter lead times are often necessary. This increased competition asks of the organization structure that quick detection of trends and customer demands be allowed as well as an ability to transfer the information to commercialized goods and services in time to meet the customers' new demands.

As a consequence of increased competition, dynamics and uncertainty, the big corporations may be downsized and layers of hierarchical structures broken down into smaller more autonomous units.[6] Decisions must come closer to the actual information source and be speeded up in order to cut lead times and increase precision in decision making.

Business-to-business; Low Degree of Standardization

Looking at markets where the offerings are less standardized, for instance business-to-business, a completely different marketing behaviour is to be expected according to the marketing literature. The individual customer is the focus and important marketing tasks are to find satisfying solutions to the specific customer's needs. This often requires a continuous interaction between the buyer and the seller. Traditionally, transaction-oriented firms structure themselves around the fundamental concept of strategic customer partnership.[7] In this respect there are probably not many differences between big firms and small ones.

The *business network* is a concept used for understanding this marketing behaviour. No organization can operate completely on its own – all organizations need customers and suppliers of at least energy and raw material. In reality the suppliers often contribute complex and well-developed products as well as knowledge and services. Besides traditional suppliers, most firms deal with consultants and other forms of cooperating organizations. The result is an interorganizational network in which a firm operates (Figure 4.1).

The links between the nodes in the business network are the *business relationships*. To be able to understand a firm's behaviour it is necessary to know the contextual situation in the network, aspects referred to as the *structural characteristics*[8] of business networks and their relationships. This is where a specific firm is doing business at a certain point in time. The structure may be characterized in terms of:

- continuity;
- complexity;
- symmetry; and
- informality.

The business relationships in business-to-business are often related to technology, product development and so on and involves more functions than just the marketing department in the selling company and the purchasing department in the buying organization. Interactions may take place between a large number of people before, during as well as after the actual sales process.

Representatives from different departments participate, for example the research and development (R&D) people, the design department, sometimes the production staff, the quality people and so on. Exchanges and relationships among the parties are often complex and long lasting. Figure 4.2[9] illustrates the complexity.

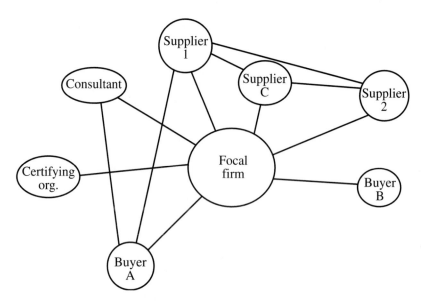

Figure 4.1   Complex relations between a selling organization and the buyer in an industrial network

In the managerial school of marketing, sales processes are regarded as a result of a seller's actions and decisions made about the marketing mix. With this view of marketing, sales emerge from the continuous contacts and interactions between the involved parties and one business transaction will lead to another and so on. It is more natural, when a firm has an ongoing relationship, to ask its present business partners if they can solve new problems as they emerge. It is more complicated, and expensive, to look for new suppliers every time it has an unsolved problem or needs to buy something. Again, this is a situation similar to the one for small businesses. The difference, of course, is the complexity – many more people and departments are involved in the case of big businesses.

In a business network there are a number of exchanges going on, in parallel and over time. Each transaction is to be understood in its context and is a part of the ongoing relationship. The exchanges of *goods* and *money* are just a part of all exchanges that go on between the parties in a business-to-business relationship. There are exchanges of *information* and sometimes different resources such as *knowledge* as well as *personal sentiments* among the people involved in the interaction.

The exchanges are either *symmetric* – both parties gain equally – or *asymmetric* – one party gets more from the relationship than the other. In an ongoing relationship some symmetry is expected. Otherwise the losing party

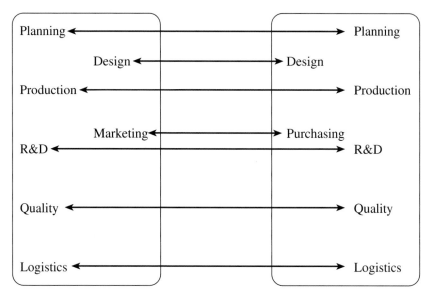

Figure 4.2   Complex relations between a selling organization and the buyer in many business-to-business situations

will leave the business relationship. The win–win case, often mentioned in relationship marketing, is easy to understand in this context.

The Uppsala school[10] uses three main concepts to understand marketing behaviour in industrial networks: *actors*, *activities* and *resources*. Actors control and perform activities and control the resources in the network. The actors have exchanges and develop relationships with the others. Each actor is embedded in a network and has, through relationships in the network, more or less access to the other actors' resources. Actors are goal oriented and base their activities on control over resources.

The activities, actors and resources can be understood in at least three levels in the network in parallel: the individual company level, the relationship level and at the level of the network as a whole, as shown in Figure 4.3.[11]

Relationships must be regarded as something to be handled, especially the critical ones. The main task from a marketing perspective is to keep all important relationships productive to the company's value-creation ability, and, if possible, improve their contribution to this ability. This is directly linked to the customers' preferences.

The company's position in the network is a strategic issue. The position directly affects the economic outcome of a company over time as well as its ability to develop and maintain relationships with other partners. Different dynamic processes must be identified and evaluated and strategies need to be

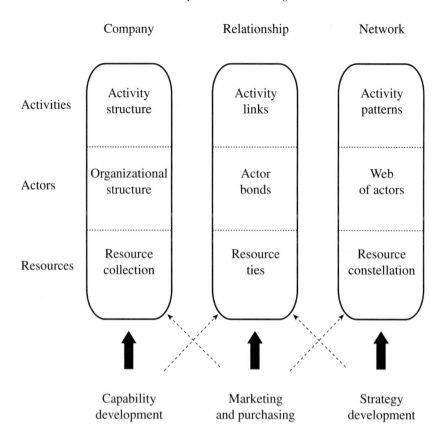

Figure 4.3   Activities, resources and actors and critical issues in coping with relationships in business networks

developed to meet changes. It is also important to produce changes when needed.[12]

> Handling the single relationship, that is, managing the dyadic function, is a condition for exploiting the potential of relationships and for taking economic advantage of business relationships. It is a condition for developing capabilities and for the strategy development in a company. Conversely, to pursue a change in the strategy of the company requires that the development effects on the relationship are monitored and adjusted.[13]

A firm cannot be involved in too many relationships. As soon as a company decides to engage a certain supplier, a certain customer, and a certain cooperator, some of its resources will be tied up, thereby limiting the company's resources to be engaged in other relationships. People need to be engaged, inventory space will be occupied, production facilities will be used to produce goods or to service this specific customer and so on. *Resource ties* emerge because there is a certain structure (certain relationships) of the business network.

As soon as two firms start to engage in business relations, different activities need to be performed both in and between the two companies. These activities link the two firms together. The activities can be anything from a single order and a flow of material and money to continuous activities where different technical, administrative subsystems in each firm are linked together and adapted to each other. Therefore the *activity links* are aspects which are important in order to understand what is happening in a business network.

Finally, when the interaction continues, bonds will emerge between the actors involved because the two parties understand and mutually interpret what is going on. These *actor bonds* are phenomena such as personal sentiments, trust, commitment and identity.

Important knowledge gathered from the behaviour of big firms in networks is developed within research in industrial marketing and purchasing – to quote from Håkansson and Snehota:[14]

> Coping with relationships, exploiting them economically, requires an awareness of their effects and insights to the interdependence that accounts for their dynamics. ... Compared with the traditional determinants of a company's performance, the relationship perspectives yield rather different implications. The main points in our argument so far are as follows:
>
> - In numerous companies, relationships have an overwhelming impact on their economic performance. When that is the case, i.e., when single specific relationships matter, they have to be managed.
> - Companies cannot unilaterally control and decide the development of relationship; they are now part of relationships and of a larger whole that affects both their outcomes and their development potential. Awareness of this interdependency is needed in order to cope with relationships successfully.
> - The time dimension becomes more important as conduct and its outcome are rooted in the past and its effects become manifest in time. Interdependence and awareness of interdependence in the company and its counterparts will be decisive to the outcome of joint action. Insight into the dynamics of business networks is required in order to cope with relationships effectively.

An important concept in this context is *trust*. As a concept, trust is prominent in many subjects, for example, the social sciences, philosophy and the business literature. In marketing, trust is today regarded as important glue that binds parties together and facilitates business in a business network. If one's business partner is trusted, business becomes easier. Trust is gained by meeting expectations and fulfilling promises made in the interaction with other organizations. To quote Blau: 'social exchange relations evolve in a slow process, starting with minor transactions in which little trust is required because little risk is involved and in which both partners can prove their trustworthiness, enabling them to expand their relations and engage in major transactions'.[15]

This statement is valid in business relationships. There are many studies on business behaviour where buying firms testify that one of the most important reasons for having relations with a particular firm is its reliability to deliver goods or services with the correct specifications on time and at the right place.[16]

Trust and commitment are becoming more prominent as concepts in understanding business relationships; to quote researchers from the Uppsala group:

> Commitment is central to the development of relationships between two companies which brings us to the issue of trust and the time dimension of the relationships.
>   Trust is a necessary condition for commitment and commitment only makes sense if tomorrow matters. Trust, on the other hand, takes time to develop between two actors. The trust-building process has been labelled social exchange. ... The interaction process that characterizes relationships can be said to be productive for the actors involved in the sense that they correct and develop their knowledge (picture of attributes) of the counterpart and learn to exploit each other (and the relationship) better. What an actor can and will do depends on the reaction of the counterpart, and vice versa. What they can do for each other is reflected in their mutual identities in their mutual commitments. Both are here summarized as bonds that arise and exist between the parties. The bonds that develop in a relationship limit or empower the parties.[17]

To summarize the picture of marketing in the business-to-business context we can say that sales emerge and take place in relationships. The business-to-business literature clearly stresses this fact and focuses on marketing as an ongoing and continuous process; one thing leads to another. Businesses are linked to each other for longer or shorter periods of time and this type of marketing is very different from what is found in the managerial school and consumer marketing. Grönroos's relationship definition[18] of marketing offers a good illustration of this:

> The purpose of marketing is to identify, establish, maintain and enhance, and when necessary terminate relationships with customers (and all other parties) so that the objectives regarding economic and other variables of all parties are met. This is achieved though a mutual exchange and fulfilment of promises.

MARKETING AND SERVICES

Marketing of services and the marketing of goods are something that cannot be described or labeled in a single form.

However, in the literature there are a number of general characteristics of services and their consequences for marketing. Services may be standardized but are often *customized*, produced and consumed by a particular customer. As a consequence, quality issues were focused on early in the development of service marketing literature although modern quality thinking has its roots in the manufacturing industry.[19] Quality in service marketing is often related to softer aspects such as customer satisfaction and whether the services offered meet the customers' expectation. The correct quality arises when expectations and various claims are met, when needs are satisfied: those of the customer, the staff and the owner.[20] Service quality is subjective, not only for the customer but for the others involved in the service process!

It is often impossible to distinguish between the production, the delivery and the consumption of the service. This *inseparability* leads to an integration of different subprocesses, totally or partly. The French word '*servuction*'[21] is sometimes used as a term for the 'production process of a service' (to distinguish this process from the process of manufacturing goods).

For most service companies, all employees are of utmost importance because service emerges in the interaction between representatives from the staff and the customer. As a marketing instrument, this interaction is key because the perceived value of the service is heavily influenced by the appearance, skills and knowledge and actions made by the service-providing personnel.

The traditional roles of producer and customer are often mixed in service marketing situations. The customer participates in the *servuction* process. The service provider must therefore interact with the customer and treat the buyer as a co-creator of the service:

> Services marketing is more fundamentals than fanciness, more common sense than science, more perspiration than promotion. Services marketing is execution, not just strategy; inspiration, not just mechanics; promise keeping, not just promise-making.[22]

Some central characteristics of service that may influence marketing decisions are as follows:[23]

- Services are processes consisting of activities or series of activities rather than things.
- The intangible service must be made tangible and concrete to make the customer understand the value of the service and what added value will be the result.
- The customer is able to evaluate the tangible aspects but the intangible aspects are more difficult to estimate. Consequently the staff in the

service company, their competency, skills and commitment will be
judged more than the service itself.

● The customer evaluates much of the service and the service company
during the process of providing the service, the *servuction*. The
servuction is regarded as the most critical part of marketing services.

It is, however, important to note that there is no consensus among
researchers in service marketing about what the differences and their
implications to marketing really are. In particular, the intangibility aspects are
criticized as it is difficult to distinguish a service from a physical product.[24] In
later chapters we shall concur with this criticism.

Grönroos described early the main components of service marketing, as
shown in Figure 4.4.[25] Shown in the top of the figure is the corporate image,
which, if it is favourable, can be supportive of the marketing effort and vice
versa. At the bottom are the needs of the target customers, which should be the
basis for planning. In the centre are the means of competition, the interactive
marketing function. The means of competition are related to the buyer–seller
interactions. The rest of the figure includes the firm's traditional means of
competition. These are pricing, traditional selling (field selling), non-
interactive communication (advertising, brochures and so on), sales promotion

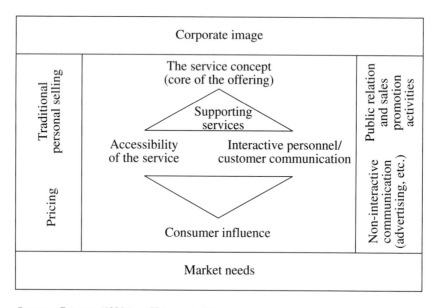

Source: Grönroos (1984a), p. 79 (see note 25).

Figure 4.4   The means of competition in service marketing

and public relation activities. The service concept is immaterial as such. By developing the other four elements of the interactive marketing function – accessibility, interactive personnel/customer communication, supporting services and consumer (buyer) influence – this intangible core can be turned into concrete services.

In contemporary service marketing literature the concepts are more elaborated (Figure 4.5).[26] Here the traditional marketing activities are regarded as the tool for giving promises to the customers, the internal marketing activities enable the firm to meet the expectations by the customers in the form of employee motivation and skills. Further, in the moment of truth, the *servuction* process, the interactive marketing function is the meeting-point between the employees' effort to produce the service and the customers' expectations and experience determine whether the firm is able to keep its promise to the customers or not.

Traditionally, goods and services are regarded as two separate and different marketing situations. As discussed in Chapter 2, marketing research started as an answer to the need for increased knowledge of what influenced demand of specific commodities such as agricultural products. In the 1970s, pioneers such as Shostack, Normann, Gummesson, Grönroos and Berry launched service marketing as a separate school of marketing because marketing services deviated from marketing of goods and required different concepts.

Today we find that these differences diminish. The tangible parts of the customer value in goods become less and less important. Instead imaginary values such as the image of the brand name, in combination with service issues such as just-in-time distribution, after-sales services and financing increased in importance.[27] The value added in pure manufacturing is often only 10–15 per cent of the final price and may sometimes be close to zero as is the case in the production of compact discs (after the first copy is produced).

Similar arguments are now to be found among researchers in service marketing, to quote Gummesson:[28]

> We have learnt that goods and services are partially different; that the interactive service encounter includes the customer in a partially simultaneous production, delivery and consumption process; that customer-to-customer interaction is important; that customers evaluate service quality in the service encounters; that all offerings consist of both goods and services; that goods and services can be both substitutes and supplements; that the service content of manufacturing firms is often higher than the goods content; and more. …
>
> Services are perspectives rather than categories. So it is never goods *against* services; it is always services with goods. Services first, because it is value-enhancing services we are looking for, irrespectively of the medium that carries them, a thing or an activity.

Consequently, concepts of service marketing may be very valid in the

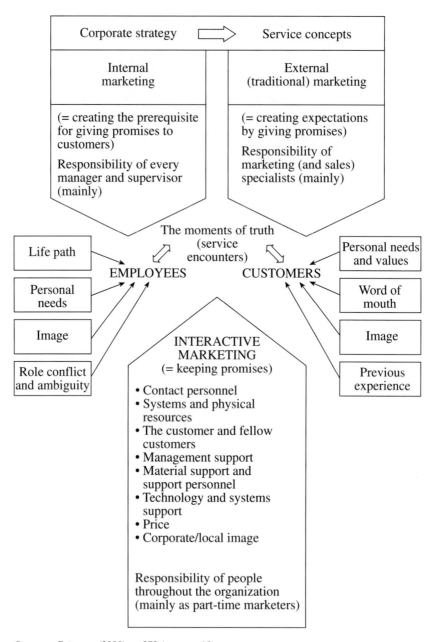

Source: Grönroos (2000), p. 373 (see note 18).

Figure 4.5   Overview of a market-oriented strategy

context of marketing goods. For example, Gummesson and Grönroos argue for the need of a new paradigm with roots in service marketing as a general marketing paradigm.[29] Marketing is to be regarded not as a specialist business function but as a general responsibility of management. This was discussed in Chapter 2. Later chapters will return to this discussion when entrepreneurial marketing is discussed more directly.

There is not much evidence that the size of the firm makes a difference as far as services are concerned, although the number of studies of small and medium-sized firms in the service sector is limited.[30] Much of the concepts in service marketing seem to be valid for small firms (growing entrepreneurially or not) as well as for big firms.

MARKETING AND ELECTRONIC COMMERCE

The developments in information technology open tremendous opportunities for businesses. Parallels have been made to the invention of the printing press by Johannes Gutenberg in the fifteenth century. The same revolutionary impact on human beings can be expected from further developments in information technology.

The Internet offers at least two primary opportunities. First, as an instrument for decision making – with almost unlimited information. Second, as a very quick and low-cost channel to actual and potential buyers.

In the 1960s, complex management information systems (MIS) were constructed. The use of these complex systems was limited to big corporations. Due to the cost of the system, only big organizations could afford the development costs and were able to host the expertise needed to run the MI systems. In reality these complex systems did not seem to be used much by the decision makers they were designed to serve.[31] Today there is information about markets and almost all sectors and places available and affordable for every business, both big and small. The problem is not the cost or the knowledge needed. Instead, information overload is the largest problem for users with limited time to choose and evaluate information.

Business via the computer is expected to revolutionize some industries. Change has been very rapid and today consumers find it possible to buy a broad variety of goods over the Internet, from expensive things such as flats and cars, to convenience goods such as books and cigarettes.

The Internet has created both a new marketplace and a completely new type of marketing channel. Effects are expected to emerge on buying behaviour in many sectors and commodities – convenience, shopping and speciality goods as well as services – for both individual consumers and organizational buyers. Expanding firms often have continuous interactions with stakeholders:

customers, partners and up-stream suppliers.[32] The Internet allows interactive contacts with a large number of individuals and/or organizations every day.

Successful stories like the fantastic growth of Amazon.com and Dell Computers are today a reality to be shared with growth-oriented firms. With an initial investment of $1.6 million, Amazon.com was able to challenge bookstores in most countries. Dell sells computers for a value of over $3 million every day using electronic communication via the Web. Companies like these are built on a close linkage between marketing and MIS[33].

The existence of electronic commerce (e-commerce) allows both big and small firms to use, for example, *one-to-one marketing*, in itself a type of relationship marketing. To be a genuine one-to-one marketer, a firm must be able to change its behaviour towards an individual customer, based on what is known about that customer; it involves more than just sales and marketing and includes loyalty and trust. It is fundamental to understand the various ways the customer is different and how these differences should affect the firm's behaviour.

There are several ways to accomplish this. In Figure 4.6, the 'New Marketing Model', developed by a consulting company, the Gartner Group, illustrates how one-to-one marketing can be practised in the concepts of traditional managerial marketing. Data are collected and stored in a database. The firm's actions are based on the stored information continuously updated

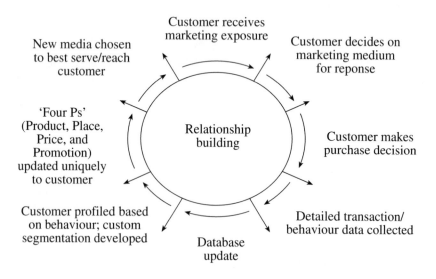

Source: The Gartner Group; Turban et al. (2000), p. 85 (see note 34).

Figure 4.6   New marketing model

with actual customer behaviour related to the 4 Ps. This goes on and on in a continuous process.[34]

From a marketing perspective the Internet offers:

- A cheap and fast route to potential and actual customers. The Web is instantly available for millions of people and companies. All changes in information may be distributed globally in fractions of a second.
- Rational handling of orders, order confirmation and other documents related to sales as well as after-sales services.
- Identification not related to size. The Web is neutral when it comes to how customers perceive firm size. However, image created by other means can be expected to influence e-commerce.
- Almost indefinite growth potential not related to the initial investment and with very limited additional costs.

Brännback and Puhakainen[35] have developed the service marketing model[36] into an *electronic marketing model* (Figure 4.7). Besides the original triangle with customers, the selling company and its employees, an additional triangle is now included. In this triangle, stakeholders of auxiliary service providers are included. To quote Brännback and Puhakainen:

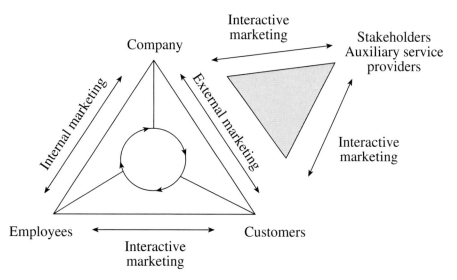

Source: Brännback and Puhakainen, Journal of Market Focused Managment, **3** (1), p. 52 (1998) Kluwer Academic publishers (see note 35).

Figure 4.7   Electronic marketing model

To our minds the emphasis, from a marketing management perspective, is now on this new triangle (shaded). The new situation is such that it is necessary to manage both triangles and understand how the customer operates in this new situation.

We use the term stakeholder because auxiliary service provider has become a beneficiary of the service offered by primary service provider. The company can have provided link-access to this stakeholder. For example, when a customer decides to buy something at a Web-site, payments can be made with a credit card. However, credit card payment over the Internet is not allowed in all countries. Some companies have solved the problem by linking their services to a Web-based banking service on-site (an auxiliary service). Thus the customer can use the same security codes for payment as he does when accessing his bank account. In this case there are three beneficiaries, the customer, the company and the stakeholder (the bank). ... [A] smaller circle is presented within the initial triangle. The circle signifies the Intranet/Extranet applications that many companies are using today. (See note 35, pp. 52–3)

In providing auxiliary services at the company's web-site, the company is building a value-adding network for the customer. This is an example of effective use of the special features of the Internet, which aims at customer bonding by linking auxiliary service to the product. The customer will come to regard this service as part of the product offer and as a function of quality.

E-commerce is also an instrument to improve efficiency in ordering and to delivery systems. Computers may do substantial parts of the interaction between a buyer and a seller, once the actual relationship has been established. Staff can be used to improve customer service, make it better and quicker.

Today it is hard to forecast the speed of the future growth of electronic commerce. Buyers, still surprisingly unaware of the benefits of the new technology, are unable to evaluate their future behaviour as electronic commerce evolves to a more and more integrated part of standard market behaviour.

CUSTOMER RELATIONSHIP MANAGEMENT (CRM)

Relationship marketing has evolved along several paths. One such path, much in focus today, is the concept of customer relationship management (CRM). The idea is that all actions taken to handle relations to customers are to be coordinated, integrated and managed with a holistic perspective to obtain a customer dialogue and as profitable long-term customer relations as possible. CRM includes actions such as identification, creation, retention and termination of customer relations. If the firm has a better understanding of the customers' behaviour, preferences and buyer behaviour, the lifetime value of the relationship will be more profitable.[37]

The fast developments of modern information technology (IT) have indeed had influence on the rapid evolution of CRM. As a consequence CRM is often identified by the various tools used in computerized and IT-related customer handling. Sometimes the term eCRM is used as a label for CRM involving a substantial number of IT and other electronic tools.

Five elements are important in CRM: the integrated (sales, marketing and service) strategy, segmentation, technology, process and organization. The customers are to be *identified*, *differentiated* and all customer communication as well as the offer are to be *customized* accordingly. In other words there must be an *interaction* between the three components. This is called the 'CRM process'.[38]

The identification is based on a flow of information about customer behaviour. The more the firm knows about its customers, the better is the ability to customize the offer and the communication.

The relationship as well as the offer to each customer is unique, or at least maximum customized to the customer's requirements and habits. The firm must be a learning organization and continuously interact with its customers to be able to tailor-make the offer and the communication through the dialogue. Further, almost everybody in the organization has to understand the benefits and requirements of CRM and actions should be coordinated among all departments involved.[39]

The customer dialogue is maintained through a number of different alternative or supplementary channels of communications such as call-centres, the Internet, databases as well as traditional mail systems, salespeople and distributors. To be able to optimize the value, all customer information should be centralized in a single database available 24 hours a day.

CRM can be used as a tool to create customer value. By the gathering of information of the customer's needs and habits, the ability to create customized and high customer value will increase. It is the main task for the company to meet and exceed customers' expectations by offering the goods and services that really are in demand and optimize the customer value. The customers' expectations are developed by a combination of the market communication of the various seller's (the promise) and the customers' own knowledge and needs.

Both big and small firms can use CRM. The philosophy of CRM does not require heavy investments, but many of the systems do. In some small firms the magnitude of the investments in systems is not justified by the increase in marketing efficiency.

MARKETING AND SMALLER ORGANIZATIONS

So far marketing has been discussed in different markets and in various organizational contexts – and specific implications for small firms have been mentioned only peripherally. A relevant question is to what extent size-related differences in market behaviour among firms are found. This will be the topic for the rest of this chapter.

What is marketing by a small entrepreneurial firm when compared to marketing by a big corporation?

> [I]t is becoming apparent that marketing in SMEs is fundamentally different and more successful in SMEs than in large firms (not just a simplified version of the more 'sophisticated' marketing practices used by larger companies). This is partly because marketing implementation can be more important to success than planning and strategy.[40]

In the remaining part of this chapter size-related differences will be discussed in marketing contexts one at a time. First some general differences to marketing by the big corporations will be identified.

Few Dominating Decision Makers: Influence of the Entrepreneur

In big corporations, decision making includes a large number of people. In smaller organizations, one single individual may make all the important decisions. If there is no controlling owner or board of directors, it is expected that the borderline between the organization and the individual may disappear. This is well accepted in the field of entrepreneurship. For example Birley[41] suggests that goals are not based on analysis of opportunity, but determined by actions which appeal to the owner/manager.

Among those successful entrepreneurs we have met and interviewed there are many examples of influential individuals who made marketing decisions that can be linked directly to specific personal goals. One of the successful family-controlled Australian firms we have talked to, started exporting to the US just because the entrepreneur had a love affair in that country. This does not necessarily mean that there was no action taken to perform market research. On the contrary – the entrepreneur soon identified potential business opportunities and in the end the operations were very successful. An interesting reaction from the entrepreneur occurred when we asked about the US operation, why and how it was initiated. We received a description of the process almost identical to what is found in every textbook on international marketing, that is, a rational choice of export market, based on evaluation of opportunities and very sequential in nature. The only thing that was left out was the original reason why this particular market was selected and analysed.

This story illustrates how some firms can make a marketing decision with a very influential individual. Business and personal considerations often walk hand in hand during the different phases of an operation in a small firm.

Besides personal goals it is to be expected that the psychology in general of the influential individuals has a higher impact on the marketing decision making when compared to big corporations.

The *interaction* between personal characteristics and goals of an influential entrepreneur and standard business considerations are very important aspects of marketing in both entrepreneurial firms and in small firms in general. In the growing firm it is the motivation to grow that is behind the decisions and such firms both actively identify opportunities and exploit opportunities regardless of whether these are generated internally or externally by other actors in the environment. The non-growing firm may have identified the same opportunity, been exposed to the same external chances, and still did not expand. Because the motivation to grow was lacking among the influential individual(s) in the latter type of company, growth never takes place.

The influence of the owner is, of course, 100 per cent in a solo firm. But in reality this single individual may be in the hands of different external stakeholders, especially if the company depends on outside financial sources. In reality, there may be tight restrictions in the autonomy in small firms' marketing decision making made by a bank or some other financial agency. Successful business opportunities may not be exploited because the bank says so!

However, it can be expected that when a company grows, the number of individuals involved in marketing decision making will increase and the personal influence on the firm's behaviour will be reduced. Nevertheless, in many fairly big companies, one particular individual may strongly influence the marketing decisions and his or her personal goals may explicitly or implicitly affect the outcome of many marketing decisions. This is the case in many entrepreneurial firms.

Rational, Structured or Non-rational, Unstructured Decision Making?

Hertz and Mattsson[42] claim that most small firms seem to lack a long-term-oriented strategy for their internationalization (export, import and/or production in a foreign country). Instead, one thing leads to another; one action leads to another action. The matchmaking, the contacts between firms occur in combinations in more or less unplanned initiatives, both the firm's and others.

The initiative for these relationships has sometimes come from the small firm itself but sometimes from the counterpart to be, for example, an agent. Since the business network contains companies that the focal, small firm only has indirect relations with, for example, customers to a distributor that use the focal small firm's products, a firm can become internationalized without its own direct influence. When internationalization has been the result of a firm's own direct influence and of the dynamics of its own network, the internationalization process may become very complex and difficult to grasp. Finally, small firms with indirect exports to an internationalized big company may gradually become more and more internationalized without taking active steps on their own. A contributory factor to this is sometimes the problems of adaptation and the direct link to the customer created by modern logistics.

Within the Interstratos (Internationalization Strategies of European SMEs) research programme conducted among small and medium-sized enterprises (SMEs) in member states of the European Union, SMEs' internationalization behaviour is being studied. One of many interesting observations was reported by Havnes (1998).[43] The models for describing and analysing developments of SMEs were dominated by what can be termed 'incremental change models'. The change mechanisms were depicted as a series of incremental changes; their accumulated effects were observed as developments of the enterprise. The incremental change paradigm was not compatible with the innovative process central to entrepreneurial theories. In the Interstratos project, observations have been made over 5 years. A proportion of the observed enterprises followed paths that are largely consistent with the incremental change models. There were, however, a significant number of enterprises (around 40 per cent) which developed their international engagement along paths more compatible with entrepreneurial models, where an *irregular and intermittent change* pattern has been found. This was the same over all investigated categories of SMEs.

From a traditional marketing perspective this behaviour may look non-rational and intuitive. But management theory provides the explanation. Mintzberg and Water[44] have classified different strategies. In this context the planned strategy and the entrepreneurial strategy were here the most relevant ones from their classification. The planned strategy consisted of deliberate actions realized as intended. This is what can be seen – or at least expected to be found – in big firms. The entrepreneurial strategy was different.

Formalization of Marketing

In modern marketing textbooks and education, the marketing plan takes a central part. Marketing actions and thinking are to be decided and written in a formal plan. This plan is central for joint implementation of marketing throughout the organization's different parts.

Carson et al.[45] make the observation:

> In an entrepreneurial SME marketing planning or decision-making is again intuitive, loose and unstructured. It is simple in comparison to formal approaches and it is almost always short-term focused. It is characterized by frequent change and flexibility. It is often unconsciously or subconsciously performed and is merged

with the intuitive decision-making practices of the entrepreneur. It certainly does not conform to dictates of conventional planning models.

Hills and Hultman[46] found that the use of formal marketing research was comparatively unusual among US entrepreneurs in general and even among extremely successful entrepreneurs. Hultman[47] found a similar pattern in Sweden where expanding firms were compared to non-expanding firms in the same industry.

Resources and Capabilities

But is it only the entrepreneur's motivation that will determine the firm's behaviour at the market? The capabilities that a firm controls, possesses and creates during the relationship to its market are another vital aspect that may totally determine how a firm can perform at the marketplace.

Capabilities are of different kinds. Day[48] has classified them as outside in, inside out and spanning capabilities, all necessary for successful marketing.

Birley[49] claims that small firms lack resources and/or knowledge which preclude decision making based on the classic strategic marketing approach of analysing markets, selecting a long-term growth strategy and optimal management in detailed plans.

Lack of management expertise and a limited customer base are further suggested[50] to influence the strategic marketing process employed by owner/managers. For example the well-known SWOT analysis (Strengths–Weaknesses–Opportunities–Threats) is, according to Carson et al.,[51] not to be found in an entrepreneurial SME. Instead:

> An inherently similar process (to formal marketing's SWOT analysis) is followed but without structure and clear purpose. Indeed, it is likely to be an unconscious process. Evaluations are based on intuition, supposition and the whole process is dominated by the desire and sometimes the need to find a circumstance which is ripe for exploitation. It is easy to see here why entrepreneurial risk is a characteristic of entrepreneurship.

However, not using many of the 'scientific' marketing models applied by big corporations may not necessarily restrict the actions of an entrepreneurial small firm. In the previous section alliances were discussed. Through cooperation a small firm may acquire the capabilities needed.

Advantages of Being Small

Small organizations have generally some major marketing advantages due to their size. In a small firm, the access to information is better because of its closeness to the customers. Few organizational layers make the links between the actual information and the final decision maker short. This opens up an important capability: *flexibility* towards customers. Flexibility makes customization possible and in general increases a company's ability to deliver superior value to each customer.

Another important capability directly linked to flexibility is the *speed of reaction* on changes in customer preferences. Not only can a small organization be expected to be more flexible but also to react more quickly than big competitors.

The small size of operations makes it profitable to *exploit smaller market niches*, perhaps targeting a specific sector of the market that is too small for a big corporation to focus upon.

Different actions possible for small firms, such as reducing the cost gap between themselves and bigger competitors or persuading customers that only they can produce real quality and that the cost difference remaining is worth it, may insulate a small firm from the direct competition of bigger organizations.

SOME ASPECTS OF MARKETING ARE SIZE-RELATED

When analysing the nature of marketing in big versus small firms, it can be regarded as containing three main categories of theories or models.

First, there are a number of *general statements* of how marketing is to be performed in all types of organizations. One such example is customer orientation, where Levitt's[52] famous article about marketing myopia clearly indicated the tragic ending of all companies that failed to focus on the customers' needs and instead focused their methods or products to satisfy their own needs. There are a number of examples of marketing myopia, such as the quick decline of Facit Corporation in Sweden when they failed to adopt electronic calculators in time. Instead they continued to produce complicated mechanical calculators totally inferior (when it came to satisfying the needs of the customers) to the new Japanese electronic machines, rapidly affordable for everybody in the early 1970s.

Second, there is a category containing all of the *different decision models* developed within marketing theory. The decision models guide the decision maker to decide which actions to take, given a number of facts. There are models of pricing, allocation of advertising budgets, design of sales people's territories, screening of new products and so on.

Finally, there are models of how marketing is to be *implemented* in organizations. Kotler[53] defines marketing implementation as 'the process that turns marketing plans into action assignments and ensures that such assignments are executed in a manner that accomplishes the plan's stated objectives'.

Within the managerial school, marketing is regarded as a functional speciality normally found only in a marketing department and performed only by specialists such as sales people, advertising experts, marketing research experts and so on. Within the relationship schools marketing, it is instead considered to be 'everybody's job' and marketing related activities are done by almost everybody in the company – at least to some extent.

By definition, the general statements are regarded as being valid in all types of firms while on the other side decision models and implementation models are valid only under one condition and not valid under another condition.

Size-related contextual influence in marketing often refers to how marketing is implemented in organizations. Implementation of marketing is expected to be very different due to the context, and size is, of course, one such context – it is obvious to everybody that a small subcontractor and the big multinational perform and organize marketing differently in many respects, for example:

- formalization (planning, decision making);
- speed of actions and flexibility, organizational structure; and
- reduced level of in-house resources (money, knowledge, information-handling capacity and so on).

SUMMARY

There are important differences in how marketing is implemented and performed in a big corporation compared to a small firm, especially when referring to marketing as visualized through the spectacles of the managerial school. In other aspects there are no or very limited differences.

Modern information technology and efficient worldwide distribution systems allow small firms to cooperate in alliances and networks. Within these networks, economies of scale may be combined with small-scale operations because each partner may be very specialized in a certain area and niche. The size-related disadvantages are quickly reduced in importance in many sectors of the economy.

This is important to keep in mind when discussing the nature of marketing in big versus small firms. We do not say that this will lead to a situation where marketing becomes more and more uniform, as contextual factors will still be there to contend with.

But size may not restrict a small firm that wants to grow. In cooperation with other organizations, big or small, it can create efficient global marketing operations and become competitive with big operators. These operations may be even more efficient because they may combine large-scale economies with the benefits of small-scale operations. The local barbershop, the small subcontractor or grocery store will not take advantage of these opportunities. Marketing in these forever-small firms will deviate from the small but growing entrepreneurial gazelles.

Neil Borden[54] raised the question 'is marketing a science or an art' in 1964. At first glance it seems easy to answer this question, especially in a discussion of marketing in big versus marketing in small firms. In the big bureaucratic multinationals, the formal aspects – how marketing is analysed, planned and decided – may be more important than the real actions. In the entrepreneurial firm, however, the formal aspects are definitely subordinated to 'the doing'; where the action is. But it is an oversimplification to believe that marketing in big firms is more of a science and marketing in small firms is closer to art.

As shown in this chapter we both agree and disagree with the view that marketing in small firms in general and in entrepreneurial growing firms in particular is different from marketing in big firms. It is a matter of which perspective is chosen – what kind of spectacles to wear when looking at marketing.

If we talk about marketing as viewed within the managerial school, we find that implementation of marketing in small firms is very different from what we find in the big firms. But when we talk about marketing in business-to-business networks, in strategic alliances and in the service sector we believe that the similarities between big- and small-firm marketing are more important than the differences.

As a matter of fact, we find that bigger firms instead try to acquire marketing capabilities that generally are to be found in smaller organizations, capabilities such as closeness to customers, quick reactions to changes in customer preferences, flexibility, low overhead costs and so on.

If we go back twenty years, marketing may have been an area where small firms were regarded as having a disadvantage. In many of the dynamic markets in the new millennium, and with the breakthrough of information technology in mind, marketing may instead be an area where small firms have advantages, and may even excel. Cooperation is a solution in situations where an economy of scale is important. In other contexts 'the economies of small-scale operations' may be the advantage to explore.

This will be further discussed in the forthcoming chapters of this book.

NOTES

1. Howard, J.A. (1957), *Marketing Management: Analysis and Decisions*, Homewood, IL:

Richard D. Irwin; Kotler, P. (1997), *Marketing Management*, Englewood Cliffs, NJ: Prentice-Hall; McCarthy, E.J. (1960), *Basic Marketing*, Homewood, IL: Richard D. Irwin.
2. See, for example, Håkansson, H. (ed.) (1982), *International Marketing and Purchasing of Industrial Goods - An Interactive Approach*, Chichester: John Wiley & Sons; Håkansson, H. and I. Snehota (eds) (1995), *Developing Relationship in Business Networks*, London: Routledge; Ford, D. (ed.) (1998), *Managing Business Relationships*, Chichester: John Wiley & Sons.
3. See, for example, Webster, F.E. (1992), 'The Changing Role of Marketing in the Corporation', *Journal of Marketing*, **56** (October), pp. 1-17.
4 . Kotler, P. (1973), 'The Major Tasks of Marketing Management', *Journal of Marketing*, (October), pp. 42-9.
5. See, for example: Kotler, P. (2001), *A Framework for Marketing Management*, Upper Saddle River, NJ: Prentice-Hall, p. 56.
6. Jacob, R. (1995), 'The Struggle to Create an Organization for the 21st Century', *Fortune*, 3 April, pp. 90-99.
7. Webster (1992), p. 9.
8. Håkansson and Snehota (1995), p. 7.
9. Axelsson, B. (1996), *Professionell marknadsföring* [Professional marketing], Lund: Studentlitteratur, p. 191.
10. See, for instance, Håkansson (1982) or Håkansson and Snehota (1995).
11. Adapted from Håkansson and Snehota (1995), pp. 45, 47.
12. See, for example, Nilsson, T.H. (1995), *Chaos Marketing*, Maidenhead: McGraw-Hill.
13. Håkansson and Snehota (1995), p. 48.
14. Ibid., p. 46.
15. Blau, P.M. (1964), *Exchange and Power in Social Life*, New York: John Wiley & Sons, p. 454.
16. Research from the IMP group in Europe (IMP = Industrial Marketing and Purchasing), see, for example, Ford (1998).
17. Håkansson and Snehota (1995), pp. 198-9.
18. Grönroos, C. (2000), *Service Marketing and Management - Customer Relationship Management Approach*, Chichester: John Wiley & Sons, pp. 242-3.
19. Shewhart, W.A. (1931), *Economic Control of Manufactured Products*, New York: Van Nostrand.
20. Arnerup, B. and B. Edvardsson (1992), *Marknadsföring av tjänster* [Marketing of services], Lund: Studentlitteratur, p. 99.
21. Eigler, P. and E. Langerad (1987), *Servuction*, Paris: McGraw-Hill.
22. Berry, L. and A. Parasuraman (1991), *Marketing Services - Competing Through Quality*, New York: Free Press.
23. Zeithaml, V.A., A. Parasuraman and L.L. Berry (1985) 'Problems and Strategies in Services Marketing', *Journal of Marketing*, **52** (April), pp. 33-46. Four service characteristics often quoted are: 1. Intangibility, 2. Inseparability, 3. Perishability, and 4. Heterogenity; Zeithaml, V.A., A. Parasuraman and L.L. Berry (1990), *Delivering Quality Services - Balancing Customer Perceptions and Expectations*, New York: The Free Press, p. 678. The discussion about marketing implications is from Arnerup and Edvardsson (1992), pp. 38-9 (in Swedish).
24. See, for example, Grönroos (2000), pp. 48-9, 59-60; Lovelock, C. (1991), *Services Marketing*, Englewood Cliffs, NJ: Prentice-Hall.
25. Grönroos, C. (1984a), *Strategic Marketing and Marketing in the Service Sector*, Lund: Studentlitteratur, p. 79.
26. Grönroos (2000), pp. 373-8.
27. Christopher, M., A. Payne, D. Ballantyne et al. (1991), *Relationship Marketing: Bringing Quality, Customer Service, and Marketing Together*, Oxford, UK: Butterworth-Heinemann.
28. Gummesson, E. (2001), 'Practical Value of Adequate Marketing Management Theory', manuscript under review, pp. 8 and 12.
29. Grönroos, C. (1994a), 'Quo Vadis, Marketing? Toward a Relationship Marketing Paradigm', *Journal of Marketing Management*, **10**, pp. 347-60; Grönroos, C. (1994b),

'From Marketing-Mix to Relationship Marketing: Towards a Paradigm Shift in Marketing', *Asia-Australia Marketing Journal*, **2** (1), and reissued in *Management Decision*, **32** (2), 1994, pp. 4–26.

30. Blois, K. (1997), 'Are Business-to-Business Relationships Inherently Unstable?', *Journal of Marketing Management*, **13**, pp. 367–82.
31. Zinkham, G. and R. Watson (1998), 'Electronic Commerce: A Marriage of Management Information Systems and Marketing', *Journal of Market Focused Management*, **3**, pp. 5–22.
32. Hultman, C., C. Gunnarsson and F. Prenkert (1998), *Marketing Behaviour and Capabilities in Some Swedish SMEs – Expanders versus Non-expanders*, Stockholm: FSF.
33. Zinkhan and Watson (1998).
34. Turban, E., J. Lee, David King and Michael Chung (2000), *Electronic Commerce - A Managerial Perspective*, Upper Saddle River, NJ: Prentice-Hall, pp. 84–6; Peppers, Don et al. (1999), *The One-to-One Fieldbook*, New York: Currency & Doubleday; Peppers, D. and M. Rogers (1999), *The One-to-One Manager, Real-World Lessons in CRM*, New York: Currency & Doubleday.
35. Brännback, M. and J. Pukakainen [sic] (1998), 'Web Marketing: Has the Distinction Between Products and Services Become Obsolete?', *Journal of Market Focused Management*, **3** (1), pp. 47–58.
36. Grönroos, C. (1984b), 'A Service Quality Model and its Marketing Implications', *European Journal of Marketing*, **18** (4), pp. 36–44.
37. Harvard Business School (2000), 'A crash course in customer relationship management', *Management Update* (March), p. 5.
38. Strauss, J. and R. Frost (2001), *E-marketing*, Upper Saddle River, NJ, Prentice-Hall.
39. See, for example, Handen, L. (2000), 'Putting CRM to Work: The Rise of the Relationship', in Brown, S.A. (ed.), *Customer Relationship Management: A Strategic Imperative in the World of e-Business*, Etobicoke, Ontario: John Wiley & Sons Canada Ltd, pp. 7–18: 15ff.
40. Hills, G. (1995), 'Foreword', in Carson, D., S. Cromie, P. McGowan and J. Hill, *Marketing and Entrepreneurship in SMEs. An Innovative Approach*, London: Prentice-Hall, p. xiii.
41. Birley, S. (1982), 'Corporate Strategy and the Small Firm', *Journal of General Management*, **8** (2), p. 82.
42. Hertz, S. and L.-G. Mattsson (1998), *Mindre företag blir internationella* [Smaller firms become international], Lund, Sweden: Liber.
43. Havnes, P.A. (1998), 'SME Development – Challenging the Incremental Change Models', paper presented at 43rd ICSB Conference, Singapore 1998, workshop on Interstratos (Internationalization Strategies of European SMEs).
44. Mintzberg, H. and J.A. Water (1994), 'Of Strategies, Deliberate and Emergent', in H. Tsoukas (ed.), *New Thinking in Organizational Behaviour*, Oxford: Butterworth Heinemann, pp. 188–208.
45. Carson et al. (1995), p. 90.
46. Hills, G. and C. Hultman (1998), 'Is University Education Relevant to Growth Oriented SMEs', in *Employment – The Great Challenge: Small Business The Great Solution*, Proceedings from 25th International Small Business Congress, São Paulo, Brazil, 11–14 October.
47. Hultman, C. (1999), 'Lack of Formal Procedures – A Rational or an Entrepreneurial Perspective in Marketing', in Hultman, C. and L. Sanner, *Implementation of Marketing in Some Swedish SMEs – Expanders versus non-expanders*, Stockholm, Sweden: FSF 1999:1, pp. 35–44.
48. Day, G.S. (1994), 'The Capabilities of Market-driven Organizations', *Journal of Marketing*, **58** (October), pp. 37–52.
49. Birley (1982), p. 86.
50. Carson, D. (1985), 'The Evolution of Marketing in Small Firms', *European Journal of Marketing*, **19** (5), pp. 7–16.
51. Carson et al. (1995), p. 90.
52. Levitt, T. (1960), 'Marketing Myopia', *Harvard Business Review* (July–August), pp. 45–56.
53. Kotler (1997), p. 763.
54. Borden, N.H. (1964), 'The Concept of the Marketing Mix', *Journal of Advertising Research*, Advertising Research Foundation Inc. (June), pp. 2–7.

5. Marketing, entrepreneurship and culture

INTRODUCTION

Figure 3.5 presented a base model of the way we look at entrepreneurship, that is, it depends on:

- use of language;
- culture; and
- entrepreneurial capacities.

Culture, which also influences entrepreneurial capacities, depends, in turn, on use of language.

In this chapter, we discuss how marketing and entrepreneurship may differ in various *national* cultures. We do this for three reasons:

1. To deepen the readers' understanding of the importance of use of language and culture for all kinds of action among people, the same is true for marketers and entrepreneurs.
2. To provide a background to the discussion of the importance of corporate culture later in this book.
3. To prove that findings in this book are valid mainly for the Western, industrialized world.

The reason we focus on national cultures is because much research has been done about the relationship between the level of culture and business style. However, as there has been very little specific research done on entrepreneurial marketing in various national cultures, much of the discussion in this chapter will be relevant not only to small firms, but to businesses of all kinds and sizes. We shall start by specifying the meaning of culture in this book. Some general dimensions of culture and cultural manifestations will be focused on. Finally, a synthesis will be developed of what is known (which will include quite a bit of speculation) about the relationship between national culture and entrepreneurial marketing in terms of management and leadership, organization, business approach and business success. This chapter concludes by clarifying what has been learned in this chapter.

THE MEANING OF CULTURE

The concept of culture comes from anthropology. Anthropologists normally have a very broad definition of culture, covering all sorts of aspects of life, understood either as objective factual circumstances or as subjective theories. An anthropologist studying culture traditionally aims at investigating every aspect of it in order to get a complete picture of the society to which the culture belongs.

No matter which way culture is understood, it is generally seen as being based on the following:

- *The essence of culture is its values*   One common understanding seems to be that culture is related to human values one way or the other. Value could be seen as 'ideas about what is desirable'[1] or as 'beliefs about desirable end-states underlying attitudinal and behavioural processes'.[2] Human beings are evaluating creatures.
- *Culture is something people learn*   People carry around culture as acquired in the family in early childhood and later reinforced and developed in schools and other organizations.
- *Culture is the intersubjective part of life*   Culture is something human-made. It is also something which is shared in a group of people. It is common to people in a certain group or category, but different (at least partly) from people belonging to other groups or categories. The 'group' referred to has to be together long enough for its shared learning to take place and could be, for instance, a sports team, a business firm, or even a nation. The 'sharing' referred to is a result of interaction in everyday life, not a result of any formal arrangement.
- *Language is a mirror of culture*   A fundamental tenet of anthropology is that there is a close relationship between language and culture. It is generally held that it is impossible to understand a culture fully without taking into account its language and it is equally impossible to understand a language well outside its cultural context.[3] Culture influences language and language influences culture in a number of ways.
- *Culture has a powerful influence on our lives*   Culture gives an individual an anchoring point, an identity, a world view, but also codes of conduct. The manner in which people consume, the priority of needs and the wants they attempt to satisfy, and the manner in which they satisfy them are functions of their culture which temper, mould and

dictate their style of living. Culture powerfully influences everything from the materialistic to the spiritual. What people consider important or unimportant becomes dictated by culture.

A key issue in discussing culture is the degree to which a culture is conscious and open rather than unconscious and covered. This has implications for how easily a culture can be studied and, in a business context, managed.[4] If we look at culture as some kind of *shared understanding*, we can place it in a consciousness–unconsciousness continuum[5] at three levels (Figure 5.1).

Behavioural norms are the most overt parts of culture as shared understanding. These are the unwritten rules of behaviour. Norms are transmitted from senior to junior, from old to young, from one generation to the next. Examples of norms are: do not argue with your boss, do not rock the boat, and look busy even when you are not. When asked, most individuals can list, at least after having thought for a while, the norms that exist in, for instance, their work group.

At a somewhat deeper level there are hidden *values and assumptions* – the fundamental drives and beliefs behind all decisions and actions. In a business context, this understanding pertains, for example, to the importance to listen to peers, what stakeholders to prioritize, the nature of the environment, and what learning and progress is all about.

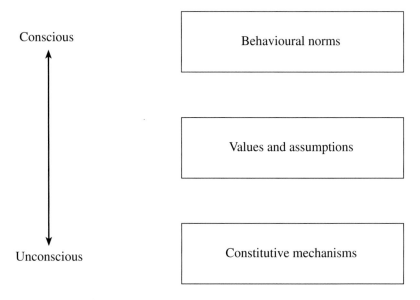

Figure 5.1 Culture in a consciousness–unconsciousness continuum

At its deepest level, shared understanding consists of the collection of *constitutive mechanisms*, those phenomenologically rooted processes of subjectification, objectification and so on, which operate existentially to create the social reality of any group and without which the other two levels of norms, values and assumptions cannot function.[6]

The reason why some values and assumptions 'disappear' into semi-awareness and why some beliefs are taken for granted and unexamined is because of *routine*. A problem that is regularly solved sooner or later becomes an underlying premise, sunk down from consciousness. This is human nature. This means, in turn, that the effect of culture on our lives is largely unrealized.[7] People are commonly unaware of their cultural blinkers.

The matrix in Figure 5.2 has been constructed to aid in the discussion of the different meanings of culture.[8] Culture (here in a business context) could be seen as some or all of the cells in the figure:

1. *Conscious behaviour*   A company may have a formal budget process which could be something every employee knows.
2. *Unconscious behaviour*   Within a company, employees might take it for granted that at a meeting the boss sits at the head of a table and those who are nearest to his or her formal position in the organization sit as close as possible to the boss at the meeting table as well.
3. *Conscious non-behaviour*   (that is, refers to values only, which in turn

CULTURE AS	Something conscious	Something unconscious
Behavioural	(1) Ex: The budget process	(2) Ex: Sitting down at a meeting
Non-behavioural (values only)	(3) Ex: The fewer accidents, the better	(4) Ex: Planning is good

☐ Culture in this book

Figure 5.2   Culture along a behavioural–consciousness continuum

may influence the behaviour of those people accepting these values). In a company there might be an official statement about the value of avoiding accidents.

4. *Unconscious non-behaviour*   There could be employees who find it 'natural' to always plan before actions are taken, even to believe that more planning is better than less planning. This might have even become a taken-for-granted value that is not questioned or debated.

Our understanding of culture in this book includes only cell (4). A definition of culture for us could be basic behavioural norms, values and assumptions (assumptions are sometimes referred to as 'beliefs'), which in an interaction between people in a group are passed on to new members and which have behavioural effects without being behavioural themselves. We refer to cells (1)–(3) as 'cultural manifestations', but not culture itself.[9]

There are three reasons for this 'restricted' use of culture:

1. As mentioned, the anthropological ambition is commonly to present a complete design for living among members of civilizations which could be marginal in a society or a historic civilization. The business researcher's ambition is, on the other hand, almost the opposite. He or she attempts, most of all, to understand the essence and core and fundamental logic of culture (of, say, a firm) which manifests itself everywhere and every day in abundance in any business setting.

2. Norms, values and assumptions are at the heart and soul of an individual when considering marketing an entrepreneurial effort. This gives a focus to this book. Culture in this book does not (explicitly) include those 'constitutive mechanisms' which are mentioned at the bottom of Figure 5.1. These 'mechanisms' are produced and are no doubt inevitable and decisive for any group in real life, but they are difficult to include (explicitly) in our general pictures of *national* cultures and their consequences.

3. Culture has sometimes come to mean almost anything. *If* a concept excludes nothing, it becomes meaningless or, at least, loses its analytical edge.

The above definition does not in any way deny those intimate relations that exist between culture and cultural manifestations.

One way to discuss the relations between national cultures and entrepreneurial marketing is by presenting research done on some general cultural values and manifestations. These cultural dimensions are not presented in any particular order but should all have some interest to marketing or entrepreneurship or both. The dimensions in question are:

- social orientation and trust;
- uncertainty avoidance and attitude to change;
- time orientation and attitude to environment;
- power and leadership style;
- problem-solving style; and
- skills being asked for and measurement of personal success.

SOME CULTURAL VALUES AND MANIFESTATIONS OF INTEREST

Social Orientation and Trust

Individualism is a central value in US culture,[10] that is, reliance on individual initiative, self-assertion, and personal achievement and responsibility. Some fundamental characteristics of individualistic cultures are:[11]

- nuclear families and independent children;
- private lives and opinions are appreciated;
- self-orientation and self-motivation;
- freedom and variety is important;
- education is promoting independence;
- individual initiative is encouraged;
- stronger ambition for individual advancement and leadership;
- individuals do the job and are rewarded as such; and
- strong feelings against collectivism.

Individualism has been described by Parsons and Shils[12] as 'a prime orientation to the self' and its opposite collectivism as 'a prime orientation to common goals and objectives'. Some cultures lean towards the individual side, some towards the collective side. Americans and those in other English-speaking countries, such as Canada, the UK, Australia and New Zealand are individualists. So are North Europeans in general. People in Latin countries, including South Americans, are collectivists and so are Africans and Asians in general. The Japanese, however, and Arabs are somewhere in between but lean towards the collectivistic side.[13]

The Japanese 'groupism' has its origins in the strong tradition of the household. Motherhood is a primary value in Eastern cultures.[14] But the term has a broader meaning in Japan: it relates to any context and is social in orientation.[15]

Trompenaars[16] refers to such a culture as the Japanese as a 'family culture'. Characteristics of a family culture include:

- It is personal with close face-to-face relationships, but also hierarchical. Many relationships are by obligation rather than by choice.[17]
- The power exerted is essentially intimate and (hopefully) benign.
- The group is the basic unit at work.[18] The group takes decisions, assumes responsibility, does the job and is rewarded.[19]
- A large part of the reason for working is the potential pleasure derived from relationships in a group. The expected reward is esteem and punishment is disappointment.
- The general happiness and welfare of all employees is regarded as the concern of the corporation.

The family is also important in the Chinese culture. However, in the Chinese system, family ethics are based on relationship between *particular individuals*. In Japan they are based on the *collective group*, that is, members of a household, not on the relationship between individuals.[20]

The importance of the family and of strong family ties among Asians in general and maybe particularly true for the Chinese, has been certified by many researchers.[21] Families are not only the bedrock of the Chinese society, they are also the bedrock of Chinese business.[22] A Chinese firm is almost always a family firm.[23] This is especially true for the Overseas Chinese business system.[24] Peter Drucker has expressed it such that 'the secret of Japan consists in Japan's ability to make a family out of a modern corporation. The secret of Chinese management may well consist in the ability of the Chinese to make a family into a modern corporation'.[25] However, a 'family' has a wide meaning for the Chinese and may include the same ethnic background and even birthplace. Overseas Chinese have built up their strength, among other factors, on an unusual ethnic solidarity.[26]

Let us consider another culture. Arabs live in a definite *class structure*.[27] The Arab class is based on the family (tribe) and its background. In a typified Arab society, privileges are unevenly distributed; Arabs live in a collectivistic culture, but it is not egalitarian.

North Europeans have *generally individualistic* cultures. However, Scandinavians do not score extremely high in individualism. They can accept rules and regulations (as long as they are fair).[28]

When Americans (to simplify, we refer to people living in the US, when we talk about 'Americans') relate to each other they are informal. They also tend to be on the expressive side.[29] Americans have a high 'willingness to communicate',[30] and American students perceive a pressure and demand for high communicative skills.[31] Americans frequently assume that informality is a prerequisite for sincerity. It has been suggested that frankness is a primary value in the American type of culture.[32]

Cultures vary in terms of how explicitly they send and receive verbal messages. Arab culture, for instance, is a *high-contextual* culture.[33] It means that communication between Arabs relies heavily on hidden, implicit, contextual cues such as non-verbal behaviour, social context and the nature of interpersonal relationships. Feedback, in the limited sense in which Westerners usually understand it, is therefore often felt by Arabs to be too blunt and lacking in finesse, regardless of truth. Frankness is of secondary value to Arabs.[34]

For the Chinese, *networking* is a natural thing to do[35] (as it is for the Arabs and, to some extent, for the Japanese). Chinese culture is famous for its *guan-xi*, which can be translated as 'relationships' or 'connections'. Everywhere in the business world you need contacts. But you have to magnify its importance many times to understand *guan-xi*.[36] Good *guan-xi* both inside and outside the firm is a guarantee of success at the personal as well as at the professional level for a Chinese person.[37] Without *guan-xi*, he or she is nothing; with *guan-xi*, he or she cannot do wrong.[38]

Several studies have shown that Japanese culture is one of the highest contextual cultures there is (competing with the Chinese and Arabs for this position).[39] What makes it hard for an outsider to get close to a Japanese is also that the Japanese value order and harmony extremely highly.

It is much easier to get close to a Scandinavian. He or she belongs to a very *low-contextual* culture (as does an American). This means that such a person is what he or she seems to be; paradoxes and surprises are few, and there is no great need to interpret him or her, his thoughts, purposes and so on. The spoken and written word is enough. But similar to the Japanese, Scandinavians do not like direct confrontation in their relations with other people. In Scandinavia, problems should be solved by open discussions leading to a compromise, not by force.[40] Scandinavian virtues include patience, restraint, moderation and emotional control, possibly partly due to its extreme egalitarianism. It is also a typified characteristic of the Scandinavian culture to trust one another.

The implications of what has been said in this section about social orientation and trust among national cultures for marketing and entrepreneurship are many. For *marketing* (to give just a few typified examples):

- In individualistic cultures consumers have their own choice; in collectivistic cultures consumers are more influenced by the group.
- In individualistic cultures a marketing slogan like 'As a consumer, you stand out from the crowd' is more successful than in collectivistic cultures.
- In informal and low-contextual cultures communication with buyers and consumers can be more direct and frank than in formal and high-contextual cultures.

- Many aspects of advanced and elaborated advertising and other promotional efforts are a waste of time and resources in high-contextual and in non-trusting cultures; networking is more the way to go in the latter case.

For *entrepreneurship* (to give just a few typified examples):

- In individualistic cultures entrepreneurship is most often the result of an individual initiative and effort; in collectivistic cultures entrepreneurship may start from an individual initiative but must have the support of the group to succeed.
- In individualistic cultures entrepreneurs are more driven by internal motives than in collectivistic cultures.
- In individualistic cultures a person is more likely to leave his or her employment to further pursue his or her own ideas in an independent new business venture than in a collectivistic culture; in a collectivistic culture a new business venture (even if in a separate firm) is often linked to and controlled by the 'father' firm.
- In trusting cultures, the entrepreneur could be almost anybody; in non-trusting cultures the entrepreneur must be somebody with connections.

Uncertainty Avoidance and Attitude to Change

Uncertainty avoidance or the need in life for structure differs among nations. On a scale where the need for structure by various countries is measured, Latin countries score very high and so do Japan and South Korea. Medium scores belong to German-speaking countries, and Asians (except the two mentioned). Africans, Americans, the British and Scandinavians score very low on the need to avoid uncertainty.[41]

The Japanese have a mixed attitude to the future. On one hand, they hate uncertainty.[42] But in another way, they can accept uncertainty, ambiguity and incompleteness. Certain things simply *are* to the Japanese – and should be accepted as such.[43] However, the Japanese are very formal and ritualistic, which is a common manifestation in cultures avoiding uncertainty.[44] They are also conservative in dress and behaviour.[45]

The Chinese are different. They are fast adapters when it may lead to business advantages[46] and they have, in general, a high respect for learning and openness to new ideas. However, willingness to learn and to change should not, here, generally be taken as creativity and innovativeness: 'Chinese culture tends to suppress individual initiative and often tames the spirit of the most resourceful individuals, rather than encouraging the sometimes erratic fire of creativity.'[47] The Asian insistence on the authority of parents and other seniors (Confucianism) may discourage creativity, competition and innovation.

Most Asians are also superstitious. When Chinese, for instance, are faced with an important decision, they may seek for auspicious signs or consult oracular books or fortune-tellers. Being superstitious is one way to 'cushion oneself' against failure in the face of risk.[48]

Related to this last point, Chinese thinking is somewhat fatalistic and very direct.[49] On the other hand, taking decisions directly, relationally and specifically as the Chinese often do, gives them a trust in themselves and in common sense, plus a high willingness to take risks and an ability to face uncertainty.[50] The Chinese not only score low in uncertainty avoidance, they also excel in risk taking.[51]

People in the US tend to be future oriented rather than oriented to the present or the past. It is one of their fundamental assumptions that the capacity to defer gratification (doing something that is not particularly pleasant today to further future pleasure) is a positive indication.[52] It is generally thought that with this concentration on the future – together with a high value placed on action and work – it is not only possible, but mandatory to improve on the present. An American future is, also, anticipated to be 'bigger and better'.[53] Americans foster a cult of progress. And belief in progress involves accepting change and the idea that change can be steered in a good direction.

In business, American managers not only value change relatively highly but also value caution less.[54] This suggests an active or dynamic orientation and a willingness to make risky decisions. Uncertainty of life is accepted as normal, and economic risks are judged by potential rewards. Many scholars claim that the American economy is very entrepreneurial, for example, Peter Drucker.[55]

One aspect of controlling today for the future is that managers in the American type of culture are more involved in strategy, and that they categorize strategic issues as opportunities, while some other cultures (like the Japanese) overwhelmingly view them as problems.[56]

Also, as part of their future orientation, Americans prefer to conform to standards that momentarily are current and up to date rather than old-fashioned.[57] On the business scene, American managers endorse 'modern' management ideas, trying to be up to date as well.[58]

We can often read that Europeans do not feel comfortable taking risks.[59] Scandinavian decision making, for instance, is commonly characterized as slow, and Scandinavian managers are often seen as indecisive and excessively cautious.[60] Unwilling to take risks may sound contradictory to Hofstede's[61] conclusion that people embracing Scandinavian cultural values have a greater willingness to take risks than most others. Our interpretation is that a Scandinavian business manager is not the stereotypical bold American loner and dare-devil who is not afraid to break into unchartered ground or the cunning

Chinese who concludes a multi-million dollar business with a handshake. The Scandinavian manager may be slow in details, but he or she (and other Scandinavians) is certainly not unwilling to change and to experiment.[62]

The implications of what has been said in this section about uncertainty avoidance and attitude to change for marketing and entrepreneurship are many. For *marketing*:

- Advertising and communicating with consumers and customers in a culture avoiding uncertainty requires messages linking to established values more than in cultures not avoiding uncertainty.
- Sales representatives in cultures avoiding uncertainty are more formal, ritualistic and conservative.
- Advertising in cultures not avoiding uncertainty is more creative and generally a more developed discipline than in cultures avoiding uncertainty.

For *entrepreneurship*:

- Entrepreneurship is more imitative in cultures avoiding uncertainty and resisting change; in cultures not avoiding uncertainty and accepting change, entrepreneurship is more innovative.
- Extrapreneurs are common in all cultures; in cultures not avoiding uncertainty, however, they can more easily cut the link with the former employer than in other cultures.
- The process to become an entrepreneur in cultures not avoiding uncertainty and accepting change is generally more direct, faster and less complicated than in cultures that avoid uncertainty and do not accept much change.

Time Orientation and Attitude to the Environment

Part of the American orientation to the future and to progress is to control nature. In short, Americans assume that the environment can be subjugated to the human will, given time, effort and money: and it should be – in the service of mankind. This American orientation is based on an economy of abundance, stemming from the immense physical and natural resources of an entire continent.[63]

Other cultures may have a more humble attitude to nature. It could be too that in some cultures the natural world is closely associated with supernatural forces and should not (or could not) be transformed by human hand. It could also be that the culture emphasizes the integration of people with the natural world, whereby the natural environment shapes people and, in turn, is shaped by people.[64] The Japanese, for instance, have learned to live with scarcity. Physical and geographic density in Japan has made its people not only to reinforce groupism, interdependence and a sense of debt and obligation, but also to excel in material handling, transportation, quality control, cutting out waste, energy conservation and convertibility.[65]

There is a considerable variation between countries and no marked pattern by continent in terms of the belief whether it is worth trying to control nature or not. Based on surveys on 15,000 managers, Trompenaars[66] came up with the following figures: only 10 per cent of the Japanese believe it is worth trying, but as much as 43 per cent of the Chinese; only 21 per cent of the Swedes but 35 per cent of the British. The British, Germans and Americans are all above the middle of the range.

Controlling the environment for a business person includes the belief in the possibility of influencing consumers and customers.

To the American, time is seen as just another part of the environment to be dealt with. And in the US, 'time is money'; it should be carefully used, properly budgeted, and should not be wasted. Cultures with this kind of attitude are usually short term in their business strategies. Also, Americans (like the Scandinavians) value promptness and punctuality highly.

In contrast, the low stress on efficiency among, for example, the Arabs is associated with the fact that their sense of time is less strict than among Westerners.[67] Punctuality is also only a tertiary value among the former.[68] A Middle Easterner does not assume or exercise a control over his time. Issues and actions are triggered by whether the time is right, not on schedule or by reference to a mechanism. Patience is a virtue among Arabs.[69]

As long as a Chinese person makes money, he or she feels that time is on his or her side. On the other hand, being so sales and money oriented makes the Chinese prone to short-term thinking.[70] However, they can be very patient when hammering out a business deal and discussing business in general, and they can be very enduring in staying with their business and building for the future for their family and children.

The Japanese have a long-term view.[71] This is shown in business by such procedures as life-long employment, slow promotion and employees being subordinated to their companies.

If Americans (and Chinese) are short term in their orientation and Japanese are long term, then North Europeans have a medium-term orientation.[72]

The implications of what has been said in this section about time orientation and attitude to the environment for marketing and entrepreneurship are many. For *marketing*:

● Preservation of nature could be a more appropriate theme in advertising and sales promotion in cultures where the attitude to the environment is less exploitative.

- Marketing planning in cultures with an exploitative attitude to the environment may include how to influence customers and consumers more than in other cultures.
- Whether a culture is short term or long term in its orientation has consequences for all aspects of marketing.

For *entrepreneurship*:

- Entrepreneurs must be more careful not to exploit the environment (including customers and consumers) in some cultures than in others.
- Quality is important for all entrepreneurs to succeed. However, it is more central and it includes more dimensions in non-exploitative cultures.
- Most entrepreneurship is a long-term commitment; however, it is more important to show short-term results in some cultures than in others.

Power and Leadership Style

Let us contrast some cultures in terms of how they look at power and in terms of what leadership style is used.

One concept commonly used to discuss power in a national culture is 'power distance'. In a culture where power distance is short, there is hierarchical fluidity, rank is decided by achievement and there is a relative equality of superiors and subordinates. Where power distance is long, the hierarchy is solid, rank is decided by background and there is inequality between superiors and subordinates.

Power distance is medium in the US. Characteristics of such a culture include:[73]

- Subordinates expect superiors to consult them but will accept autocratic behaviour.
- An ideal superior to most is a resourceful democrat.
- Laws and rules apply to all but a certain level of privileges for superiors is judged as normal.
- Status symbols for superiors contribute moderately to their authority and will be accepted by subordinates.

Common for countries having a medium power distance like the US is that they advocate participation in the manager's decisions by his or her subordinates; however, the initiative towards this is supposed to be taken by the manager.[74]

Company triangles (the organizational hierarchies) are generally very flat in the US.[75] A hierarchy in the American type of culture means inequality of roles, established for convenience.[76] The organization type is implicitly structured, managers are more interpersonally oriented and flexible in their style, and informal consultation is possible without formal participation.[77]

Organization pyramids in the Arab world are very steep – steepest of all in an international comparison made by Trompenaars.[78] They are tall and centralized.[79] What usually follows from such steep pyramids is that top-down communication is dominant and that authoritarianism becomes a primary value.[80]

Who is doing something is more important than *what* is being done among the Arabs. We could call this 'management by subjectives'.[81] The Arabs score very high on power distance[82] and Arab managers see themselves as father figures.

The Chinese are very similar in this respect. Characteristics of a Chinese business enterprise include an autocratic, centralized style of management. Authoritarianism is a primary value in Eastern cultures in general.[83]

In all this talk about centralized autocracy and tall organization pyramids among Arab and Chinese businesses, it is important to realize that they contain formal as well as informal characteristics (chaotic to many outsiders) and that they are not bureaucratic in the classic Weber sense of the word. A better word for Arab as well as Chinese businesses is that they are rather 'personalized' (by their power-holders).[84]

Chinese culture is definitely a very *power-centred* culture. All Chinese-dominated countries in Southeast Asia score high in power distance.[85] A difference between the Arab and the Chinese cultures is that the latter is more interested in control. Chinese managers want to have a hand in most things connected with their business.[86] The Chinese way is to control everything.[87] And everybody who is not a key individual (a member of the extended family, functioning more on trust) is supervised.[88] 'Chinese leaders are control freaks'.[89]

The Japanese are here (as in so many other respects) different. To the Japanese businessman, organization really means the people. Another way to express the fact that Japanese organizations really mean people is to say that Japanese companies are run for the benefit of their employees – of, by and for its people:[90]

- *Of the employees*   To never forget that a business organization is made up of people and can function no better than they do.
- *By the employees*   To organize the firm into teams, from the executive

suite to the factory floor; to encourage workers to make on-the-spot decisions rather than check their brains at the superior's door.

- *For the employees* To have a natural cooperation between management and workers, because everybody's welfare is tied up with that of the company.

In North European business organizations, unlike in Arab and Chinese ones, there is more vertical communication, and employees are less afraid of disagreeing with their boss.[91] Egalitarianism means co-determination at work in North Europe and a democratic decision-making style. Industrial democracy fits well with the North European kind of culture. Its deeply entrenched egalitarianism has made it easier to introduce less formal, more delegating styles of management.[92] It also means less centralization and flatter organization pyramids.[93]

Equality in Scandinavia has also led to a high level of *gender equality*. There are more women in qualified and better-paid jobs than in most other countries. Scandinavia has, in fact, the highest proportion of working women in the industrialized world.[94]

Scandinavians strive for consensus like the Japanese. But, instead of stressing the individual as in the American way, the family in the Chinese way, the clan in the Arab way or the group at large in the Japanese way, they tend to stress the team and personal relations.[95] In one study, Scandinavian managers saw themselves and were seen by British managers as more 'consultative' than in Britain, where a more autocratic management style is common.[96]

The implications of what has been said in this section about power and leadership style for marketing and entrepreneurship are many. For *marketing*:

- In cultures where power distance is short, people involved in various marketing activities can work more openly and informally together than is the case in cultures where power distance is long.
- Cross-functional exchange and cooperation, between marketing and other functions, is easier and more common in cultures where power distance is short than in other cultures.
- In cultures where power distance is long, control of all marketing activities from higher up the hierarchy is much tighter than in cultures where this distance is short.

For *entrepreneurship:*

- In cultures where power distance is long, initiatives for entrepreneurial activities come normally from the top; in cultures with short power distance such initiatives can come from anywhere in the hierarchy.

- In cultures where power distance is long, control of all aspects of a new venture effort by the entrepreneur could be very detailed and frequent as compared with other cultures.
- In cultures with shorter power distance, the progress of a new venture effort can be a flurry of exchange of ideas, with an intensive flow of information between participants, open disagreements about where to go next, and so on. In cultures with longer power distance this is much less likely to be the case.
- In cultures where power distance is short (and egalitarianism is the norm) the proportion of women starting a new business venture is higher than in other cultures.

Problem-solving Style

The typified American manager is expected to be very task oriented and rational, known for solving problems successfully, quickly and decisively. Efficiency is a primary value in the West in general.[97] The US emphasis on efficiency has consistently impressed observers.

It would even be descriptive to say that American problem solving is scientific rather than traditional.[98] Americans are taught to act on logic.[99] Logic and scientific methods have been internalized as the means of solving new problems and solutions are perceived as progress or improvements.

Logic and scientific thinking as understood in the West is not a generally valid, or even applicable, model for problem solving elsewhere. The Chinese, for instance, may have problems thinking in abstract terms in the sense of a mental experiment with a symbolic model and to look at events and objects as something to be manipulated in hypothetical experiments.[100]

One example of the Chinese lack of abstract thinking (the way Westerners look at it) is that they do not look at their business firms calculatively, as impersonal and purposive (which is common in the West), but more as parts of themselves, even existential.[101] The striking lack of abstracts in the Chinese language leads to different thought processes from those normal in the Indo-European languages.[102] The Chinese think of problems as deeply embedded in a context, out of which explanations cannot be torn.[103]

The success of Chinese business leaders rests very much on high flexibility and adaptability[104] and on political pragmatism.[105]

The Japanese are also suspicious of too much logic. They have a word, *rikutsupoi*, which means 'too logical' and which is used in a derogatory sense.[106] One could say that Japanese apply 'the logic of the situation', always considering circumstances and context.[107] Rationality for a Japanese is to look for consensus.

North Europeans are as rational and practical as the Americans are. Scandinavians, for instance, appreciate sensibility and matter-of-factness.[108] Managers there see themselves as practical[109] and Swedish businessmen describe themselves as 'efficient' and 'rational'.[110]

The implications of what has been said in this section about the problem-solving style for marketing and entrepreneurship are many. For *marketing*:

- In cultures where rationality and efficiency are highly valued, careful preparation and detailed planning of marketing activities are more appreciated than in other cultures.
- In cultures stressing rationality and efficiency, marketing activities are judged on their more objective merits than in other cultures.
- In 'scientific' cultures more alternatives for solving a specific marketing problem are considered from a more means–end point of view than in other cultures.

For *entrepreneurship*:

- There are fewer traditional approaches to entrepreneurship in cultures stressing rationality, efficiency and a 'scientific' approach than in other cultures.
- There is a more generally valid and officially accessible body of knowledge of how to do entrepreneurship in cultures using a 'scientific' approach to business.

Skills Being Asked For and Measurement of Personal Success

What is counted as a 'high-quality' person and what it means to succeed as a human being, is the topic of this section.

Americans consider it almost a right to be materially well off and physically comfortable. They expect convenient transport, a variety of clean and healthy foods and comfortable homes equipped with labour-saving devices.

Another much publicized aspect of the American culture is its positive appreciation of achievement – being able to reach individual wealth, recognition and self-actualization. Achievement is defined in terms of recognition and wealth in the American type of culture.[111] This money and things orientation may even make people prefer a higher salary to shorter working hours.[112] In general, US companies appear to rely much more on monetary rewards than do typified Japanese firms.[113]

There is sympathy for the successful achiever in the US. The strong people tend to be compensated and given the rewards.[114] Social status of managers is dependent on rank (not class). Americans disagree strongly that respect should depend on family background.[115] Young men (and increasingly young women) are expected to make a career; those who do not are generally seen as failures.

This is not so in all countries. Some cultures put more stress on being than on doing.[116] Among Arabs, for instance, being a caring person is more important than individual freedom[117] and being loyal to your employer is more important than acting efficiently.[118]

The status of the individual in the West is tied to education and knowledge. Relationships between employees in a firm could be characterized as 'specific tasks in a cybernetic system targeted upon shared objectives'.[119] American business education looks at management as a specialist profession using rational, 'scientific' tools.

In Japanese management, there is a generalist orientation and an elaborate educational system built into the company; Western management has a specialized orientation and if new skills are required, outsiders (temporary 'trouble-shooters') are employed. Such outsiders can serve an integrative role at the same time as they can allow individuals to develop even more in-depth skills for future use.[120]

There are many who assert that the Chinese (like the Japanese) are hard working, industrious, almost workaholics.[121] This is true for bosses as well as for workers.[122] The Chinese culture is also generally very materialistic. The Chinese way to show 'class' is through money and things. The old Chinese principle of avoiding excesses to keep a proper balance between the opposite forces of yin and yang, often seems to be neglected in our modern times. The Chinese have difficulty letting go of money;[123] there is a worship of power and money, according to some.[124] It is not greed, however, that drives the Overseas Chinese to be so money oriented, it is fear – and the yearning for the protection that money will give you.[125]

Important to the Chinese as well as to the Japanese is 'face'. Face can be protected, saved, added, given away, exchanged and even borrowed. The fear of losing face is nothing more than the fear of having one's ego and prestige deflated. It can be caused by a broad range of things: having an expected promotion fall through, one's child failing an examination, one's daughter marrying a poor man, one's brother working in a lowly position, receiving an inexpensive gift. The list goes on and on.[126]

The logical counterpart to 'losing' face is to 'gain' face. The prestige of an Asian may be inflated by working in a large company, by being surrounded by influential 'friends', by showing off materially and so on.

Asian cultures stress 'shame' and Western cultures stress 'guilt'. Shame is associated with public disgrace and loss of prestige; guilt carries a sense of individual responsibility and conscience.[127]

In his classic study on the importance of national cultures in business,

Hofstede introduced a scale he called 'masculinity–femininity', that is, whether a nation approves more of traditional male values or traditional female values. Japan scored highest among all his 40 countries in *masculinity*.[128] Characteristics of a high masculine culture include:[129]

- greater work centrality;
- a greater social role is attributed to corporations;
- larger corporations are more attractive;
- managers are less attracted by a service role;
- greater gender role differentiation;
- a money and things orientation;
- live to work; and
- fewer women in more qualified and better-paid jobs.

In the same study, Scandinavian countries scored exactly the opposite, that is, highest in *femininity*.[130] Among other things, this means for the Scandinavian culture:

- achievement is defined in terms of human contacts and a living environment;
- self-expression and self-fulfilment is important;
- motivational factor to feel part of progress and change is important; and
- there is sympathy for the weak in society.

Scandinavians describe themselves as 'reliable', 'honest', 'ethical', 'loyal' and 'correct'.[131] Honesty among Scandinavians is certified by others as well.[132] A related concept, that is, frankness, is valued highly among Scandinavians as well as among Americans.[133] However, individual Scandinavians are not supposed to be aggressive or stand out above the crowd. It is not socially tolerated for a Scandinavian to be 'uppity'; this is frowned upon. The important thing is to have what it takes – but not more.[134] The Scandinavian avoidance of setting themselves above others has sometimes been interpreted as a failure to assert themselves as individuals.[135]

Management in Europe is not seen as a specialist profession like in the US, but managers are rather 'quasi-generalists loosely and ambiguously defined'.[136]

The implications of what has been said in this section about skills asked for and measurement of personal success for marketing and entrepreneurship are many. For *marketing*:

- In a materialistically oriented culture, constantly bringing out new products and services is important. Marketing can have a big role to play here.

- In a culture where performance and individual contribution to the firm is more important than loyalty and consensus within the firm, individual roles in a marketing effort are more clearly defined.
- In a 'scientific' culture, more than in a traditional culture, the marketing approach follows the textbook version of planning, deciding and controlling as a model where optimization of resources is a norm.
- In a 'feminine' culture, marketing themes should contain values like 'caring', 'sympathy' and 'solidarity' more than in a 'masculine' society.

For *entrepreneurship*:

- In cultures where achievement is measured in terms of self-made personal results, entrepreneurs are more recognized and rewarded than in cultures where loyalty to the employer is highly recognized.
- In cultures where loyalty to the profession is more recognized than loyalty to the employer, intrapreneurship and extrapreneurship are more likely to occur.
- It is more accepted to fail in an entrepreneurial effort in a culture ruled by 'guilt' than in a culture ruled by 'shame'.

National culture can be important in explaining differences in values and manifestations in a society as far as business activities are concerned. We have illustrated how marketing as well as entrepreneurship should be understood, at least partly, in their national cultural contexts.

This book is mainly valid in a culture which comprises the US, English-speaking countries (like the UK, Canada and Australia) and Northern Europe (the Scandinavian countries, Holland and, to some extent, Germany). This culture could be referred to as 'Western culture'. Even if there are differences within this culture (we have seen some of them already and there are more to come), we think it is meaningful to discuss our subject, that is, entrepreneurial marketing, in this context as if it were homogeneous. We find the following norms, values, assumptions and manifestations in Western culture:

- individualism (even though Scandinavians could be referred to as 'collective individualists');
- informality;
- trust, honesty and frankness;
- low-contextual communication;
- willingness to learn and to change;
- future orientation and risk taking;
- short to medium-term orientation in time (more of the former in the US than in Europe);

- belief in controlling and influencing the environment (even if more exploitatively so in the US);
- short power distance (medium in the US);
- implicitly structured organizations with open communication, fairly democratic decision making and less authoritarianism;
- high equality among sexes;
- more of a 'scientific' than a 'traditional' problem-solving style;
- achieved more than ascribed status; and
- specialist to quasi-generalist managers.

Let us summarize what we think we know about (we shall have to add quite a bit of speculation here) business of relevance to entrepreneurial marketing in general cultural terms in the Western context. The desire is to answer the following questions: who is doing what, where, and with what results?

- *Who*   How do we understand management and leadership in Western culture?
- *What*   What type of approach to business is taken in Western culture?
- *Where*   What is the meaning of an organization in the Western culture?
- *With what result*   What is the meaning of business success in Western culture?

NATIONAL CULTURE AND ENTREPRENEURIAL MARKETING

Understanding of Management and Leadership

The Western entrepreneur and manager of a small firm is an individualist – but not a brute. He (or, almost as often, she) appreciates being independent, self-governed and self-sufficient. The attitude of an entrepreneur to the firm is to look at it calculatively (not so much emotionally), as a means of accomplishing his or her interest in success and personal achievement. The entrepreneur also attempts to keep his or her private life separate from the life as an entrepreneur, leader and manager of the small firm.

A manager in a Western firm *achieves* a position – it is not an appointment. A managerial position is professional, it is a 'modern' management ideal, the person in the position is expected to be task oriented and rational and to appreciate sensibility and matter-of-factness.

When building a firm, there are several rules which should guide a manager or entrepreneur in the West:[137]

Table 5.1   Skills of an entrepreneur or manager of a small firm: West versus East

In the West	In the East
Entrepreneurial characteristics	
Moderate, calculative risk taker	(Same as in the West)
Creative and innovative	Less of an innovator, more of an adapter of business concepts already existing elsewhere; technical adequacy and timing is more important than a pioneering spirit
Self-confident and optimistic	Even more self-confident and optimistic than in the West, once willing to take the plunge
Committed, persevering and hard-working	(Even more than in the West)
Obsessed by opportunities	(Same as in the West)
The SME stands and falls with the quality of the entrepreneur	(Same as in the West)
Managing a small firm as a leader	
Knowing self	Self-reliant to extremes
Looks at leadership as a model	Wants to be a role model (and the spider in the net)
Endorses modern ideas and changes style with type of business and size	Is more traditional and uses the same style independent of type of business and size
High value placed on the individual, personal initiative, self-assertion and personal achievement	High value placed on the family, social prestige and loyalty
Guilt motivates more than shame	Shame motivates more than guilt
Frank and open manager	More secretive manager
Managing a small firm – planning	
Planning can be formal, factual and detailed	Planning is more personalized, opportunistic and intuitive
Strategic planning is an edge, but senior manager only occasionally looks further ahead	Tactical flexibility is an edge, but much time is spent by senior manager on daily operative matters
No limit to growth	Limit to growth is fear of losing control
Business is seen as an isolated entity to be optimised	Business is seen as existing in a network to be fully exploited

Managing a small firm – organizing

Adapted to need of all stakeholders (outsiders as well as insiders)	Adapted to the need of founder (insiders only)
Work division may take place	The boss assumes responsibility for all business functions
Informal, involving employees, getting to know skills of organization members; delegating and trusting	A personalized and autocratic approach; more distance-taking to other organization members; less delegating and trusting
Using contacts to compensate for lack of skills and resources	Contact is all (networking as a way of life)
Less bureaucracy recommended	Less personalism recommended
Individual initiatives encouraged; employees speak their minds; honesty, sincerity and respect is expected in a professional order	Individual initiatives suppressed; employees fear to disagree; loyalty, obedience and respect is expected in a hierarchical order
Application of sophisticated structures and systems	More ad hoc, neglecting standard procedures
Personnel management necessary to motivate and to keep people	No formalized personnel policy

Managing a small firm – decision making

Scientific	Personalistic
If trust, trust in people's skills	If trust, trust in people's loyalty
Formal meetings common	Formal meetings rare
A respectful attitude to law and order	A creative attitude to law and order

Managing a small firm – controlling

Delegating control to some extent to trusted people	Problems to delegate control; control freaks
Close supervision rare	Close supervision common
Systems in filing, recording, inventory and stock control reduced to bare necessities	Systems in filing, recording, inventory and stock control commonly missing
Searching for feedback and learning from mistakes	Very flexible and willing to learn from what others have done, but look at own mistakes as loss of face
Blames mistakes on own wrongdoing	May blame mistakes on bad 'joss'
Continuous change and improvement, if for nothing else, for the sake of image	Change and improve only for financial gains

1. Try to adjust individual needs to organizational needs.
2. Introduce methods of individual incentives such as pay-for-performance, individual assessment, Management by Objectives (MBO).
3. Expect job turnover and mobility of employees to be high.
4. Seek out high performers, heroes and champions for special praise.
5. Give people the freedom to take individual initiatives.

To run a business means different things in different cultures. Peter Drucker, the grandfather of American management, has referred to it as 'getting things done through other people'.[138] But not only that, in the West, a manager is expected to be interpersonally oriented, to act democratically and to consult subordinates. This is a key to success in Western entrepreneurship and the management of a small firm.

One way of summarizing the necessary skills of an entrepreneur or manager of a small firm in the West and the East could be set out in Table 5.1.[139]

Type of Business Approach Taken

One basic idea behind entrepreneurship in the West is not to simply or passively fit in, to just exploit openings and opportunities, but to be truly a part of creating the future. The environment not only can, but should, be controlled for human convenience. This means accepting, even endorsing, change. It also means being more innovative and more risky in the entrepreneurial approach – exploiting the environment scientifically (Figure 5.3).[140]

It is a completely accepted (in fact, quite common) course of a personal career for somebody in the West to leave his (or her) employment to further pursue a career on ones own in an independent entrepreneurial (extrapreneurial) venture. This person could be almost anybody, not necessarily somebody with the right contacts, supported and connected in a business *before* entering into it.

The Western approach to business is *scientific*. How to do it is discussed in means–ends terms; timing, budgeting, trust, faith, sincerity and frankness are important. There is also a wide body of public knowledge to draw upon in the West – documented know-how to do business. It is a small wonder under these circumstances, especially in combination with the fact that markets and marketing tools are very developed, that marketing is a science, particularly in such a mass market as in the US.

A typical definition of 'marketing' in an American textbook could sound like this:[141] 'Marketing is the process of planning and executing the conception, pricing, promotion and distribution of ideas, goods and services to create exchanges that satisfy individual and organizational objectives'. This idea of what marketing is all about (to excel with an optimal 'marketing mix')

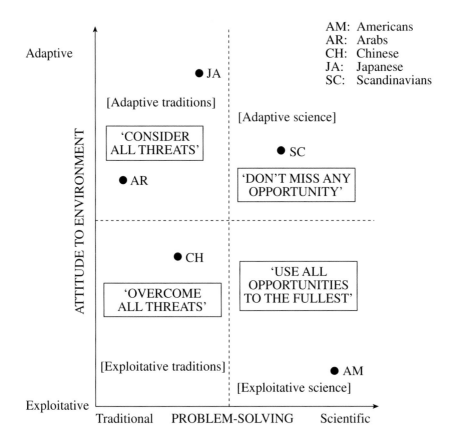

Figure 5.3   Solving business problems

fits well with stressing an approach to business called 'scientific' and a disposition for sophisticated structures and systems. But does this mean that business in less-developed countries does not work because 'they are using a less sophisticated approach'? Certainly not! And important to this book, does this mean that small firms should try to emulate the big firms' approach to marketing as much as they can? Not necessarily so![142]

There are alternative (or maybe supplementary) approaches to marketing as a strictly rational, decision-oriented optimization of the marketing mix. In the East, for instance, networking is a natural thing to do. Naisbitt[143] has even called it 'the organisational model for the twenty-first century'.

Defining *strategy* as 'external adaptation' and as 'internal integration' can be summarized using its cultural determinants (Table 5.2)[144]

Table 5.2   Cultural determinants of strategy

External adaptation	Strategy
Relationship with nature	Controlling/adapting
• Uncertainty	
• Control	
Human activity	
• Doing vs. being	Right moves vs. right stuff
• Achievement vs. ascription	Actions vs. competences
Truth and reality	Facts and figures
	Intuition and philosophy

Internal integration	Strategy
Human nature	Who is capable of making decisions
Nature of relationships	
• Power and status	Who has the right, legitimacy
• Individual/collective	Who is responsible/accountable
• Task/social	
Language	
• High context/low context	Goals are explicit
	Strategy clearly articulated
Time	
• Monochronic/polychronic	Decisions discrete
	Step-by-step action plans
• Long term/short term	Time frames for implementing

More specifically, there are reasons for starting a business in the West (and different from the East) (Table 5.3).[145]

Marketing approach among small firms also differs between the West and the East. (Table 5.4).[146]

Meaning of an Organization

We have seen already that organizations in the West are very flat, where people generally trust one another, where they are frank and sincere to one another, and where they relate to one another informally. Hierarchical roles exist, but they are established for reasons of convenience.

A Western entrepreneur, for instance, views the organization of his (or her) small firm more as a system than as a social group. This does not exclude

Table 5.3   Businesses started: West versus East

In the West	In the East
Motivated by personal achievement	Motivated by social status and prestige of family
Unsatisfied with previous work situation	More tolerant of existing work situation, even if bad
Most new businesses are marginal firms, some are lifestyle firms, and a few are high-potential firms	(Similar to the West, except definition of 'lifestyle' is not the same)
More new SMEs found in services and commerce sectors	(Depends on development of society)
SMEs may be discouraged from starting in some sectors, due to major investments required to start there	SMEs may be crowded out from some sectors because the government has earmarked the sector for major investments
No general restrictions to specific economic sectors in terms of management and marketing skills required	Avoid economic sectors requiring complex management and marketing skills

people, of course, but the Western organization has specific tasks targeted upon shared objectives. We can picture the situation in Figure 5.4.[147]

Entrepreneurship (both as an independent move or as intracorporate processes) is natural in the West. Change comes easily, deviant behaviour is not seen as a threat and there is faith in what the future may bring (with the will of Man).

There is a variation *within* Western culture, however, in the belief in how much it is possible to change an organization and how easy it is to make the change. Americans, for instance, take on culture more lightly in the sense of believing that they are more able to manage it than are Europeans:

> The very notion that culture can be 'managed' is, in itself, culture-bound. . . . American managers tend to see culture as something organizations *have*; European managers are more likely to see it as something that organizations *are* and thus more dubious about being able to change it. The American assumption of being able to control one's destiny and the propensity to take action have created quite a market for how-to, self-improvement books and for books about managing across cultures.[148]

Table 5.4   Marketing approach among small firms: West versus East

In the West	In the East
Should find market niches	(Same as in the West)
A limited *use* of marketing in practice; however, a definite customer focus	A limited *knowledge* of marketing in practice; production and finance seen as more important
The whole range of marketing management activities applied, if needed	Few standard trade marks, fewer standardized displays, almost no sales policy, little market research and less organized distribution
A broader promotional approach; promotion may even come first	Personal selling (possibly product samples given away) promotional tool of choice
Service is very important	Service is less important
What is new can sell in its own right	What is popular can sell in its own right

One model, which may be of special interest to entrepreneurial marketing, is to what extent one can look at an organization as a *decision-making* mechanism or at least a place where decisions are made. It seems to be a generally accepted conception in the West that entrepreneurship (when successful) is the outcome of some tough decisions and that the job of managers (in small firms as in other firms) is to make decisions. But this is not a model generally valid across cultures. The Japanese, for instance, have a way of co-evolving with customers.[149] This means that decision making is an act at a specific point in time and it may not make sense in the Japanese culture. The decision process and implementation overlap without any given moment of decision in between.[150] Japanese language does not even have an equivalent for 'decision making'.[151] One could say that the Japanese are more process than result or task oriented.[152]

Understanding of Business Success

Business plays a role in the centre of the stage for growth and development in the West. To succeed in the West is to be part of this pattern. This means, among other things, exploiting opportunities before or better than someone else, proving yourself (as a business manager) to be more efficient and providing (through your goods and services) more convenience than your competitors or, in general, always staying ahead of competitors.

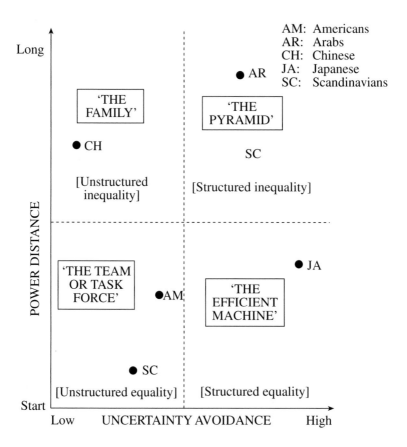

Figure 5.4   Organizational views

This means, in Western culture, that if you want to succeed in business you have to – constantly have to – bring new goods and services to the market, or at least, improved versions of old ones. The market in the West expects no less.

The implication of this for entrepreneurs and for managers of small firms is not up to this book to detail. In very general terms, *how to succeed* differs across cultures but the interest in doing it is universal (Figure 5.5).[153]

CONCLUSION

In this chapter we have seen how entrepreneurship and marketing depend on the culture of the nation where they take place. In fact, all that is stated in the

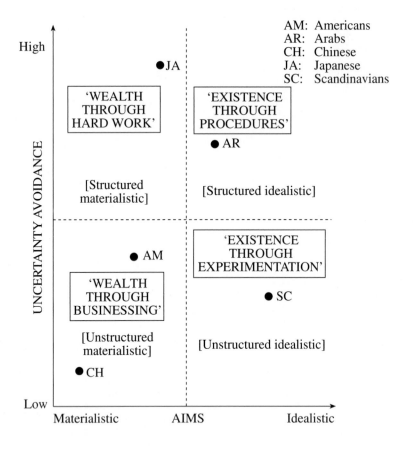

Figure 5.5   How to succeed

rest of this book can be seen in the light of this chapter. Still, this is not always explicitly stated, and neither should it be. To always point out the importance of culture would be to constantly remind ourselves of the fact that we are human beings. True, but obvious.

The reader is advised to use this chapter as a background and, if needed, go back to it from time to time. When, or if, this is done, the reader should keep a few things in mind:

- A culture never stands still; it is an intersubjective product; even if it changes slowly, it still *changes*.
- By discussing differences among cultures, we have neglected many *similarities* that exist across cultures.
- Cultures do, and should, *learn from one another*; in business, the

Western world learned about the importance of corporate cultures from the Japanese in the 1980s – in the 1990s and beyond, can we learn from the networking skills in the rest of Asia?

- Even if, by and large, we now leave *national* cultures, we shall have reason to come back to *corporate* cultures on several occasions.

NOTES

1. Athos, Anthony G. and Robert E. Coffey (1968), *Behavior in Organizations: A Multidimensional View*, Englewood Cliffs, NJ: Prentice-Hall, p. 100.
2. Conner, Patrick E. and Boris W. Becker (1975), 'Values and the organization: Suggestions for research', *Academy of Management Journal*, **18** (3), p. 551.
3. Ferraro, G.P. (1994), *The Cultural Dimension of International Business* (2nd edn), Englewood Cliffs, NJ: Prentice-Hall, p. 47.
4. Kilmann, Ralph H., Mary J. Saxton and Roy Serpa (1986), 'Issues in understanding and changing culture', *California Management Review*, **28** (2), p. 89.
5. This view of culture at various levels of explicitness and implicitness is very common. Our model is influenced by the one suggested by Kilmann et al. (1986), pp. 89–90 and it is also used by Bjerke (1999) (Bjerke, Björn (1999), *Business Leadership and Culture. National Management Styles in the Global Economy*, Cheltenham, UK: Edward Elgar). Similar models are suggested by Trompenaars (1995) (Trompenaars, Fons (1995), *Riding the Waves of Culture*, London: Nicholas Brealey), p. 23, where he places 'implicit basic assumptions' in the centre of culture and 'norms and values' just outside this centre. Schneider and Barsoux (1997) (Schneider, Susan C. and Jean-Louis Barsoux (1997), *Managing Across Cultures*, Hemel Hempstead, UK: Prentice-Hall Europe), pp. 18–19 compare culture to an ocean. Just under the waterline we find 'beliefs and values' and deep down towards the bottom there are 'assumptions'. Included as an outer layer in Trompenaars's model of culture is 'artefacts and products' and above water in Schneider and Barsoux's cultural metaphor there is 'artifacts and behavior'. However, as the reader will see later, we do not include these aspects in culture proper, but look at them as cultural manifestations.
6. Compare Berger, P.L. and T. Luckmann (1966), *The Social Construction of Reality*, Garden City, NY: Doubleday.
7. Samovar, L.A., R.E. Porter and Nemi C. Jain (1981), *Understanding Intercultural Communication*, Belmont, CA: Wadsworth, p. 25.
8. Bjerke, B. and A.R. Al-Meer (1994), 'A behavioral consciousness view of corporate culture', Association of Management 12th Annual International Conference, Dallas, TX: Proceedings of the Organizational Studies Group, Vol. 12, No. 1, p. 177.
9. Cultural manifestations in a society include all sorts of institutions as well as architecture and art; that 'group' which is of primary interest to us here is the nation or the society at large.
10. Hofstede, Geert (1984), *Culture's Consequences*, Beverly Hills, CA: Sage, p. 158; Humes, S. (1993), *Managing the Multinational*, Hemel Hempstead, UK: Prentice-Hall, p. 113; Ferraro (1994), p. 109.
11. Samovar et al. (1981), pp. 75–7; Hofstede (1984), pp. 92, 132–3, 153, 154, 166–7, 171, 173–174; Schwind, Hermann F. and Richard B. Peterson (1985), 'Shifting personal values in the Japanese management system', *International Studies of Management and Organization*, Summer, p. 71; Bjerke, Björn (1989), *Att skapa nya affärer* [Creating new business ventures], Lund, Sweden: Studentlitteratur, p. 41; Arvonen, Jouko (1989), *Att leda via idéer* [Leading through ideas], Lund, Sweden: Studentlitteratur, p. 102; Ferraro (1994), pp. 91, 109; Trompenaars (1995), pp. 51–4, 142–4.
12. Parsons, T. and E.A. Shils (1951), *Towards a General Theory of Action*, Cambridge, MA:

Harvard University Press, p. 18ff.

13. These conclusions are based on studies made by Hofstede (1984), Ferraro (1994) and Trompenaars (1995).

14. Sitaram, K.S. and Roy T. Cogdell (1976), *Foundations of Intercultural Communication*, Columbus, OH: Charles E. Merrill, p. 191.

15. See Nakane, Chie (1967), *Kinship and Economic Organization in Rural Japan*, New York: Humanities Press, and Nakane, Chie (1972), *Japanese Society*, Berkeley: University of California Press.

16. Trompenaars (1995), pp. 139–42.

17. Schwind and Peterson (1985), p. 71.

18. Pascale, R. and A. Athos (1982), *Japansk företagsledning* [The art of Japanese management], p. 123; Humes (1993), p. 112; Trompenaars (1995), pp. 51–2.

19. Arvonen (1989), p. 132.

20. Nakane (1972), pp. 1–2.

21. See, for instance, Harris, Philip R. and Robert I. Moran (1987), *Managing Cultural Differences* (2nd edn), Houston, TX: Gulf, p. 311; Chau, Theodora Ting (1991), 'Approaches to Succession in East Asian Business Organizations', *Family Business Review*, **4** (2) (Summer), p. 161; Chu, Chin-Ning (1991), *The Asian Mind Game*, New York: Macmillan, pp. 200–201; Hoon-Halbauer, Sing Keow (1994), *Management of Sino-Foreign Joint Ventures*, Lund, Sweden: Lund University Press, p. 89.

22. 'Fissiparous fortunes and family feuds' (1996), *The Economist*, 30 November, p. 69.

23. Jansson, Hans (1987), *Affärskulturer och relationer i Sydöstasien* [Business cultures and relations in Southeast Asia], Stockholm: Marknadstekniskt Centrum, No. 29, p. 27.

24. Chen, Min (1995), *Asian Management Systems*, London: Routledge, p. 84; Rohwer, Jim (1995), *Asia Rising*, Singapore: Butterworth–Heinemann Asia, p. 232.

25. Drucker, Peter and Isao Nakauchi (1997), *Drucker on Asia*, London: Butterworth–Heinemann, p. 7.

26. Seagrave, Sterling (1996), *Lords of the Rim*, London: Corgi Books, p. 17.

27. Bjerke (1999), p. 115.

28. Daun, Åke (1989), *Svensk mentalitet* [Swedish mentality], Stockholm: Rabén & Sjögren, p. 129.

29. Trompenaars (1995), pp. 65–6.

30. Daun (1989), p. 217.

31. Ibid., p. 66.

32. Sitaram and Cogdell (1976), p. 191.

33. The terms 'high-context culture' and 'low-context culture' originate from Hall, E.T. (1977), *Beyond Culture*, Garden City, NY: Doubleday.

34. Sitaram and Cogdell (1976), p. 191.

35. Seagrave (1996), p. 341.

36. Chu (1991), p. 199.

37. Hoon-Halbauer (1994), p. 89.

38. Chu (1991), p. 199.

39. See, for instance, Czinkota, R., P. Rivoli and I.A. Ronkainen, (1994), *International Business* (3rd edn), Orlando, FL: Harcourt Brace, p. 231; Ferraro (1994), pp. 51–2.

40. Lawrence, Peter and Tony Spybey (1986), *Management and Society in Sweden*, London: Routledge & Kegan Paul, p. 59.

41. Hofstede (1984), p. 122.

42. Bjerke (1999), p. 182.

43. Pascale and Athos (1982), p. 88.

44. Hofstede (1984), p. 143.

45. Moran, Robert T. (1988), *Venturing Abroad in Asia*, Maidenhead, Berks, UK: McGraw-Hill, pp. 45–6.

46. Seagrave (1996), p. 17.

47. Chu (1991), p. 190.

48. Wong, Sin-lun (1995), 'Business networks, cultural values and the state in Hong Kong and Singapore', in Brown, R.A. (ed.), *Chinese Business Enterprise in Asia*, London: Routledge,

p. 144.
49. Jansson (1987), p. 11; Weidenbaum, Murray Samuel Hughes (1996), *The Bamboo Network*, New York: Free Press, pp. 57–8.
50. Bjerke (1999), p. 163.
51. Jansson (1987), p. 22; Chen (1995), p. 132.
52. Ferraro (1994), p. 94.
53. Samovar et al. (1981), p. 72.
54. Davis, H.J. and S.A. Rasool (1988), 'Values research and managerial behavior: Implications for devising culturally consistent managerial styles', *Management International Review*, **28** (3), p. 17.
55. Drucker, Peter (1985), *Innovation and Entrepreneurship*, London: Heinemann.
56. Sallivan, J. and I. Nonaka (1988), 'Culture and strategic issue categorization theory', *Management International Review*, **28** (3), p. 9.
57. Samovar et al. (1981), p. 79.
58. Hofstede (1984), p. 174.
59. See, for instance, 'A survey of business in Europe' (1996), *The Economist*, 23 November, Survey attachment, p. 16.
60. Lawrence and Spybey (1986), p. 50; Lindkvist, Lars (1988), *A Passionate Search for Nordisk Management*, Copenhagen: Institut for Organisation og Arbejdssociologi, August, p. 55; Phillips-Martinsson, Jean (1992), *Svenskarna som andra ser dem* [Swedes as other people see them] (rev. edn), Lund, Sweden: Studentlitteratur, p. 59; Brewster, C., A. Lundmark and L. Holden (1993), *A Different Tack. An Analysis of British and Swedish Management Styles*, Lund, Sweden: Chartwell Bratt, p. 30.
61. Hofstede (1984), p. 140.
62. Bjerke (1999), p. 205.
63. McMillan, C.J. (1985), *The Japanese Industrial System* (2nd rev. edn), New York: Walter de Gruyter, p. 20.
64. Ferraro (1994), p. 98.
65. McMillan (1985), pp. 20–21.
66. Trompenaars (1995), pp. 126–7.
67. Bjerke (1999), p. 119.
68. Sitaram and Cogdell (1976), p. 191.
69. Harris and Moran (1987), pp. 62ff.
70. Jansson (1987), p. 23; Lasserre, Philippe and Hellmut Schütte (1995), *Strategies for Asia Pacific*, London: Macmillan, p. 131.
71. Humes (1993), p. 112.
72. Ibid., p. 112.
73. Hofstede (1984), p. 259.
74. Ibid., p. 258.
75. Trompenaars (1995), p. 114.
76. Hofstede (1984), p. 94.
77. Ibid., pp. 92, 216, 143.
78. Trompenaars (1995), p. 114.
79. Hofstede (1984), p. 107.
80. Sitaram and Cogdell (1976), p. 191.
81. Trompenaars (1995), p. 160.
82. Bjerke, B. and A.R. Al-Meer (1993), 'Culture's consequences: Management in Saudi Arabia', *Leadership and Organization Development Journal*, **14** (2), p. 31.
83. Sitaram and Cogdell (1976), p. 191.
84. Bjerke (1999), p. 144.
85. Hofstede (1984), p. 77.
86. 'How to conquer China (and the world) with instant noodles' (1995), *The Economist*, 17 June, p. 27.
87. 'Asia's new giants' (1995), *Business Week*, 27 November, p. 31.
88. Redding, S. Gordon (1993), *The Spirit of Chinese Capitalism*, Berlin: Walter de Gruyter, p. 217.

89. 'Information anxiety' (1997), *Business Week*, 9 June, p. 52.
90. 'How Japan puts the "human" in human capital' (1991), *Business Week*, 11 November, p. 11.
91. Hofstede (1984), pp. 92, 94.
92. 'Europe's new managers. Going global with a US style' (1982), *Business Week*, 24 May, p. 79.
93. Hofstede (1984), p. 107; Trompenaars (1995), p. 144.
94. 'Home sweet home' (1995), *The Economist*, 9 September, pp. 21-2.
95. Humes (1993), p. 121.
96. Brewster et al. (1993), p. 93.
97. Sitaram and Cogdell (1976), p. 191.
98. Bjerke (1999), p. 92.
99. Hodgetts, R.M. and F. Luthans (1991), *International Management*, Singapore: McGraw-Hill, p. 37.
100. Jansson (1987), p. 21.
101. Bjerke (1999), p. 163.
102. Redding (1993), p. 141.
103. Ibid., p. 77.
104. Jansson (1987), p. 28.
105. Seagrave (1996), p. 17.
106. Pascale and Athos (1982), p. 96.
107. Bjerke (1999), p. 193.
108. Daun (1989), pp. 162-3.
109. Hofstede (1984), p. 92.
110. Phillips-Martinsson (1992), p. 19.
111. Hofstede (1984), p. 200.
112. Ibid., p. 201.
113. Boulton, William R. (1984), *Business Policy: The Art of Strategic Management*, New York: Macmillan, p. 168.
114. Hodgetts and Luthans (1991), p. 27.
115. Trompenaars (1995), p. 94.
116. Ferraro (1994), p. 97; Trompenaars (1995), p. 92.
117. Trompenaars (1995), pp. 47-8.
118. Muna, Farid A. (1980), *The Arab Executive*, London: Macmillan, p. 156.
119. Trompenaars (1995), p. 159.
120. Nonaka, I. and J.K. Johansson (1985), 'Japanese management: What about the "hard" skills?', *Academy of Management Review*, **10**, (2), p. 186; Negandhi, A.R., G.S. Eshgi and E.C. Yuen (1985), 'The management practices of Japanese subsidiaries overseas', *California Management Review*, **27** (4) (Summer), p. 94; Lindkvist (1988), p. 40; Trompenaars (1995), p. 4.
121. For instance, Harris and Moran (1987), p. 312; Jansson (1987), p. 10.
122. Rohwer (1995), p. 52.
123. Jansson (1987), p. 26.
124. Yang, Bo (1991), *The Ugly Chinaman and the Crisis of Chinese Culture*, St. Leonards, Australia: Allen & Unwin, p. 111.
125. 'A survey of business in Asia' (1996), *The Economist*, 9 March, Survey attachment, p. 12.
126. Chu (1991), p. 197.
127. Lasserre and Schütte (1995), p. 273.
128. Hofstede (1984), p. 189.
129. Ibid., pp. 200-201, 205, 207-8.
130. Ibid., p. 189.
131. Phillips-Martinsson (1992), p. 19.
132. Lindkvist (1988), p. 29; Daun (1989), p. 56.
133. Sitaram and Cogdell (1976), p. 191.
134. Bjerke (1999), p. 203.
135. Lawrence and Spybey (1986), pp. 124-6.

136. Humes (1993), p. 112.
137. Trompenaars (1995), p. 62.
138. Schneider and Barsoux (1997), p. 29.
139. These results come from Bjerke, Björn (1998a), 'Entrepreneurship and SMEs in the Singaporean context', in Toh, M.H. and K.Y. Tan (eds), *Competitiveness of the Singapore Economy*, Singapore: Singapore University Press/World Scientific, pp. 278-9, and from Bjerke, Björn (2000), 'A typified, culture-based, interpretation of management of SMEs in Southeast Asia', *Asia Pacific Journal of Management*, **17** (1) (April), pp. 103-32.
140. Bjerke (1999), p. 244.
141. Bennett, P.D. (ed.) (1995), *Dictionary of Marketing Terms* (2nd edn), Chicago: AMA.
142. For this discussion, compare Bjerke, Björn (1998b), 'Some aspects of inadequacies of Western models in understanding Southeast Asia entrepreneurship and SMEs', paper presented at 43rd *ICSB World Conference*, Singapore, 8-10 June.
143. Naisbitt, John (1995), *Megatrends Asia*, London: Nicholas Brealey, p. 7.
144. Schneider and Barsoux (1997), p. 115.
145. Bjerke (1999).
146. Ibid.
147. Bjerke (1999), p. 235.
148. Schneider and Barsoux (1997), p. ix, emphasis added.
149. Trompenaars (1995), p. 174.
150. Söderman, S. (1983), *Japan och industriell marknadsföring* [Japan and industrial marketing]. Lund, Sweden: Studentlitteratur, p. 8.
151. Hofstede (1984), p. 27.
152. Pascale and Athos (1982), p. 95.
153. Bjerke (1999), p. 239.

6. Growth, learning and co-creation

INTRODUCTION

The purpose of this chapter is to prepare some of the background of our conceptual framework for entrepreneurial marketing suggested in Chapter 8. Let us first, however, briefly summarize the background provided in Chapters 1–5 before proceeding.

We started in Chapter 1 by characterizing the new economic era. This 'era' seems to enter an increasing number of business sectors and industries, at least in the industrialized world. This led naturally to our interest in:

- small firms;
- entrepreneurship;
- marketing; and
- growth.

We ended the first chapter by separating two kinds of growth, that is, managerial growth and entrepreneurial growth. We also stated that entrepreneurial growth can be based on partial entrepreneurship or complete entrepreneurship.

In Chapter 2, we learned that the discipline of marketing of today contains a variety of theories, concepts and even paradigms. Although we feel very humble to all efforts spent by great minds in figuring out how to run successful businesses, we are critical of mainstream marketing theories in some important aspects. In our opinion, mainstream marketing:

- is trapped in its own paradigm, rigid in perspective. General textbooks are still very similar to those the authors read 20 years ago;
- fails to adapt to the changing conditions in the business world of the twenty-first century, such as unstable conditions and non-linear growth;
- is narrow in perspective, focusing on marketing only within and from the lines of a legal definition of a firm with a distinct and clear interface between itself and its environment; and
- gives too much attention to marketing as a function in big corporations, thereby enlightening too few of the new and important developments.

We find *limitations* in the ability of traditional mainstream marketing theories to serve as the sole framework for understanding marketing behaviour of fast-growing entrepreneurial firms in the new economic era.

We are to some extent critical of the advocators of relationship marketing. However, the problem with traditional marketing, as well as with relationship marketing, is not that it is obsolete or non-relevant – the problem is that it covers only a part of the complexity of marketing behaviour of the entrepreneurial firms in this new economic era. Therefore, we do not believe that any of the two marketing orientations should be given a monopolistic position.

In Chapter 3, we noted that entrepreneurship research has a long history even though it is rather new from a business research point of view. We also noted that the subject is very popular today and has become an integrated part of modern life, particularly in those business sectors touched by the new economic era.

Traces of the history of entrepreneurship research can be seen today. In particular, four characteristics are commonly associated with entrepreneurship at present:

- risk taking;
- management;
- innovation; and
- exploiting opportunities.

We found the last two of these four, in particular, of major interest in the new economic era.

We classified our present understanding of entrepreneurship in four groups and had something to say about each as far as its relevance in the new economic era is concerned. We also noted the important difference between explaining and understanding. We claimed to use an explanatory approach, where the independent variables are 'use of language', 'culture' and 'entrepreneurial capacities'.

We ended this chapter by discussing management, leadership and entrepreneurship, and concluding that entrepreneurship should be more associated with leadership in the new economic era than, as has traditionally been the case, with management. We also pointed out that over the life of a firm, different combinations of management, leadership and entrepreneurship are necessary.

In Chapter 4, we stated:

1. Small firm marketing is not, and should not be, a mini-version of big firm marketing.

2.   There are advantages to gain for small firms by using their own marketing approach.

In Chapter 5 we brought to the attention of the reader one important variable in our base model of marketing, that is, culture. We did this in order to:

1.   deepen the understanding of the fundamental importance of culture (and use of language) in all kinds of business, including marketing and entrepreneurship;
2.   provide a background to discuss culture at the level of individual firms later on; and
3.   prove the fact that the findings in this book are mainly valid in the Western, industrialized world (the world mostly touched by the new economic era, anyway).

The rest of this chapter will move in steps. These steps are: (a) various kinds of growth; (b) learning in focal and virtual organizations; and (c) the concept of 'co-creation'.

MODES OF GROWTH

One area of research which has attracted researchers and politicians as well as decision makers in recent years is growth among small firms.[1] For politicians and decision makers there is a problem. It is normally true that a very small share of small firms will grow and provide new employment.[2] Most small firms do not want to grow.[3]

What makes some firms grow while others do not? This question is not easy to answer. Storey[4] has summarized some of the existing knowledge on this matter. He discusses growth of small firms as generated by three factors (a) the entrepreneur in the firm, (b) the character of the firm, and (c) the strategy of the firm. Examples of results according to this author are as follows.

The entrepreneur   Results show that the entrepreneur who has a positive attitude to business establishments and growth has a higher probability of accomplishing growth of the firm, while entrepreneurs who are forced into starting a business due to unemployment have a lower probability in succeeding in running the business and, even less, in developing it. Results indicate further that high education and previous management experience will influence the probability for growth in a positive direction. Businesses started by more than one person have a higher probability of surviving and growing.

The character   Young and small firms tend to grow faster than established and bigger firms, but there are large differences between industries. The type of firm, from a legal point of view, makes a difference, as incorporated firms grow faster than unincorporated firms.

The strategy   Growing firms have more external owners who contribute with financial capital as well as knowledge. Results indicate that fast-growing firms often focus on a specific market segment or position. The introduction of new products is important for growing firms. The firm, however, does not have to be overly innovative. Furthermore, fast-growing firms are often more willing to recruit external managers and members of the board, and to delegate decisions to non-owning managers.

Nevertheless, it is safe to conclude that whether a firm will start to grow or not *depends mainly on the entrepreneur.*[5] The entrepreneur's attitude towards growth and his or her appreciation of the impact that successful growth will have on the new firm will be crucially determining factors. A number of issues will, however, have a bearing on the entrepreneurial decision to remain proactively entrepreneurial or to exercise a degree of control over the amount of growth and change that the enterprise undergoes:[6]

1. The owner may desire to remain independent and maintain ownership of his or her firm.
2. The owner may be driven, after the initial taxing effort to launch the venture, by an impulse to simplify life by keeping the firm small and more easily manageable.
3. The owner may harbour a genuine concern about his or her ability to manage successfully in a fast-growing, increasingly complex enterprise.

The truly entrepreneurial firm does not stand still:

> Constantly in search of new opportunities, entrepreneurs focus primarily on the external environment of customers, competitors and markets – after all, the growth of any enterprise is achieved through effective action in the markets for its products.[7]

Therefore, a small firm's growth, if you like, its ability to cope with change, is determined by *new* sales. This brings us to a classic table (Table 6.1).

Table 6.1   Four ways of growing

	Same market	New market
Same product	1	3
New product	2	4

1. *Grabbing a larger share of an existing market with an existing product*
    This has traditionally been called 'penetration'. This kind of business
    growth does not, generally, involve much of innovation and,
    consequently, not much of entrepreneurship either, at least not the way
    entrepreneurship is normally understood. We may call this 'linear
    growth', that is, doing 'more of the same in the same market'.
2. *Acquiring a share of an existing market with a new product*   Developing
    a new product (for an existing market or for a new one) is generally
    understood as one kind of entrepreneurship. This means that a firm is
    changing internally (or even being started in the first place) as well as
    externally.
3. *Entering a new market with an existing product*   This means that a firm
    grows externally, but does not change much internally. Nevertheless, it
    may be referred to as entrepreneurship (even if only in a limited sense).
4. Growing in the first or third fashion could be referred to as 'quantitative'
    (in the first even a linear) growth. Another kind of growth is to grow more
    qualitatively (that is, internally as well). One such growth is noted in cell
    2 above. Another, more radical version (also entrepreneurially more
    radical) is by creating a new market with a new product.

Growth in cell 1 may also be referred to as 'managerial' growth. Growing in
cells 2–4 may be referred to as 'entrepreneurial' growth (even if 3 is more
limited and cell 2 and, above all, 4 represent complete entrepreneurship).

As noted, successful pursuit and exploitation of opportunities emanating
from the external market may, or may not, have an impact on an existing small
firm by creating pressure for internal change. We may separate imitative new
business ventures from innovative new business ventures in this respect (Table
6.2).[8]

Let us explore the differences between managerial and entrepreneurial
growth further and do it by applying one of the variables in our entrepreneurial
base model, that is, *use of language*.[9]

There are several reasons to separate managerial growth from
entrepreneurial growth. Basically, these two situations are quite different as
far as what recipes to use for success, especially in marketing. More
fundamentally, the two are based on two separate ways of looking at the
business situation in question. The language we use provides our ways of
looking at things. In other words, managerial growth and entrepreneurial
growth should use different terms (different language in a wide sense) when
applied properly (Table 6.3).

The list could be made longer, but it is long enough to prove the point that
two different ideas of growth are at hand. The idea behind *managerial growth*
(compare Table 6.3, left column) is to plan united, structured systems,

Table 6.2   Consequences of innovative new business ventures

Imitative new business ventures	Innovative new business ventures
Few changes from before	Many changes from before
Using existing knowledge and methods	Creating new competencies
Administrative influence	Administrative and cultural influence
Centralization	Decentralization
Do things right	Do the right things
Listen to the economic rhythm	Listen to the customers
Marketing	Networking
Planning	Learning
Systems	Actors
Capital	Entrepreneurs
Good ideas	Adequate culture
Stability	Manoeuvrability
Economies of scale	Small start-ups

Source: Bjerke (1996), p. 13 (see note 8).

controlled by business concepts. What is important is to be efficient, gain from economies of scale, apply various standards, be financially better off and to have educated managers at the top. The idea behind *entrepreneurial growth* (compare Table 6.3, right column) is to learn from variety and to act in processes guided by visions. It is important to change, to become, to be committed in small but beautiful units where surprises are welcome. Entrepreneurs within this situation act as leaders and promote an adequate business culture.

This is not the place to discuss the pairs of terms in Table 6.3 in any detail (several of them have appeared already in this book, and some will come back again later). One pair could be worth some elaboration here, however: *planning* versus *learning*.

It seems to be a common, often implicit, understanding that the more we plan in business, the better. Planning is seen as a way to control, to 'simulate' future possibilities, to coordinate, to reduce uncertainty, to inform, just to mention a few advantages of planning often advocated.

According to Vesper,[10] planning, whether mental or in writing, can be used for designing, negotiating, testing, and learning about the new business venture. Its payoffs may include the following:

Table 6.3   Two vocabularies in matched pairs

For managerial growth	For entrepreneurial growth
• planning	• learning
• unity	• variety
• systems	• actors
• structure	• process
• business concepts	• visions
• we are	• we become
• efficiency	• commitment
• economies of scale	• small is beautiful
• standardization	• surprises
• financial capital	• entrepreneurs
• education	• culture
• management	• leadership

- to test all or pieces of the venture concept and make 'go/no go' decisions about them;
- to find ways of refining aspects of the product and the start-up process so they work better;
- to look for ways to improve upon the design goals and concept of the venture itself;
- to look for other venture opportunities;
- to anticipate needs that may require advance preparatory time;
- to anticipate and head off potential problems in the start-up
- to prethink future decisions so they can be made faster and better later;
- to get started on the long lead time part of the task in a timely fashion;
- to get the benefit of others' thinking;
- to reach a common understanding of cooperative tasks; and
- to learn about venturing by thinking through what may be involved in it.

With so many potential reasons in favour of planning, why do not entrepreneurs do more of it and why do so few entrepreneurs produce formal plans at all? Reasons may include the following:[11]

- the opportunity cost of the time to gather more information, rather than reprocessing what is already known, and of having to redo the plan as conditions change and new information makes the old obsolete;

- danger of reinforcing misleading fantasies about how things will develop, thereby producing poor decisions;
- risk of becoming discouraged by envisaging so many complexities that it all seems impossible;
- drudgery of abstract activity with no real-world feedback or results until action is taken;
- discouragement from review by others who are better equipped to discover weaknesses than to add reinforcements and reveal directions for further opportunity; and
- pain of being wrong, a likely experience in planning.

Basically, planning is meaningful only when circumstances permit, that is, when at least some aspects are stable and not everything is changing all the time, when there is a structure to be seen, when things are related in some kind of a system, when there is a standard against which improvements can be measured and so on.

Generally speaking, in managerial growth, the advantages of planning are more visible, while in entrepreneurial growth, its disadvantages are more prominent. Also, generally speaking, quantitative changes (especially meaning growth) can be achieved by long-term strategic planning ('more of the same'). When external development takes qualitative leaps, responding with too much planning is more harmful than useful. *Qualitative change requires learning.* Let us explore learning in more detail.

LEARNING IN FOCAL AND VIRTUAL ORGANIZATIONS

During the 1990s, the number of studies applying the *network metaphor* within entrepreneurship research grew.[12] This was partly a reaction to using psychological variables trying to explain entrepreneurship; instead, network research focused on how business opportunities are being created and organized in the field.

Starting from this view, Johannisson[13] described the entrepreneurial process as a gradual institutionalization of the entrepreneur's personal network. To start with, the venture involves the family and later encompasses more external actors. From this point of view, establishing a business is about operating a network.[14] To put it differently: 'It's simple. ... We either get used to thinking about the subtle processes of learning and sharing knowledge in dispersed transient networks. Or we perish.'[15]

Formerly, we treated knowledge within the framework of the 'traditional', what we refer to as 'focal', organization. However, many organizations are increasingly changing their ways of acquiring and creating knowledge by relying on more opened and more closed partnerships. This will have implications for how knowledge may be created and how organizational learning may take place.[16] Thorelli[17] regards networks in general as something between markets and hierarchies.

So, increasingly, scholars have acknowledged that an organization's learning and value making are inescapably embedded in various forms of partnerships. There have been many theoretical approaches to the rise of organizational partnerships,[18] including imaginary organizations,[19] strategic alliances,[20] virtual organizations,[21] networks,[22] dynamic networks,[23] strategic networks[24] and regional networks.[25] We prefer the term 'virtual organizations'. This term is primarily used to refer to systems that are interlinked by advanced information technology,[26] and it mostly refers to a very temporary constellation.[27] Unfortunately, there is little agreement on the definition of a virtual organization.[28] However, Zimmermann[29] gets to the point by claiming that a virtual organization is an organization 'which is lacking some structural characteristics of real enterprises, but nevertheless functions like an enterprise in the imagination of the observer'. So, a virtual organization (like an imaginary organization) is an artificial representation of what we see, conceived and directed by one or more actors using the virtual organization perspective. The people who design these organizations do so consciously and with a fairly explicit vision of the final result in mind.[30]

We think 'virtual organization' fits nicely what an entrepreneur with a vivid mind can do in the new economic era. Another description for a virtual organization could be a 'personal contact network'.[31] One could make a distinction between *personal* networks and *social* networks. Another possible distinction is between *moral-support* networks and *professional-support* networks.[32]

Social-oriented networks are called 'weak-tie' networks and business-oriented networks are called 'strong-tie' networks.[33] Strong-tie peer networks may provide the following functions:[34]

1. grounded vision in reality;
2. increased level of aspiration;
3. enhanced opportunity identification through stimulation of ideas, creativity, and so on;
4. practical assistance; and
5. an emotional support system.

Holmqvist[35] offers an interesting distinction between two interrelated, yet disparate ways of organizational learning. One is to create variety in experience. This is called 'exploration'. The other is to create reliability in experience. This is called 'exploitation'. Experiential-learning theory of organizations has primarily taken the *focal* organization as the unit of analysis. When conceptualizing *virtual* organizations, actors and/or firms may share experience with each other, even building a new reality together. Relationships between exploitation and exploration on one hand, and focal and virtual organization on the other are shown as a model in Figure 6.1.

This means that exploitation mainly takes place in focal organizations, while virtual organizations provide excellent opportunities for exploration. In general, the frequency, nature and type of relationship between individuals or organizations influence the manner in which business is carried out between them.[36]

> While networks generally define the type and totality of relationships between people and organizations, personal contact networks (PCNs) are seen as particularly relevant in the context of the entrepreneurial SME with its centralized, independent and personalized style of management. Personal contacts are also significant for marketing in the entrepreneurial SME from its pioneering days of intuitive marketing through subsequent periods of greater structure and control when marketing might be described as sophisticated. Such contacts play a critical role in maintaining the entrepreneurial efforts of those managing the enterprise's development end ensuring its continued commitment to opportunity and change.[37]

Possibilities offered by virtual organizations include:[38]

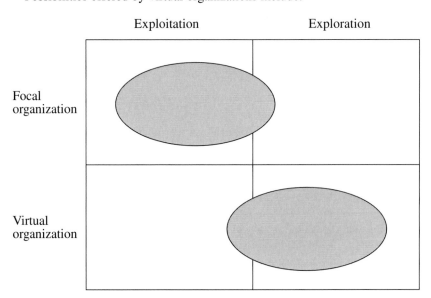

Source: From Holmquist (2000), p. 56 (see note 35).

Figure 6.1 A model for studying learning within and between organizations

- helping the entrepreneur develop a company even when conventional resources, particularly capital, are very limited;
- providing a model for growth without expanding, for linking synergy to energy, and for involving many more people than just the employees in the service of the company's concept of business.

Perhaps the most intriguing aspect of virtual organizations 'is their potential capability of creating a field where partners' tacitly hold organizational knowledge, which may be "brought to the surface"'.[39]

Networking is important for intrapreneurs as well, then (at least in the beginning of a new venture differently from the independent entrepreneur) inside the focal firm where he or she is employed. Pinchot III[40] identifies four stages of intrapreneuring: solo phase; network phase; bootleg phase; and formal team phase.

Kanter[41] discusses the same phenomenon in three stages: definition of the project; coalition building; and action.

The tricky part in creating a new business venture, particularly when growing, is to know when to emphasize the focal organization, when to emphasize the virtual organization, when to focus on exploration, when on exploitation and so on. We shall come back to this concept later. We shall also be back with more about networking and strategic alliances in the context of marketing in the next chapter, especially as a tool for pooling resources among small firms.

CO-CREATION

We have talked about two types of growth, that is, managerial and entrepreneurial, two types of organizations, that is, focal and virtual, and two types of learning, that is, exploitation and exploration. It is likely that managerial growth is more associated with focal organizations and exploitative learning, entrepreneurial growth more with virtual organizations and explorative learning (Figure 6.2).

In other words, when a firm intends to grow managerially ('doing more of the same'), it should try to improve on what it knows already (exploitative learning) and concentrate on its own (focal) organization. If, on the other hand, a firm intends to grow entrepreneurially, in other words, establish itself as an independent business venture in the first place or add a new business venture to those which exist already ('doing new things'), it needs to learn new things (explorative learning). This takes place, to a large extent, together with other business vendors, including future customers and more social and political types of stakeholders (in the intrapreneurial case also with the established

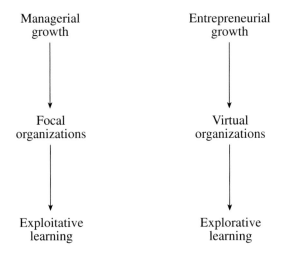

Managerial growth	Entrepreneurial growth
Focal organizations	Virtual organizations
Exploitative learning	Explorative learning

Figure 6.2   Growing, organizing and learning

business ventures and powerholders that exist in the firm already), that is, in virtual organizations.

Growing and learning always means creation of some sort. However, entrepreneurial growth in virtual organizations where explorative learning takes place means, above all, creation of something *genuinely new* (even a new reality) – and this is done together with other actors (outside of established business vendors). We refer to this as 'co-creation'[42]. One interesting aspect of this, and of particular interest to this book, is how co-creation of customer value takes place. This is the topic of the next chapter.

NOTES

1. Landström, Hans (2000), *Entreprenörskapets rötter* [The roots of entrepreneurship] (2nd edn), Lund, Sweden: Studentlitteratur, p. 91.
2. Storey, David (1994), *Understanding the Small Business Sector*, London: Routledge.
3. Davidsson, Per (1989), *Continued Entrepreneurship and Small Firm Growth*, Stockholm: EFI Stockholm School of Economics.
4. Storey (1994).
5. Carson, D., S. Cromie, P. McGowan and J. Hill (1995), *Marketing and Entrepreneurship in SMEs*, Hemel Hempstead, UK: Prentice-Hall International (UK) Limited, p. 159.
6. Carson et al. (1995), p. 160.
7. Ibid., p. 163.
8. Bjerke, Bjorn (1996), 'Understanding or explaining entrepreneurship', paper presented at UIC/AMA Research Symposium on Marketing and Entrepreneurship, Stockholm, 14–15 June, p. 13.
9. The discussion will follow Bjerke, Björn (1989), *Att skapa nya affärer* [Creating new business ventures], Lund, Sweden: Studentlitteratur, Chapter 3.

10. Vesper, Karl (1993), *New Venture Mechanics*, Englewood Cliffs, NJ: Prentice-Hall, p. 25.
11. Ibid., p. 26.
12. Landström (2000), p. 109.
13. Johannisson, Bengt (1996), 'Personliga nätverk som kraftkälla' [Personal networks as a source of power], in Johannisson, B. and L. Lindmark (eds), *Företag, företagare, företagsamhet* [Ventures, venturers, venturing], Lund, Sweden: Studentlitteratur, pp. 122-50.
14. Compare Sexton, D.L. and N.B. Bowman-Upton (1991), *Entrepreneurship: Creativity and Growth*, New York: Macmillan, p. 206.
15. Peters, Tom (1994), *Tom Peters Seminar*, London: Pan Books, p. 174.
16. Holmqvist, Mikael (1999), 'Learning in imaginary organizations: creating inter-organizational knowledge', *Journal of Organizational Change Management*, **12** (5), pp. 419-38: 424.
17. Thorelli, H.B. (1986), 'Networks: Between Markets and Hierarchies', *Strategic Management Journal*, **7**, pp. 37-51.
18. Holmqvist (1999), p. 419.
19. Hedberg, B., G. Dahlgren, J. Hansson and N.-G. Olve (1997), *Virtual Oganizations and Beyond*, Chichester: John Wiley & Sons.
20. Bengtsson, L., M. Holmqvist and R. Larsson (1998), *Strategiska allianser. Från marknadsmisslyckande till lärande samarbete* [Strategic alliances. From market failure to educative cooperation], Malmö, Sweden: Liber; Harrigan, K.R. (1988), 'Strategic alliances and partner asymmetries', *Management International Review*, **28**, pp. 53-72.
21. Davidow, W.H. and M.S. Malone (1992), *The Virtual Corporation*, New York, NY: Harper Collins; Hale, R. and P. Whitlam (1997), *Towards the Virtual Organization*, London: McGraw-Hill.
22. Powell, W.W. (1990), 'Neither market nor hierarchy: network forms of organization', *Research in Organizational Behavior*, **12**, pp. 295-336.
23. Miles, R.E. and C.C. Snow (1992), 'Causes of failure in network organizations', *California Management Review*, Summer, pp. 53-72.
24. Jarillo, J.C. (1988), 'On strategic networks', *Strategic Management Journal*, **9**, pp. 31-41.
25. Hanssen-Bauer, J. and C.C. Snow (1996), 'Responding to hypercompetition: the structure and processes of a regional learning network organization', *Organization Science*, **7** (4), pp. 413-27.
26. Arnold, O. (1998), Untitled, 6 March, http://www.teco.uni-karlsruhe.de/ITVISION/virtualEnterprisesMain.html#virtCorp; Greiner, R. And G. Metes (1995), *Going Virtual Moving Your Organization into the 21st Century*, Englewood Cliffs, NJ: Prentice-Hall.
27. Goldman, S.L., R.N. Nagel and K. Preiss (1995), *Agile Competitors and Virtual Organizations*, New York, NY: Van Nostrand Reinhold; Hale and Whitlam (1997).
28. Holmqvist (1999), p. 426.
29. Zimmermann, F.O. (1997), ' Structural and managerial aspects of virtual enterprises', 29 June, http://www.teck.uni-karlsruhe.de/IT-VISION/vu-e-teco-htm/p. 2.
30. Hedberg et al. (1997), p. 14.
31. Carson et al. (1995), p. 200.
32. Hisrich, R.D. and M.P. Peters (1992), *Entrepreneurship: Starting, Developing, and Managing a New Enterprise* (2nd edn), Homewood, IL: Irwin, pp. 64-5.
33. Granovetter, M. (1973), 'The strength of weak ties', *American Journal of Sociology*, **78** (6), pp. 1360-80.
34. Sexton and Bowman-Upton (1991), p. 207.
35. Holmqvist, Mikael (2000), *The Dynamics of Experiential Learning. Balancing Exploitation and Exploration Within and Between Organizations*, Stockholm University: School of Business Research Report No. 2000: 12
36. Johannisson, Bengt (1986), 'Network strategies: Managerial technology for entrepreneurship and change', *International Small Business Journal*, **5**, pp. 19-30; Mastenbroek, W.F.G. (1993), *Conflict Management and Organization Development*, Chichester: John Wiley.
37. Carson et al. (1995), pp. 199-200.
38. Hedberg et al. (1997), p. 15.

39. Holmqvist (1999), p. 435.
40. Pinchot III, Gifford (1985), *Intrapreneuring*, New York: Harper & Row, pp. 181–4.
41. Kanter, Rosabeth Moss (1983), *The Change Master*, London: Unwin Paperbacks, pp. 217ff.
42. For a conceptual discussion of 'co-creation', see Bjerke, B. and C. Hultman (1998), 'Marketing and Entrepreneurship. A Conceptual Discussion', *Swedish Foundation for Small Business Research*, FSF 1998: 2.

7. Marketing as co-creation of customer value

INTRODUCTION

The roots of traditional marketing in rational decision theory and planning theory make it hard to relate it to dynamically changing environmental conditions in a new economic era. Business plans do not generate customer value, nor do marketing plans! As mentioned earlier, planning is a tool for coordination and not a tool for business development. At its best a plan is a roadmap of how to administer and implement various actions that can be anticipated and foreseen in advance. However, formal marketing analysis may conserve traditional thinking in conceptualizing markets, goods and services. Instead, flexibility and rapid reaction to exploit perceived opportunities are rewarded in dynamic markets.

A BROADER VIEW OF MARKETING

The Future Role of Marketing: A Scenario

Rapid change and increased competition in the new economic era require high flexibility in the output in the value-creating processes of a firm. By necessity, all parts of these processes must be linked to the market and to relevant customers. The environment must be brought into the crucial processes of the organizations, where people feel committed to the market. Competition and change will force companies to let the whole organization be market focused and customer oriented much more than today.

What consequences will this have for marketing as a discipline and as a function in the business world? We foresee two different effects. First, we expect a disintegration of marketing as a specialist function. Marketing will probably not survive as a planning specialist functional area or department, as defined within the managerial paradigm. The specialist functions related to marketing may well be selling, advertising, market research, market communication, logistics, e-commerce, selling, quality assessment and control and so on. However, these functions need to be linked to the environment (not to each other) more tightly in the future and may well be 'outsourced'. In a way, this turns the clock back to the situation of the early days, before separate specialist functions were brought together under a vice-president for marketing.

The second consequence that we expect, which is a direct result of the first consequence, is that marketing will be spread across all other functions of the firm. Changes of the basic market conditions in the new economic era will force marketing to take a new and broader role as competition and market-demand forces arouse a need for close links between all parts of a firm and its customers. Because of competition and a high level of accessible information about alternatives, buyers will be able to make better decisions and become more goal oriented compared to what was possible in the 1960s, 1970s, 1980s and even the 1990s.

As buyers are able to distinguish between alternatives, 'value for money' will be more important in the new economic era. A successful firm must therefore be very oriented both to the customers' subjective perception of what they find as a 'best buy' and to technology and other necessary resources to create better and better customer value. This is not a functional task for the marketing department; instead it is a matter of survival as well as growth strategy for the firm at large, small or big, starting with the top management.

Marketing as Interrelated Value-creating Processes

In Chapter 3 we looked at entrepreneurship as a process. We use the same perspective on marketing. A process view allows us to capture and better explain some of the growth-related aspects of marketing in general and of entrepreneurial marketing in particular.

First we need to focus on the ultimate purpose of marketing. The creation of customer value is in our opinion the ultimate goal of all (marketing) actions taken by a firm. The customer value is what the buyers pay for and what, in the long run, secures survival.

All definitions of what marketing is should contain aspects of value creation. Our standpoint is not controversial. In their résumé of marketing theory, Sheth et al. state:[1]

> [T]he main purpose of marketing is to create and distribute values among the market parties through the process of market transactions and market relationships. The concepts of creating and distributing value inherently implies that marketing objects, functions and institutions must create a win–win market behaviour. In game theory language, marketing should be a positive sum game rather than a zero sum (or negative sum) game.

Customer value is a key concept here, indeed. It is important to state that *customer value is subjective* in the sense that it is the customers' perception of the value that counts. The value is in the eyes of the beholder, the customer and not the supplier. This seems to be obvious but it is a very important fact, neglected in too many marketing situations. As Nilsson[2] points out, buyers evaluate both *concrete* and *abstract* attributes! To understand how customers think, the value provider must learn what key dimensions of value the market uses when judging offerings.

McKinsey & Company[3] use a framework called the 'value delivery sequence'. It consists of three simple logical steps:

- choose the value;
- provide the value; and
- communicate the value.

A manufacturer or a service firm can only provide *potential* customer value. True customer value emerges when all three steps above are successfully completed and the customer has transformed its full potential into real value. Hence, real customer value emerges in the customer's context first and last, and true customer value is culturally related.

We have now set the stage for the forthcoming discussion. The task for marketing is to transform, through the marketing processes, input such as information and other resources such as money, knowledge and material into superior customer value, as perceived by the customers.

MARKETING AND VALUE CREATION IN ALLIANCE

In Chapter 6 we described networking in general and virtual organizations in particular. The step is not far from what is often called 'strategic alliances'. The differences between a virtual organization and an alliance are more linguistic than reflecting a clear distinction. A virtual organization is a more imaginary (even if real in effect) type, and alliance is a concept that gives the flavour of tighter relationships. Virtual organizations and strategic alliances are both to be regarded as networks. The special reason why alliances are focused on here is that specific opportunities for pooling resources are opened to cooperating small firms in such alliances. However, in the very beginning of the creation of a new business venture, networks are probably more often a virtual type than a more formal alliance type. At this stage of the business venture, the latter has not yet been developed and structured.

Alliances in a Resource-dependency Perspective

The resource-dependency perspective[4] is an excellent explanation of the phenomenon of strategic alliances. In essence, all organizations are dependent upon resources such as *knowledge*. For example, research knowledge, production knowledge and skilled labour, energy, production facilities, money and access to customers are the key ingredients of alliances. These are needed for all kinds of purposes related to an organization's performance. The overall goal for all organizations is (naturally) survival. Some resources are more important for survival and/or success. Such resources are especially important to possess or at least to control.

The big corporations possess most of their own vital resources. This gives such organizations an advantage over smaller organizations, unless smaller organizations are able to control vital resources without ownership.

Highly successful strategic alliances have emerged during the last decades. These alliances may take almost any form, from very loosely related cooperating organizations, so-called virtual organizations, to strong formal links in franchise agreements of joint ventures (Figure 7.1).

Not only do small firms work together in alliances but also big firms do as well. Small and big firms may ally themselves with each other. The rationale for the cooperation is that resources may be pooled. Resources needed by the partners in the alliance are made available (almost) as if possessed.

Sometimes it is better not to possess but to have access to certain resources. Ownership ties the organization to this particular resource and reduces flexibility. In an alliance, an additional partner with resources can be easily included and, at the same time, if necessary, older partners can be excluded from the network if and when their contributions are too small. The looser an alliance is, the easier to include and exclude partners.

Vital scarce resources like R&D can be made available in exchange for other scarce resources. Buyers or similar resources may in the cooperating organizations be exploited better, leading to leaner organizations and cheaper production, marketing and so on.

For an entrepreneurial firm, alliances open up all possible opportunities. With modern information technology and the well-developed global logistic systems of today a small firm can work together with other companies on almost any place on the earth. The best suitable partners can easily be in interactive communication in real time and shipments between the cooperators can be done in one or two days, worldwide.

What is seen in the form of virtual organizations and other types of alliances are combinations of both the economies of scale with the economies of small-scale organizations. This opens the way for the ultimate marketing dream – to provide world-class, superior customer value at lowest possible costs. What is done *in-house* are all the things that a particular focal company can do better and more cheaply than anybody else can. Virtually all the rest can be *outsourced* to other companies, who have the capabilities to produce and

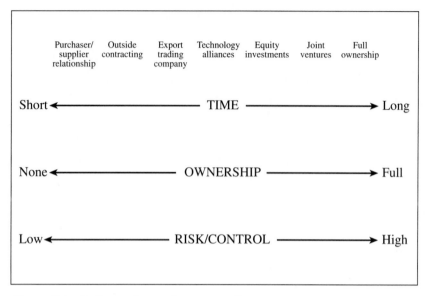

Figure 7.1   Different forms of strategic alliances

perform better in those specific aspects in question. A small firm can then be a world-class master in a particular market niche and still be small and flexible.

Furthermore, resource alliances between small firms (and others) increase the flexibility and the ability to deal with dynamic and uncertain markets. Adaptations to changes can be done quickly and different morphologies of the alliances may serve different customer segments or geographical areas.

Quasi-corporations

Achrol[5] discusses the evolution of new types of marketing organizations:

> ... the marketing function's environmental openness, flexibility and adaptive agility are constrained in the conventional organization by the extent to which the firm invests resources and facilities in indigenous products, R&D and production technology. The post-industrial era could take the principle of division of labor and task specialization a giant leap forward to the division and specialization of business functions. Organizations of the future are likely to be vertically disaggregated, with many of their functions performed by a network of specialized organizations.[6] These functionally specialized firms will be held together and co-ordinated by *market-driven* focal organizations, organizations that may be the closest yet to a true 'marketing company'[7] ... They involve complex exchange relationship among partner firms, to manage which 'quasi-corporation' will evolve sophisticated and socio-political systems.

Achrol identifies two main types of marketing organizations. The *market exchange company* is organized around buyers and markets in the form of a giant information system. It is hooked into a worldwide directory of suppliers of products with all relevant information on product specification, custom design possibilities, prices, current inventories and locations, production times, terms of trade and so on. The market exchange company is, in a way, a quasi-market. Examples are the highly successful organizations using the Internet as channels to customers, like Amazon.com. The strategic core – primary source of power – of such a company is its worldwide links to customers, its information centres of suppliers and the quality of its market information network.

The other type of market organization is the *market coalition company*, that is, one able to adjust to the changing conditions in the environment by developing multiple structures, each of which is better adapted under a given set of environmental conditions. The market coalition company is a quasi-corporation containing a functionally specialized marketing firm acting as the coordinating nucleus of a network of strategic alliances. The focal organization will outsource all or large parts of its functional needs in technology to alliance firms specializing in various areas.

The exchange and coalition models of market alliance organizations are shown in Figure 7.2. The flexibility in combination with the possibility of 'incorporating' world-class capabilities makes a well-organized strategic alliance very competitive. What is the result of a change from production (to marketing) to information- and relationship-handling capabilities is the ability to create a superior and functional network as the source for adding superior customer value. Here is where the entrepreneurial small firm has as good a chance as any other organization – regardless of size – to compete successfully in the global markets.

Marketing: Joint Creation of Customer Value

Marketing in this type of situation is far from finding the optimal marketing mix as in mainstream marketing discussed in Chapter 2. Instead, relationship skills exist in combination with technology and production capabilities, which enable the organization to perform the best offer available – the *best customer value* which is the resource requested by the parties in the alliance. As an example, what are regarded as good or ideal suppliers[8] are those that:

- deliver reliably;
- contribute substantially to the cost advantage;
- are seen as reliable and dependable and responsive;
- have an awareness of joint interest;

- have a potential for synergy;
- are characterized by a superior technical and aesthetic fit of their product; and
- show their joint interest by taking a functional approach to conflict resolution.

Further, reciprocal exchange of information is important, both formal and informal, and that information exchanges are expected to contain all types of necessary information.

In the traditional marketing literature, especially from the managerial school, customer value is regarded as being produced within a firm. The suppliers deliver goods and services needed, but the value to the customer is created within the firm. Cooperation in virtual organizations or more formal alliances gives a different picture as explained below.

The term 'co-opetition'[9] is relevant for situations when firms may act in different roles – or may be regarded as acting in different roles. The big industrial corporations as well as the small firms interact in multiple roles and may be suppliers, cooperators and competitors to one another because what they offer the market is, or can be regarded as, supplementary. Firms cooperate when their offerings to the market are supplementary; when they compete the offerings are not supplementary but overlapping.

Think of increased sales by cooperation, to create better customer value together instead of competing over the same markets; that is the essence of co-opetition. Instead of going to war over an existing market, joint actions may lead to market enlargements and sales improvements. An example which is common today is global alliances among airlines, such as Star Alliance. The airlines do compete with one another, but try to reduce the efforts of competition towards efforts to create better alternatives and services – better value – to the customers. It is all a matter of perspective: from one perspective the companies are competing; from nother perspective they are supplementary and offer better customer value through joint actions.

This phenomenon has little if anything to do with the size of a company. Instead it has to do with the companies' capability to create customer value in a *value constellation*.[10] Traditionally, value creation is regarded as a sequential process, as shown in value chains.[11] A firm at the first stage in the value-adding system adds value and then sends the goods downstream to the second stage and so on to the final customer. In markets where the products are complex and/or the service components are large, the value creation is probably not sequential. A firm may be involved in the development of a specific offering, later produce parts of the offering and may continue to be involved in improving the offering to the customer and so on. Another reason why value may be created in a non-sequential order is the need for flexibility and

Quasi-corporation:

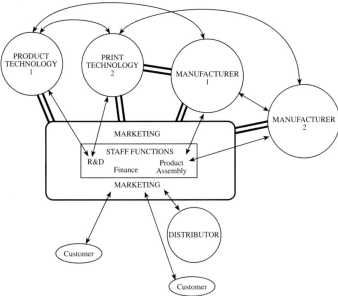

Quasi-market:

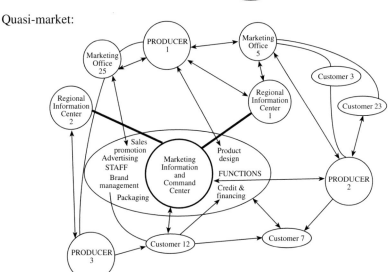

Source: Reprinted with permission from *Journal of Marketing*, published by the American Marketing Association, Achrol, R.S. (1991), 55 (October), p. 88.

Figure 7.2 The coalition and exchange models of market alliance organizations

adaptation. Each customer requires specific customizations and the specifics may change over time.

A value constellation may take almost any morphological form and be more or less stable over time. In dynamic situations, almost constant reconfiguration may go on. In more stable situations, the structure of the value constellation may be of a more permanent nature. This is fundamental in the modern view of a firm's marketing capabilities, and provides another component in discussing differences between managerial and entrepreneurial growth (Figure 7.3; compare Figure 6.2).

It is probably more fruitful to look at creation of customer value when growing entrepreneurially as taking place in value constellations rather than in value chains. When, on the other hand, growing managerially, circumstances are more structured and certain. Therefore, value chains may be the more appropriate model.

When a big corporation tries to break up into smaller, flatter and more autonomous units, it aims to create the same benefits as found in the quasi-corporations – small business units that are related to but still independent of one another. The difference is that the traditional corporations have more activities and the results are still developed and produced in-house instead of being outsourced to any meaningful degree.

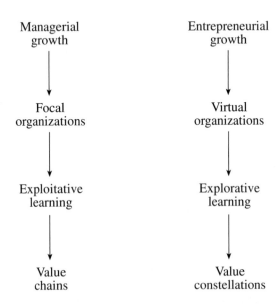

Figure 7.3   Growing, organizing, learning and creating customer value

VALUE CONSTELLATIONS: SETS OF COOPERATING VALUE CREATORS

To summarize from the last section, in the business literature of today we read about a new type of organization, set up in cooperation with other firms. Such a phenomenon is often described in colourful language: a shamrock company, a spider organization, a starburst organization, a strategic alliance, a network, or an imaginary or virtual organization, to give some examples. Such structures are contrasted against the traditional view of focusing on a *single firm* as the organization.

It is surprising that there is still so much focus on a single firm, as defined by law, as a unit of observation and conceptualization! Only historic reasons can justify that. If we want to understand the creation of customer value in growing entrepreneurial firms in the new economic era, the relevant object is not the single individual or focal firm! It is the group of actors or firms which together co-create value for a specific market in interaction between three levels, as shown in Figure 7.4.

In a value constellation the *interaction* between the three levels is crucial. In this interaction, parties involved have different tasks and a number of different roles must be performed[12] to create the customer value. When we talk about a certain constellation there is a specific casting of actors at each level. In other contexts, each actor may participate in other constellations and play other and

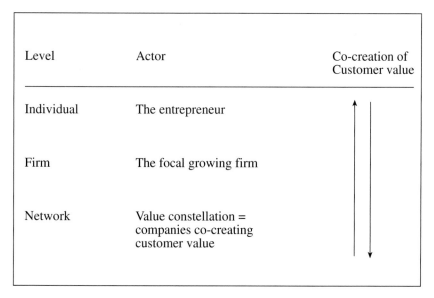

Level	Actor	Co-creation of Customer value
Individual	The entrepreneur	
Firm	The focal growing firm	
Network	Value constellation = companies co-creating customer value	

Figure 7.4   Levels in the value-creation process

different roles. Further, over time the individuals as well as individual firms participating in the constellation may change, but the roles are more stable.

We identify three main roles, one in each of the three different levels in the value constellation (Table 7.1). Primarily, the role of the individual entrepreneur (or the entrepreneurial team) is to find innovative solutions to create outstanding customer value. There must be someone who starts the process and possesses the capacity to come up with new and better solutions.

Table 7.1   Roles in the value-creation process

Level	Actor	Roles in the value-creation process
Individual	The entrepreneur	To initiate and drive the process
Firm	The focal growing firm	To coordinate and take the leading role in the value constellation's efforts (constellation captain) and host the core capabilities in a particular set of value creators
Network	Value constellation	The individual firm in the constellation may be a niche specialist, able to produce (world-class) goods and or services needed in the total value-creating processes. As a total, the constellation should be able to act as a world-class player in international markets

Second, there needs to be a coordinator and a hub in the value constellation. Here we find similarities in research in the sets of cooperating firms performing value to customers in the marketing channels. To illustrate that a particular organization takes the role of leadership to improve efficiency in marketing channel flows, the concept of 'channel captain' was introduced in the distribution literature in the 1960s. The channel captain was the party in a marketing channel that took a lead in structuring and organizing the channel between manufacturers and the customer. This may be a dominant firm at any level in the channel.

Similar concepts are used in the alliance literature, for example Hedberg et al.[13] specifically mention the importance of an IO leader (IO = imaginary organization). In a value constellation there must be a champion or a captain that takes the lead and coordinates the efforts to create customer value. Again, this is an entrepreneurial effort, although it is not a role at the individual level. Instead it is the focal company of the entrepreneur that plays this role.

Finally, the third level is the set of cooperating firms in the whole value-creating system constituting the value constellation. The main role here is to produce the total customer value of a specific offering. The value of what is offered to the market is to be ultimately assessed by the end-user. However, the end-user may play an important part in the value-creation process as well. This is the second meaning of the concept of co-creation.

In the previous discussion, co-creation was used to illustrate the point that customer value is created by a set of cooperating partners. Within service marketing, the customer's contributions to the production of the service have a significant impact on productivity and quality.[14] The customer is a co-producer of value.

Co-production of customer value also takes place in contexts other than traditional service industries. In the automotive industry, for instance, subcontractors are required to follow the customer's hard demands but are assisted in their efforts to meet these demands. In complex industrial business-to-business relations, joint development between sellers and buyers is commonplace. In long-term relationships, both parties learn to improve regardless of the content of the offering.

Further, in e-commerce, to take another example, the buyer must take an active part both in seeking information and in learning how to use the product after shipping. The customer-related activities in the value processes are probably increasing, as e-commerce becomes more widespread.

In some marketing contexts, relationships and offerings are simple. The customer is more of a passive receiver of the customer value. When, say, cigarettes are bought, there are few different ways of smoking them. If, on the other hand, a cigar is bought, personal smoking habits have an impact on the smoking experience. If the cigar is smoked too quickly the burn will be too hot, thereby reducing the aromatic sensation. The customer's behaviour during consumption has a direct impact on the value. As this simple example illustrates, in more complex consumption situations, the customer becomes an important part of the value-creation process regardless of the product.

Normann and Ramirez[15] argue that interactive value creation is becoming more common in future complex markets. Hence, in complex contexts, in durable buyer–seller relationships, and when the interactivity between the customer and the seller increases, the customer should be seen as a co-creator of customer value.

Let us discuss the three levels of the value-creation process as presented in Figure 7.4 and Table 7.1, that is, the level involvement of the individual/

entrepreneur, the level of involvement of the (coordinating) firm, and the level of network/co-creation.

CHARACTERISTICS OF THE LEVEL OF THE ENTREPRENEUR

Roles of the Entrepreneur

Outstanding value creation often starts with entrepreneurial action. To find the basic opportunity to create new rules of the marketplace games asks for a different kind of thinking compared to the conventional one, an ability to find something new and, sometimes, revolutionary. Traditional marketing theory does not give much guidance here. A simple explanation would be to claim that growing firms make better combinations of the Ps of the marketing mix, which of course is true in a way, but is not sufficient to understand why some firms grow and others do not.

By introducing the concept of *entrepreneurship* in the discussion we identify the missing link, the entrepreneur, who is able to create innovative new combinations and drive the new business venture process to success. Therefore, the *initiator* of a new value-creation process is the entrepreneur using his or her capacity to find new economic combinations where other individuals do not, thus providing innovation, spotting and exploiting opportunities, thereby creating new value to customers. This is important. It is on the level of the *individual* entrepreneur (or the individuals in the entrepreneurial team) that the superior value-creation process starts, and it is the entrepreneurial process that generates the necessary forces to drive further development of the value-creating processes. Regardless of circumstances, there must be somebody that drives this superior process. The level of the entrepreneurial process will consequently need to be included in entrepreneurial marketing.

Like the entrepreneurial processes, other processes related to value creation in this context do not take place sequentially, nor are they possible to plan in advance. Some need to be coordinated as we go, while others may even be impossible to anticipate.

Influences from the Individual on Marketing Processes

This will lead to a different way of looking at marketing processes. Characteristics of *individual* interpretations of reality and decision-making behaviour become important tools if we want to understand entrepreneurial marketing.

There are several reports in the literature about how small, fast-growing firms do not act in their long-term interests; nor are they sequential in their marketing behaviour, for example when becoming internationalized. Instead things happen, which, in the eyes of an outsider, look very random.[16]

In an entrepreneurial firm the individual entrepreneur has a strong influence on important actions taken by the firm. His or her way of understanding and implementing what is perceived as interaction with the market and other parts of the business environment, will have a direct impact on the business. The *entrepreneurial strategy*[17] is characterized by intermittent and changing behaviour caused by new information. The entrepreneur interprets the environment and instantly wants to act upon these interpretations to enhance customer value.[18]

Growing firms are often opportunity driven and take chances as opportunities appear.[19] Further, we know from the management literature that individuals in general continuously perceive and interpret new information into mental constructions of reality.[20] This interpretation process goes on as long as the individual is exposed to new information and as a consequence, the mental construction of reality changes with the information. Whenever an entrepreneur finds a better path to value creation and customer satisfaction he or she will use his or her organization to implement the new vision.

What is sometimes irregular and intermittent behaviour of entrepreneurs is functional in small, growing entrepreneurial firms in dynamic environments, such as those that exist in the new economic era. Furthermore, growth in such firms does not take place in a managed way but (to a large extent) through constructing virtual networks and other kinds of alliances, where the entrepreneur plays a leadership role, not acting primarily as a manager.[21]

Marketing Benefits of Entrepreneurial Influence

The turbulence of today's market has often been characterized by non-linear changes, sometimes even as chaotic situations.[22] Such conditions are more disadvantageous for the big corporation than for the growing entrepreneurial firm. In dynamic situations, quick actions are needed. Closeness to customers, flexibility and ability to adapt to customer demand may create the culture necessary for very sensitive marketing actions as well as for quick response. As a catchphrase, we noted earlier in Chapter 1, that 'survival of the fastest' is sometimes used to illustrate what kind of companies are the potential winners in the new economic era.

Dynamic and chaotic new situations are better handled with quick feedback loops and a mental capacity and predestination to take new actions to deal with what is unforeseeable than by trying to meet such changes with planning, even if the plans are flexible. Indeed, to create chaos has even been suggested as a marketing strategy[23] for a growing company.

The entrepreneur lives with the market as well as the company almost 24 hours a day and gets new information every day. This information is constantly interpreted in the entrepreneur's mind.[24] As a consequence of continuous interpretation of new and additional information, the vision of how to create better customer value is reevaluated and soon put into action to accomplish better customer value.

Entrepreneurial marketing benefits from:

- continuous exposition to and interpretation of market information;
- a few actors which have great impact on the organization and have the power to impose their visions and ideas on the organization;
- quick action and response to changes; and
- an ability to make new combinations, thereby changing the rules of the game at the marketplace by creating better customer value.

CHARACTERISTICS AT THE LEVEL OF THE COORDINATING ENTREPRENEURIAL FIRM

Entrepreneurial Spirit and Capability

It is too simple to say that growth can be explained simply by taking the correct marketing actions. A firm that grows takes the correct actions, of course. That is why they grow! But to create growth in a company there is a need for something more. This is the entrepreneurial drive and motivation to create growth. The concept of 'entrepreneurial capacity' is what we use to describe such individuals, and 'entrepreneurial spirit' (or capability) describes the firms.

For growth to continue, an entrepreneurial spirit must live in the company. This is the engine that takes a lead, motivates and stimulates key individuals in the focal entrepreneurial firm and in its virtual networks. If a company has a goal to continue this type of growth, this entrepreneurial spirit must be kept vital. There are many firms that stagnated because the spirit to achieve something extra died. In a growing firm, the process of keeping the entrepreneurial flame alive is an important task for everybody.[25]

The constellation captain takes the lead in the value-creating constellation. It is hard to imagine the type of value-creating system discussed in this chapter without some kind of leadership; and the reason for a particular organization to take this lead is entrepreneurship. The individual entrepreneur (or core group of entrepreneurs), who organizes a team, spreads the entrepreneurial spirit to others and makes things happen, making his or her organization take the lead in value-creating constellations.

The second aspect of entrepreneurial spirit is *entrepreneurial learning*. Entrepreneurs continuously interpret the environment and reevaluate in this process the paths to customer satisfaction, which is why the entrepreneurial strategy is more intermittent and opportunity oriented than the planned strategy of the large corporations. Entrepreneurs see opportunities and believe in their own ability to create whatever they want.[26]

The new idea and action taking go hand in hand for an entrepreneur. The academics may say whatever they want, but many successful entrepreneurs take actions when they find what they believe to be a viable idea. The idea must be implemented instantly. In such a context the learning process becomes crucial. *Learning by doing* is a very important process in an entrepreneurial firm.

We have found many examples of entrepreneurs taking orders from clients and customers without really knowing how to solve their problem. They afterwards admitted that many of the problems were not even possible to foresee in advance. But faith in their own ability and ability to motivate others was enough.

Market analysis and marketing planning have another meaning under these circumstances. This does not mean that entrepreneurial firms do things randomly. There is just no perceived need for formal marketing analyses because the entrepreneur lives with the market virtually around the clock. Entrepreneurs in general have a high degree of knowledge of their market, technology and market offerings.

To Access and to Balance the Necessary Resources

To secure the access to necessary resources is crucial in a growing company. But in the new economic era the possession or ownership of resources is without meaning. Instead it is enough to be able to utilize all necessary resources, owned or not. Hence, a shift from ownership to utility in the view of necessary resources is what we advocate; as a consequence, the focal firm has lost its meaning as the prime target for analysis. The important task for the coordinating entrepreneurial firm, the constellation captain, is to secure the utilization of resources necessary for fulfilment of the business vision of the entrepreneur.

In the early stages, choices are limited and the entrepreneur may have to take whatever he or she can find in the environment. Later, there may be opportunities to choose which resources to possess in-house and to secure what is necessary from outside partners. This may occur when the company, after initial growth, is able to control the financial flow. This process is called 'resource balancing'.

Resource balancing can be viewed both at the level of an individual focal firm and at the level of the whole value constellation. At the level of the value constellation, the decision is what specific partners to include in the constellation and what distribution of resources there will be.

In reality this is not a decision that can be dealt with as a rational choice. A growing firm may have a reduced set of partners to choose from and imperfect knowledge leads to a more opportunity-driven choice. Further, it is not a decision made once and for all.

Previously we have stated that what is needed most in the new economic era is intellectual resources. Other resources and partners are there in abundance. What is required is the intellectual capacity to persuade other actors to participate in the value-creation process on a win–win basis. In a value constellation, all partners must be winners (and, in the new economic era in particular, hopefully have fun as well). At any given time the set of potential partners may be limited but over time the world is open to everybody, *if* the world is viewed that way!

In a stable environment the need for changes in the value-constellation is limited. In most markets in the new economic era, however, the turbulence created by new breakthrough techniques and frequent launching of new goods and services, requires a *continuous update* of participating parties and a functional and adequate resource balance between these parties in the value constellation.

These changes may vary from minor replacements of a marginal supplier to complete reconfiguration of the firm's value-creating system. The former type of evolutionary change is a normal activity to improve the present value-creating ability. The latter type of change is a consequence of a radically altered business concept or a consequence of entrepreneurial activities and innovation. Examples are:

- new customer offers;
- new technologies;
- new forms for distribution; and
- new material.

We see more of the latter in the new economic era.

Ownership, Utilization of Resources and Core Capabilities

The balance between internal or external resourcing (ownership versus utilization) is to be determined primarily on the basis of availability and what critical capability is needed for long-term success and growth in potential markets. Again, the only necessary resource to host in-house, is the ability to organize the value-creating system, to reconfigure the value constellation when necessary, and to make things happen.

However, in reality some parts of value-creating activities can be expected to be in-house in the coordinating entrepreneurial firm. Barney[27] has identified four criteria that guide a firm's evaluation of resources: value, rareness, imitability and organization. A resource that meets all four criteria, a resource that is valuable in the eyes of the customers, is rare, hard to imitate and possible to exploit within the organization, will probably generate sustainable competitive advantage and consequently should be hosted in-house.

An important concept in this context is *core competency*, which is based on those resources which an organization exploits in order to gain sustainable strategic competitive advantages.[28] In its general meaning a core competency can be any important resource, human, financial, physical or organizational, such as knowledge, individual capacities or collective capabilities, physical assets, anything to be used to gain competitive advantage within the scope of the organization's vision. We shall use the concept of *core capability* for an organization's ability to create strategically competitive offerings to a market.

Quinn formulates the relevant, fundamental question: 'What critical skills do we need to develop to be the best in the world from the customers' viewpoint?' – and to provide the answers:[29]

Maxim One: For maximum long-term strategic advantage, companies focus their own internal resources on a relatively few basic sources of intellectual or service strength – or classes of services activities – which cerate and maintain a real and meaningful long-term distinctiveness in customer's minds.

Maxim Two: The key to competitive analysis and competitive advantage is to approach the company's remaining capabilities as a group of service activities that could be either 'made' internally or 'bought' externally from a wide variety of suppliers specializing or functionally competing in that activity.

Maxim Three: For continued success companies actively command, dominate, and build barriers to entry around those selected activities critical to their particular strategic concept. Concentrating more power than anyone else in the world on these core competencies as they affect customers is crucial to strategic success.

Maxim Four: Strategists plan and control their outsourcing so that their company never becomes overly dependent on – or later dominated by – their partners.

According to Quinn, knowledge-based service activities are the most crucial ones to master and consequently to host in-house.

CHARACTERISTICS OF THE LEVEL OF CO-CREATION IN VALUE CONSTELLATIONS

Structures of Co-creation

Co-creation may take almost any morphological form depending on its purpose. Co-creation (as well as virtual organizations and value constellations) is a system only in the eyes of the beholder, in this case especially the coordinating, leading firm (and hopefully to partners), and it can be anything from totally loose couplings to tight, long-lasting ties.

It is the leading coordinating firm, the value constellation leader that designs the structure by taking in or excluding partners and arranging for the conditions for exchange within the structure. We have seen from research in industrial marketing that firms tend to rely on existing partners. Co-creation is therefore not only momentary but takes place for shorter or longer periods of time. The differences and similarities between more visual structures are only in the eyes of the beholder and co-creation becomes a *structure* in the eyes of the focal coordinating firm, a structure which is linked together with visual ties such as a flow of goods or money or non-visual ties such as information and knowledge.

The components of virtual organizations are a pool of partners, a pool of customers, the focal organization (the leader of the virtual organization), and core competencies of the participants. Some main structures of virtual organizations identified in the literature are:[30]

- the spider web;
- the interconnected island;
- united front towards the market;
- the clockwork; and
- the missing link.

In the spider web, the partners are chosen to participate in a specific business context. The parties are all centred around the constellation leader, who coordinates and drives the structure, like a spider in the centre of a web.

In the interconnected island structure one or several companies join forces with other enterprises in order to achieve economies of scale or scope, geographic coverage or an effective infrastructure. The use of a unifying factor such as a joint trade mark, concept or customer base are bases for synergy in another type of structure, all getting synergy by showing a united front towards the market. The clockwork means a number of components closely intermeshed like the cogwheels of a clock. Finally, the missing link is when previous systems are combined in a better, more efficient way, thereby producing better value than before. Many growing firms emerge as the missing link, the parts and the technology are there, it is just the value-creation leader that is missing. In other words there is no one who has yet identified the possibilities or at least not found it worthwhile to exploit them.

The desire to create outstanding customer value dictates what the final constellation will look like. The traditional concepts of upstream and downstream in the value chain may be obsolete in a value constellation with interactive value creation. Nevertheless the concept can be used to illustrate that partners are to be taken in for all roles, besides leadership. Partners can be used to get closer to the customer, to provide customer image or to leverage customer value because of synergy effects between the offerings. On a parallel or upstream level the reasons for partnership are almost infinite.

The value constellation is more or less stable. As environmental or other conditions change, the constellation needs to be reconfigured. For the leading organization, this is an important process. To look for better partners, to develop the skills of the partners is necessary for superior value creation in dynamic situations. The value constellation is hardly ever optimal or perfect, only satisfactory or unsatisfactory at a certain point.

In Chapter 2 the institutional school was outlined and Butler's concept of the four utilities[31] was summarized as:

- *elementary utility* (what is fundamentally performed for the buyer);
- *form utility* (to develop the goods and make them palatable to the consumers);
- *place utility* (transportation, the buyers normally need the goods in other places than the location for production); and
- *time utility* (storage during the time lag between production and consumption).

The concepts of the four utilities are important both in marketing and in logistics to understand the distribution of roles and the interchange ability between those roles in marketing systems such as, for example, marketing channels. Supplemented with *possession utility* (the transfer of ownership from seller to buyer) these concepts can be used to understand the distribution of tasks when co-creation takes place in a value constellation. In the value constellation there is a distribution of tasks and as in channels of distribution, several independent firms act to co-create customer value. By doing so, they perform certain utilities. The distribution of tasks is to be done so that no other arrangement can produce the same or better customer value at a lower cost. The level of co-produced customer value is decided by the focal leader organization.

Each partner exploits its own special core capabilities. Elementary utility comes from the original business vision in the focal organization, form utilities come from co-producers, place and time utilities come from third-party logistics and possession utility comes from partners such as call centres, e-commerce consultants, web-hotels, sales companies, brokers or middle-hands in the distribution channel. As a consequence, a buyer may in reality have little contact with the focal coordinating organization that 'owns' the concept because a niche specialist performs possession utility as a sales company or as a web-broker.

We argue that most of what we traditionally conceptualize as processes related to value creation within a focal organization are also valid when we neglect the organization's borders and use the whole value constellation as a unit for distribution of tasks for co-creation of customer value. However, forms of leadership as well as the strategic aspects of core capabilities transfer are more complicated.

THE VALUE CARRIER: THE OFFERING TO THE MARKET

Importance of the Offering

In the following sections we shall concentrate on the outcome of marketing processes, the output created by the value constellation taken as a whole, but first the offering to the market will be discussed.

In the early 1960s, before the focus on the marketing mix became prominent. Frey[32] proposed that marketing decision variables could be categorized into two groups: the *offering* and the *methods and tools* used. The former was the product as some kind of goods, packaging, brand, price and service, and the latter was channels of distribution, personal selling, advertising, sales promotion and publicity.

Let us carry on where he ended. In the following sections the offering to the market will be regarded as one important concept which is conceptually separated from actions taken to create transactions and/or customer relationships. The offering is conceptually what carries the potential value to the customer and what is formally transacted in a business deal. However, value emerges first when the customer gains some utility when the suppliers and sellers combine their efforts. Therefore, customer value is always co-created with the customer because customer value rarely emerges without customer participation.

The Customer and Levels of Customer Focus

First we need to establish the role of a customer. In the perspective of a value constellation, cooperation when serving a particular client must take place, the whole constellation must be centred at the hub to serve the specific customer and not only the single focal firm. However, the meaning of customer focus then becomes more complex. For each firm included in the value constellation, the customer is not simply the closest downstream firm that adds value (if we can talk about downstream value creation). The prime customer is instead the buyer of the output from the whole value constellation as identified by the focal entrepreneurial firm. This complex view of customer focus may be broadened even further. We find a complex network where not only the roles of buyers and sellers are blurred, but where some partners (especially the constellation captain) have more influence on the buying decisions than the actual receiver of a particular constellation partner's output may have.

At least four different customer levels can be identified. First, we have the actual buyer of the output from the whole value constellation. Second, we find the customer of this buyer (the customers' customer); third, we have the firm that leads the value constellation (the constellation leader) and makes the decisions of which partners to include; and fourth, the actual receiver of the output of a particular constellation partner. Hence, the concept of a customer can be specified in terms of first-order customer, second-order customer and so on.

When we talk about the customer, we refer to the buyer of coordinated output from the value constellation in terms of a specific offering to the market, what in traditional marketing literature is regarded as the firm's customer. Note that the offering does not have to be standardized or pre-manufactured. An offering is something somebody offers another party to buy or is asked to sell. As soon as there is something that may cause a transaction between a seller and a buyer there is what we call an offering.

Goods or Services: The Similarities are Important!

Above we described how successful entrepreneurs have the ability to create outstanding offerings to the market. We regard the offering as the single most important outcome of the value-creating processes and it is the carrier of customer value. The offering is the manifestation of the entrepreneur's vision and what the customer ultimately will evaluate and choose or not choose. However, we prefer to talk about offerings rather than goods or services.

As mentioned earlier, looking at the marketing literature we believe that too much attention has been given to the *distinctions* between goods and services during the last decades. Historically, service marketing emerged as a new school in relation to mainstream marketing. The rationale was that services in general show distinct differences to goods such as intangibility, production and consumption being closely related and so on, all together justifying a specific theory for marketing of services.

There are of course several differences. However, we like to focus on the *similarities*. An important aspect has to do with what we call 'value time'. It is often said that an important distinction between services and goods is that only goods can be stored. In a physical sense this is true. But from a marketing point of view even goods have a limited time for value. If you store fresh fruits, time will limit its value very rapidly. The same goes for fashion goods, computers, and so on. In the same way, a service may be postponed in time. The standard example of a non-storable service offer is the airline seat. At the time the plane takes off the service is not there anymore. Today, however, we find that planes do not take off until a certain number of seats have been sold. Hence, value is related to time, and value time is an important dimension to consider when we focus on customer value, regardless of whether we offer what traditionally would be classified as services or goods.

Today, most of what is offered to the market contains both aspects of goods and aspects of services. For example, cars include both the physical car and finance arrangements, maintenance programme, and so on. Leasing a car is classified as a service offering, including almost the same components as a car sold by contract with instalments. Hence, the differences may be subtle but the similarities are many and need to be kept in mind.

To be critical, the prevailing perspective, with much of the focus on the distinctions, is the differences between goods and services from the eyes of a seller. If we look at goods and services from the buyer's point of view, the differences may be less important. Buyers buy goods and services because they perceive a need. This perceived need may be based on a long mental process or just a result of an impulse. Nevertheless, there is a perceived need. We should focus on what the buyer buys instead of what the seller sells.

Buyers buy something that they expect will satisfy their needs regardless of whether they are goods or services or a combination. They buy *value* and *utility* (Table 7.2).

Table 7.2   The offering can be understood from two viewpoints: the buyer's and the seller's

Seller's view	Buyer's view
Set of tangible elements Set of intangible elements	Perceived value and utility

Drucker[33] realised this early:

It is a customer who determines what business is. It is the customer alone whose willingness to pay for a good or service converts economic resources into wealth and things into goods. What a business thinks it produces is not of first importance, especially not to the future of the business and its success. What the customer thinks he/she is buying, what he/she considers value, is decisive – it determines what a business is, what it produces, and whether it will prosper. And what the customer buys and considers value is never a product. It is always utility, meaning what a product or service does for him. The customer is the foundation of a business and keeps in existence.

The Offering Contains Tangible and Intangible Elements

The offering to the market must be described by its *value* and understood in its *perceived* value. The value emerges from a set of tangible and intangible components produced in the value constellation and offered to the market by the seller. The mix between tangible and intangible elements may differ between industries, even between offerings, but it is to be understood from the viewpoint of the buyer. The set of elements is the offering from the seller's point of view.

Note that the offerings are the manifestation of all activities and processes that a complex set of actors within the value constellation has co-created, regardless of whether we talk about what traditionally has been labelled goods or services. The tangible elements constitute goods and the intangible, services. Offerings contain elements of both kinds.

The buyer may not always be aware of the complex set of co-creators that jointly produced the customer value. Nor may the customer acknowledge the focal entrepreneurial firm, the constellation leader as the real seller or producer. The venture the buyer buys from, the seller in his or her eyes, may be just another niche specialist in the value constellation. Examples of such specialists are telemarketing companies, agents, specialist sales companies and web-based brokers.

The value, manifested in the tangible and the intangible elements, constitutes the offering. Normann and Ramirez[34] argue that an information code is included in the view of what the offering is, and this information code is the third component. This code tells the buyer 'how to use' the offering. In its simplest and most tangible form this is just the manual, like the manual enclosed with a camera or a computer. But the code can also assume an abstract form. An example of this form of code is 'lifestyle-advertising' about cigarettes, fashion and alcohol. We include such aspects in the intangible elements, however this is an essential part of the offering.

Actions to Create Transactions and Relations

We find the offering to the market the single most important value carrier. But offerings seldom sell themselves. Firms need to take action to induce the customer to buy. Such actions may be very apparent, marked and explicit or discrete and intangible. A transaction is a necessary part of sales and cannot be neglected in any commercial system.

Besides creating transactions, firms take actions to create relationships and customer retention. The creation of the offering, as well as the transactional and relationship actions, are important categories of output from the processes in the value constellation. This will be discussed further in the following chapter.

SUMMARY

In this chapter, marketing has been seen as the customer value-creation processes. There are three levels of actors that co-create customer value: the level of the entrepreneur, the level of the coordination firm and the level of co-creation itself (firms directly taking part in a value constellation).

In Figure 7.5 parts of this chapter are integrated. Information and all forms or resources are transformed into customer value and actions to create transactions and relationships through interactions and processes at all three levels.

We have argued:

- The level of a single focal firm is not enough to understand the value-creation process. Instead the value constellation and the various interactions between the three levels in the value constellation are crucial.
- Resources are crucial to create customer value, but an extreme, human, brain capacity is necessary to host the in-house resource. The rest can be acquired in various forms of cooperation with external partners.
- The entrepreneurial way of doing business can be very functional in a dynamic environment while on the other hand a planning philosophy may create a less flexible marketing behaviour.
- The focus on superb customer value is crucial for growing firms. Lack of true customer value can never be compensated with marketing cosmetics.
- The customer buys certain utilities. The distinction between goods and services is of less importance when customer value and utility are focused upon. Nobody cares what the seller sells; only what it can do for the buyer, the customer and the end-user. In this respect everything could to be regarded as 'services'.
- To be able to deliver the necessary utilities that create the customer value, the market is offered something that often contains both tangible

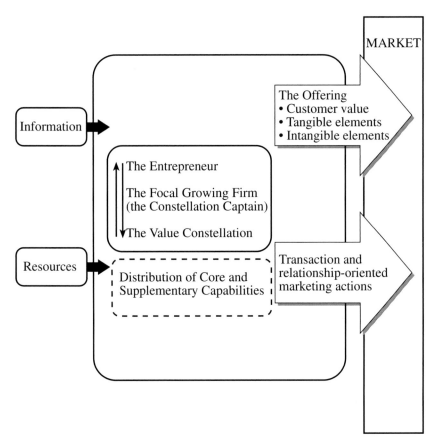

Figure 7.5   The value constellation and its levels of actors

(goods) and intangible (services) components as well as information on how to use it. With this in mind the difference between marketing of goods *vis-à-vis* marketing of services diminishes.

NOTES

1. Sheth, J., D. Gardner and D. Garrett (1998), *Marketing Theory, Evolution and Evaluation*, New York: John Wiley & Sons, p. 196.
2. Nilsson, T.H. (1991), *Värdeladdad marknadsföring* [Value-laden marketing], Malmö, Sweden: Liber-Hermods, pp. 71, 76–9.
3. Bower, M. and R.A. Garda (1985), 'The Role of Marketing in Management', *McKinsey Quarterly*, Autumn, pp. 34–46.
4. March, J. and H. Simon (1958), *Organizations*, New York: Wiley; Aldrich, H. (1976), 'Resource Dependence and Interorganizational Relations between Employment Service

Offices and Social Service Sector Organizations', *Administration and Society*, **7** (4), pp. 419-54; Pfeffer, J. and G.R. Salancik (1978), *The External Control of Organizations*, New York: Harper & Row.

5. Achrol, R.S. (1991), 'Evolution of the Marketing Organization: New Forms for Turbulent Environments', *Journal of Marketing*, **55** (October), pp. 77-98.

6. Miles, R.E. and C. Snow (1984), 'Fit, Failure and the Hall of Fame', *California Management Review*, **26** (Spring), pp. 10-28.

7. Keith, R.J. (1960), 'The Marketing Revolution', *Journal of Marketing*, **24** (January), pp. 35-8.

8. Håkansson, H. and I. Snehota (eds) (1995), *Developing Relationship in Business Networks*, London: Routledge, pp. 236-9.

9. Nalebuff, B. and A. Brandenburger (1996), *Co-opetition*, Garden City, NY: Doubleday/ Currency.

10. Normann, R. and R. Ramirez (1994), *Designing Interactive Strategy - From Value Chain to Value Constellation*, Chichester, UK: John Wiley.

11. See, for example, Porter, M.E. (1985), *Competitive Advantage*, New York: Free Press.

12. In the 1960s, the concept of roles was introduced in the channel literature. A similar approach is taken here; see, for example, McCammon, B. (1963), 'Alternative Explanations of Institutional Change and Channel Evolution', in Greyser, Stephen A. (ed.), *Toward Scientific Marketing*, Chicago: AMA, pp. 477-90; Gill, L. and L. Stern (1969), 'Role and Role Theory in Distribution Channels', in Stern, L. (ed.), *Distribution Channels - Behavioural Dimensions*, Boston, MA: Hougton Mifflin, pp. 22-47.

13. Hedberg, B., G. Dahlgren, J. Hansson and N. Olve (1997), *Virtual Organizations and Beyond: Discover Imaginary Systems*, London: Wiley.

14. Gummesson, E. (1998), 'Productivity, quality and relationship marketing in service operations', *International Journal of Contemporary Hospitality Management*, **10** (1), pp. 4-15.

15. Normann, and Ramirez (1994), pp. 28-30.

16. Havnes, P. A. (1998), 'SME Development - Challenging the Incremental Change Models', paper presented at the 43rd ICSB World Conference in Singapore 1998, workshop on Interstratos (Internationalization Strategies of European SMEs).

17. Minzberg, H. and J.A. Water (1994), 'Of Strategies, Deliberate and Emergent', in Tsoukas, H. (ed.), *New Thinking in Organizational Behaviour*, Oxford: Butterworth Heinemann, pp. 188-208.

18. Hultman, C.M. (1999), 'Nordic Perspectives in Marketing and Research in the Marketing/ Entrepreneurship Interface', *Journal of Research in Marketing and Entrepreneurship*, **1** (1), pp. 54-71.

19. Carson, D., S. Cromie, P. McGowan and J. Hill (1995), *Marketing and Entrepreneurship in SMEs*, Hemel Hempstead: Prentice-Hall International (UK) Limited, p. 55.

20. Tsoukas, H. (1994), 'Introduction: From social engineering to reflective action in organizational behaviour', in Tsoukas, H. (ed.), *New Thinking in Organizational Behaviour*, Oxford: Butterworth-Heinemann, pp. 1-22; Weick, K.E. (1979), *The Social Psychology of Organizing*, Reading, MA.: Addison-Wesley; Weick, K.E. (1995), *Sensemaking in Organizations*, Thousand Oaks, CA: Sage.

21. Compare our discussion about differences between managers and leaders earlier in this book.

22. Nilsson, T.H. (1995), *Chaos Marketing - How to Win in a Turbulent World*, Maidenhead, UK: McGraw-Hill.

23. Ibid.

24. Tsoukas, H. (ed.) (1994), *New Thinking in Organizational Behaviour*, Oxford: Butterworth-Heinemann.

25. This does not mean that a firm always has to be entrepreneurial in order to grow. There is also managerial growth, see further Chapter 8.

26. Hultman, C. (2000), *Affärsprocesser i växande företag - Om marknadsföring för tillväxt* [Business processes in growing companies – about marketing for growth], Stockholm: FSF.

27. Barney, J. (1997), *Gaining and Sustaining Competitive Advantage*, Reading, MA: Addison-

Wesley, p. 145.
28. Prahalad, C.K. And G. Hamel (1990), 'The Core Competence of the Company', *Harvard Business Review*, May/June, pp. 79-91.
29. Quinn, J.B. (1992), *Intelligent Enterprise*, New York: Free Press, pp. 53-55.
30. Hedberg et al. (1997), pp. 39-44.
31. Butler, R.S. (1923), *Marketing and Merchandising*, New York: Alexander Hamilton Institute, pp. 20-21.
32. Frey, A.W. (1961), *Advertising* (3rd edn), New York: Ronald Press, p. 30.
33. Drucker, P. (1973), *Management: Tasks, Responsibilities and Practices*, New York: Harper & Row, p. 61.
34. Normann and Ramirez (1994).

8. A conceptual framework for entrepreneurial marketing

INTRODUCTION

One could say that our framework for entrepreneurial marketing is based on four pillars (Figure 8.1). Entrepreneurs are able to use their entrepreneurial capacity to formulate the visions of how to create customer value. Consequently *entrepreneurship* is one key element in the framework and it explains *why* and *how* opportunities are recognized and implemented into customer value through transactional and relationship marketing actions.

Second, *resources* are needed to create customer value contained in the offering to the market, the value carrier. Resources are either possessed or acquired by cooperation with partners in the value constellation. Information is also a resource, and in the forthcoming framework, information is separated from the offering.

Third, customer value is co-created by the different *processes* in the value constellation.

Fourth, the *actors* that run the processes and co-create customer value are partners in the value constellation. Because of the frequent use of outsourcing, the traditional concept of a single, focal firm as the core for value creation has lost its relevance.

In the previous chapters, entrepreneurial behaviour as well as the three levels of actors in a value constellation have been thoroughly discussed.

This chapter starts by discussing two of the above four pillars, that is, resources and processes. These two will be combined with the other two pillars in three steps:

1. presenting an integrated view of marketing as transactions and as relationships;
2. discussing various growth patterns of small firms, including the entrepreneurial marketing firm; and
3. providing a content to our entrepreneurial base model, that is, the three variables: use of language, culture and entrepreneurial capacity.

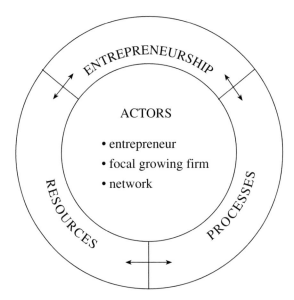

Figure 8.1　Four pillars of the entrepreneurial marketing framework

The chapter will end by developing a model for analysing the entrepreneurial marketing firm.

RESOURCES AVAILABLE AND CO-CREATION OF CUSTOMER VALUE

In the growing entrepreneurial firms that we have studied, customer value was not created solely by actions taken by a single firm. Instead a number of firms were involved. This is not a very surprising finding. In Chapter 7, we discussed how outstanding customer value is to be co-created by the best players to be found and business networks were discussed in Chapters 6 and 7 as well.

There are several reasons why growing firms in particular need to rely on a whole set of cooperating partners, all potential co-creators of value to their customers. Some examples are:

- production of superior customer value requires the best players; economies of scale and scope favour niche specialists;
- lack of an alternative: no competency for in-house production is available;
- flexibility, changing or uncertain customer demands;

- time; the lead time to market launch does not allow time for in-house competency creation; and
- lack of one's own resources.

We shall, again, focus on the last issue and discuss the phenomenon of co-creation of customer value and its conceptual consequences from a resource perspective.[1] This focus is justified by the fact that the potential for more resources is the single most important reason why networks are critical to the small growing entrepreneurial firm.

Infinite Amount of Resources Available by Co-creation

Resources such as raw materials, energy, money, machinery, highly developed components, semi-finished goods and services (the list can be almost endless of all types of resources) are needed in modern value creation. Further, regardless of industry and type of output, it takes *human knowledge* at all stages of the life of a firm in the new economic era to exploit and add value to all other required resources.

All resources can rarely be hosted in-house. Instead, value creation is always partly done in cooperation with external partners such as subcontractors, consultants and of course traditional suppliers. In reality, co-creation is the regular form of value creation. Even big corporations like Ericsson use cooperation with a large number of firms, just to get access to innovation, and smaller entrepreneurial growing firms in particular must cooperate with others in the environment to get what they need.

In the new economic era, cooperation in virtual networks is a necessity to survive; in the old economic era, cooperation in some form or another has been going on at least since the beginning of industrialization. Hence, to understand value creation we must move away from focusing on what is happening in an individual firm. Very few firms produce value on their own! Instead, almost all firms cooperate with customers, suppliers, original equipment manufacturing (OEM) manufacturers, consultants and so on.

Our chosen perspective leads to a very important conclusion that concerns how we look at the individual firm and its resources. When customer value is co-created on a regular basis the relevant resources to consider, is the sum of all resources of all the firms involved in the value constellation. We must realize that the tradition to focus one company as only an isolated entity, only restricts our perception of what resources and capabilities really are available to create customer value.

Instead, there are no restrictions at all, besides the organization's own capability to determine the right formula in finding the necessary resources and creating vehicles to tie these resources together in a value-creating system.

This formula must contain three important parts, in addition to the original business vision of what value to offer the market. First, capabilities to identify what resources are needed, second, capabilities to find the relevant partners and third, the capabilities to successfully drive and coordinate the value-creating constellation that co-creates the relevant customer value. In an entrepreneurial firm, these capabilities depend on the individual entrepreneur and his or her team.

Consequently, it is irrelevant to discuss differences in the possession of resources between small and big firms. When Birley[2] stated that SMEs lack resources and/or knowledge which preclude decision making based on the classic strategic marketing approach of analysing markets, selecting a long-term growth strategy and optimal management of a detailed plan, she had a legal definition of the company in mind.

Again, the opportunity to use resources is open to everybody with the intellectual capacity to have a virtual view and to take the correct actions and create relationships and alliances with all necessary partners that possess the resources required for the production of customer value in any sector. Kirzner[3] noted early that entrepreneurship in itself only requires human knowledge. In his spirit we state that the only resource really needed in-house, is human brain capacity to put it all together.

A PROCESS VIEW OF VALUE CREATION

One important part of our view of entrepreneurial marketing is the concept of *processes*. Processes are generally less focused in marketing literature compared to, for example, the fields of business process re-engineering and of quality management, where improvements of the business processes are regarded as a crucial tool for successful value creation.

The traditional definition of a (business) process is as follows: 'A process is a logical, related, sequential (connected) set of activities that takes an input from a supplier, adds value to it and produces an output to a customer'.[4] When analysing a real venture it is up to the analyser to decide what set of processes and subprocesses to include. A process may contain several subprocesses and it is the purpose of analysis and the ingenuity of the analyser more than anything else, that dictates what is to be included as processes:

> Companies have thousands of processes, not 'ten or so', and for obvious reasons I call the immensity of these processes the 'process swamp' – a complex, dynamic, and seemingly formless assortment of processes, some closely connected to others, others related only slightly or not at all.[5]

At the lowest, operational level there are an almost endless number of subprocesses going on, all constituting what can be called the 'process swamp'. A few examples are:

- creating customer service;
- inventory management;
- shipping;
- meeting with business vendors;
- channel management;
- public relations;
- supplier relations;
- staff training;
- budgeting of marketing costs;
- production planning;
- product launching;
- joint action with competitor for breaking up new markets;
- branding, credit controlling; and
- co-development of a new product with customer.

To create customer value involves a complex set of related business processes, including planning and executing.

Creating as well as driving the processes are other fundamental aspects often neglected in previous marketing theory. The essence of the marketing processes is the creation of better value to the customer, especially in entrepreneurial marketing.

If we try to identify all the processes related to value creation we would soon get lost and drown in the swamp, as we would do by focusing on all activities performed in an enterprise. Also, the breaking down of the main processes into subprocesses is based on the division of labour and/or the organizational hierarchy. Instead, it is the process perspective that is important as well as a discussion of what types of relationships between the processes we can expect to find in growing entrepreneurial firms in dynamic environments like the new economic era.

Entrepreneurial Marketing as Related Value-creating Processes

We prefer to see marketing as a set of interrelated business processes, connected in different types of dependencies with the ultimate purpose of creating customer value.[6] Inputs to these processes are information, various tangible resources as well as intangible resources such as intellectual capacity. Output is primarily what is offered to the market as tangible and intangible customer benefits as well as actions taken to generate transactions and relationships.

As a consequence, we should like to replace the well-structured marketing management model described in Chapter 2. Marketing in general and entrepreneurial marketing in particular could better be characterized as blots of oil in water, some well tied together, others with very loose couplings (see Figure 8.2). These processes take place in a context of human culture, as discussed in Chapter 5, as well as in the context of the particular business logic relevant for each industry in which the firm is doing business. The benefit of the marketing management planning model is its simplicity. It is easy to identify the components as well as the relations between the components.

With a process view we cannot offer such simplicity. Instead, there is a complex and changing pattern of various processes and much of it is in the eyes of the beholder. However, Benson[7] gives theoretical support for a hierarchical perspective, that is that some of the processes are subordinated to others. His argument is that many of the observable, operational inter-organizational processes are dependent on more general visions, forces and processes, such as innovation and R&D or structuring and maintaining the focal and virtual organizations.

Based on this perspective, Hultman[8] differentiates between forms of interaction in marketing channels. On a more general level is the interaction and competition of scarce resources within the marketing channel. On the operational level is the daily interaction to create efficiency in the flows and

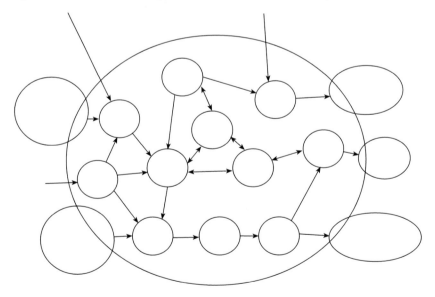

Figure 8.2   Business processes

promotional activities in the channel. Processes on these two levels go on in parallel as two different games.

We shall take a similar standpoint in the further analysis of entrepreneurial marketing. A marketing channel is in itself a special form of value constellation where the parties cooperate to perform different utilities related to distribution. Further, especially in a value constellation, driven by an entrepreneur, some main processes have a strong impact on the daily work in all of the participating organizations.

In particular, this is valid for processes concerning how the leading entrepreneur/organization acts as decision maker and how resources as well as the capabilities are distributed in the value constellation. Examples are how entrepreneurs make sense of market opportunities, how the entrepreneurial capacity affects the organization's behaviour[9] and how resources for value creation are distributed in the constellation.

This hierarchical view, that is, to regard some of the processes as strongly influencing the others, allows us to understand the relationships between traditional marketing activities and entrepreneurial growth. On the operational level we find all processes related to marketing activities. These are related to and depending on processes on the general level, how the leading entrepreneur thinks and/or how significant actors in the coordinating organization act.

The processes on the general level are normally hard to outsource to the value constellation while the more specialized processes on the operational level are to be carried out by the partners with the best capabilities. However the perspective must be the same in both cases, that is, that of the whole value constellation.

CREATION OF TRANSACTIONS AND CUSTOMER RETENTION: BALANCING MARKETING AS TRANSACTIONS AND AS RELATIONSHIPS

The offering has an exclusive position in all outbound activities undertaken. All of the very successful entrepreneurs we have talked to, have been able to create a high customer value in their offerings to the market. However, besides creating the value-carrying offering, firms undertake many outbound activities. In essence, activities are undertaken to create transactions and relationships to the markets and other business vendors.

In mainstream marketing the focus is on transactions and how the seller creates transactions by taking various actions, and using combinations of the marketing mix. Transactions are here of course equal to sales; the ownership of something is transferred from the seller to the buyer, normally in exchange for money. The main concept for these actions is the marketing mix.

In Chapter 2 we referred to some critics of the marketing-mix concept. The concept was, in fact, heavily criticized.[10] The advocates for relationship marketing are, as mentioned, among the critics. They suggest instead that marketing is much about relationships. Both schools take the standpoint that their opinion better reflects the essence of marketing. However, we pointed out in Chapter 2 that neither transactional nor relationship marketing is, on its own, enough for our purpose.

Christopher et al.[11] characterize transactional and relationship marketing as follows:

Transactional marketing:

- focus on single sales;
- orientation on product features;
- short time-scale;
- limited customer commitment;
- moderate customer contact; and
- quality is primarily a concern of production

Relationship marketing:

- focus on customer retention;
- orientation on product benefits;
- long time-scale;
- high customer service emphasis;
- high customer commitment;
- high customer contact; and
- quality is a concern of all.

Transactional marketing is obviously more immediate in the time dimension. The focus is on the transaction itself and how to get the customer to buy. Firms take actions to make a specific customer make the decision to buy at a certain time. In relationship marketing the purpose is to retain the customer. The time-scale is longer. Firms take actions to retain the customer and to build trust and other sentiments that tie the specific customer to the selling firm.

In our contact with successful entrepreneurs we have found that they practise both transactional and relationship marketing.[12] However, and this is important, they rarely do both with equal extent and intensity at the same time.

This fact is illustrated in Figure 8.3. This figure is meant to be more of a nominal and conceptual sketch than a descriptive or prescriptive model. We

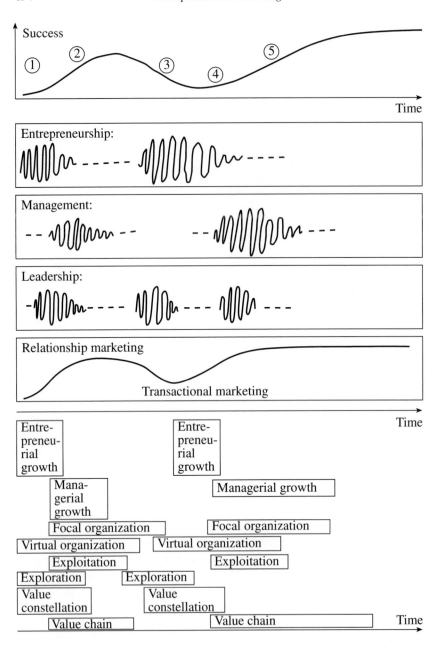

Figure 8.3   Transactional and relationship marketing

use it in order to put various concepts developed in this book in their proper place, that is, entrepreneurship, management and leadership, two kinds of marketing (transactional and relationship), two kinds of growth (managerial and entrepreneurial), two kinds of organizations (focal and virtual), two kinds of learning (exploitative and explorative) and, finally, value chain and value constellation. It is done by placing these concepts in specific periods over time for a hypothetical firm, the development of which, in terms of success (or lack of it), is drawn at the top of the figure. This development is divided into five stages.

Stage 1 The firm is born. This is done by (independent) entrepreneurship, that is, it is a matter of entrepreneurial growth. What is needed, is more leadership than management. The entrepreneur must be a leader while building up virtual organizations (and all kinds of alliances) and, if the entrepreneur is not alone in his or her focal organization, to be a leader for his or her employees. There is more relationship marketing than transactional marketing, above all to configure the new value constellation. Learning is more of an explorative kind than of an exploitative one, that is, it is more important to learn what is genuinely new than to learn more about what is known already.

Stage 2 The firm has taken off and grows 'on its own'. This is more of a managerial growth than an entrepreneurial growth (but still growth). Management is more important than being a leader. There is transactional marketing more than relationship marketing, that is, to secure growth by managing a positive cash flow and by managing the marketing mix. Most of the interest is on the focal organization (the virtual one is, more or less, established). It is possible to see a value chain and learning is more of an exploitative kind than an explorative one, that is, concentration is on learning the details of a pattern, which seems to lead to success.

Stage 3 Stage 2 cannot go on for ever. Competitors and other market forces, including changes in consumer taste, will prevent unlimited growth with one unchanged success pattern. Things will start to go wrong. It is necessary to take the lead again in order to motivate 'the troops' in bad times for the extra effort needed to turn around the negative trend and in order to develop, at least partly, a new value constellation. In other words, it is necessary to start a second round of entrepreneurship (what in our terminology should be called 'intrapreneurship'). It is also necessary to explore new learning and to concentrate on relationship marketing again.

Stage 4 The second wave of entrepreneurship has had a positive effect. The firm starts to grow again (entrepreneurially) and a new success seems possible. But there is still some leadership (in the virtual organization) to be undertaken. Transactional marketing is, again, starting to take over from relationship marketing.

Stage 5   This is, in principle, a repetition of Stage 2. However, this second wave of entrepreneurship might be more sustainable than the first one.

In other words, when entrepreneurship is driving the firm (at the independent phase or at the intrapreneurial one), it is a matter of entrepreneurial growth, more of relationship marketing, applying leadership (building up a virtual organization, where learning takes place through exploration) in a value constellation (which is, at least partly, reconfigured). On the other hand, during the management phases, it is a matter of management growth, more of transactional marketing, applying management (in the focal organization, where learning takes place through exploitation) in a value chain.

One reason why we want to disassociate entrepreneurship from transactional marketing is that the latter is dominated by the management paradigm, which is not of prime importance to entrepreneurship in the new economic era.

These two situations of transactional and relationship marketing are presented as extremes, which are, strictly speaking, never separated from each other in real life. It is all a matter of priorities as to which one to concentrate on (which one depends on the stage of the firm). To prioritize is necessary in order to succeed in the new economic era, where nothing is for free and no slack is allowed!

It should be understood that transactional as well as relationship marketing are both necessary in the long run. For instance, transactions could even be crucial for a firm in the short run, especially after a hectic, sometimes chaotic, entrepreneurial phase (as we have seen from the collapse of many internet-based businesses lately).

Regardless of whether a firm has a very short- or a long-term relationship with its customers, or combinations of both, there must be at least a transaction of something. If the firm is to survive in the long run, the transaction(s) must be made at a price exceeding the seller's costs. Normally there are a number of transactions over time and, in very many of the long-term relationships between all buyer/seller dyads or networks, there are numerous transactions.

Firms, especially growing firms, need to monitor cash flow carefully. Lack of financial resources can demolish a healthy firm very rapidly. In the growth stage the depletion of cash can be severe. Situations occur frequently when the growing firm needs cash. Particularly in these cases, the orientation towards transactional marketing is necessary.

It is obvious that a number of transactional-oriented actions must be taken; prices must be set, goods must be delivered and so on. Buyers react to these actions, at least to some extent. Although heavily criticized, the marketing-mix concept is here suggested as a useful tool for understanding some parts of an entrepreneurial firm's marketing behaviour. However, by reducing the number to a few 'Ps', the level of simplification in the marketing-mix concept is so high that we only capture a small part of all actions taken by entrepreneurial (and other) firms.

For a more holistic analysis, we should include other actions, more *transaction-supportive* actions in a framework for marketing in growing companies, to be in alignment with the entrepreneur's thinking. Theoretically this can be justified. We need to go back to the early Nordic research in the area to find that the basic meaning was that there were a number of business actions besides price that have an impact on the buyer's decision making. Firms take a number of different actions in order to influence the market, and Mickwitz[13] states: 'We have therefore tried throughout to pay attention to the presence of a number of different methods which firms employ in order to increase their sales'.

However, and this is the point, as in the case of transactional marketing above, we could equally well argue for the necessity to build and sustain business relationships in the long (and sometimes even short) run. So, the two perspectives in marketing – transactional marketing and relationship marketing – are in our opinion indeed *supplementary*. The marketing-mix concept is useful for describing and analysing some aspects of small firm marketing behaviour, but only during some of its phases. Other aspects such as trust, personal relations, and so on, must be included in a more elaborate framework. In one study of firms,[14] the relationship aspects seem to work more as some kind of transaction-supportive actions. A useful metaphor is that they act like catalysts in a chemical process! Both transactional and relationship aspects are needed over time for successful transactions. The transactions are facilitated by relationship actions – but we still do not know much about the interactions between marketing actions in these two categories.

Hence, a more complex perspective is needed, including both marketing-mix-related actions as well as actions such as the creation of reputation (referral marketing) and goodwill, long-term personal relations, trust and so on, where transactional as well as relationship orientations are captured. Therefore, such actions need to be included in the analyses at the same level as the marketing mix.

Below we have examples of actions taken by an entrepreneurial firm to influence the market. Some of these actions are directly oriented to create sales, the 'transaction creators'. Others are taken without a particular sale in mind. If the purpose is to keep and retain customers (to create relationships) the actions can be labelled 'relationship creators'.

Examples of transaction creators are:

- price cuts/discounts (or price increases when possible; price related to

  demand rather than customer value);
- extended offers on specific occasions due to demand;
- special adjustments and adaptations;
- sales promotion activities; and
- adaptations.

Other actions are taken with the purpose of creating relationships and retaining customers in the long run, the relationship creators. Examples are:

- hospitality;
- handling and quality of work;
- building personal sentiments;
- bartering exchanges;
- flexibility to changes in customer requirements; and
- trust building.

  Hence, we advocate that marketing must contain actions of *both* aspects. Which one is focused on depends on whether the firm is in an entrepreneurial drive or not. As a consequence, transactional and relationship marketing are both important as concepts – and action. The classification of transactional or relationship is due to the purpose of the action, and whether the firm is in an entrepreneurial or a management phase.

  The *balance* between transactional and relationship orientation in actions taken towards the market may vary due to the marketing context, but is primarily due to whether the firm is becoming entrepreneurial or not. To master both transactional marketing and relationship marketing is important for a growing company as well as to master the balance between the two types of actions.

GROWTH PATTERNS

From Figure 8.3, we can derive some 'typical' growth patterns. We have presented six such patterns in Figure 8.4.

  We refer to Pattern A as 'The minnow that never took off'. This means that even if the firm tried to achieve growth, it never occurred. Possible reasons based on our conceptual framework could be that the firm is doing too much transactional marketing and too little relationship marketing, that the firm applied the wrong type of learning at the wrong time, or that the firm never really understood its proper role in its value constellation.

  Pattern B is called 'Icaros'. Icaros, from Greek mythology, invented a device that made it possible for him to fly: a pair of wings, covered with wax.

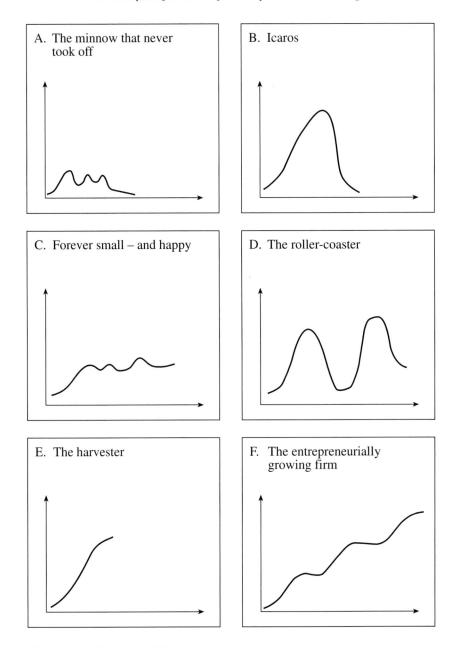

Figure 8.4   Some possible growth patterns

Unfortunately, Icaros flew too high. The wax on his wings was melted by the sun and he fell to the ground and was killed. In our terminology this could be an entrepreneur who was never able to become a manager (or enter into a partnership with one). This entrepreneur was entrepreneurial for too long, applied too much of relationship marketing for too long, and was never able to generate enough transactions to survive.

Most small firms are like Pattern C, that is, 'Forever small – and happy'. They start their business by finding a market niche of their own. However, they never had the ambition to grow, and they concentrate on exploitative learning, their own focal firm, management and transactional marketing, occasionally applying a bit of exploitative learning, networking, entrepreneurship and relationship marketing in order to survive.

'The roller-coaster' (Pattern D) is not good at timing various actions, applying each of the two sides of learning, focal and virtual life, management and entrepreneurship, and each of the two kinds of marketing for too long, thereby running a very volatile business. If there are any employees in the firm, labour turnover is probably very high.

Pattern E, that is, 'The harvester' is like Pattern B (Icaros) with a happier ending. Business was founded on a good idea, but the entrepreneur was able to sell his or her business to another, possibly bigger firm, cashing in before things turned bad. What happened to its business after the firm was sold is not part of this pattern.

Pattern F, which we refer to as 'The entrepreneurially growing firm' is an excellent example of what can be done in the new economic era, applying a well-balanced and timely mix of various types of learning, growth and marketing. It is about concentrating on explorative learning when necessary, on exploitative learning when necessary, on the virtual organization when necessary, on the focal organization when necessary, and so on.

Let us explore two of these patterns in further detail, that is, 'the roller-coaster' and the 'entrepreneurially growing firm'.

In Figure 8.5, we can see the roller-coaster growth patterns together with some of our conceptual pairs. The horizontal bars in the figure are supposed to indicate when various activities such as 'management' and 'relationship marketing' are focused on. Figure 8.5 shows that the firm is entrepreneurial for too long, management comes in too late, leadership should have come earlier the second time. Focusing on relationship marketing for too long and transactional marketing for not long enough leads to entrepreneurial growth only (when there is growth).

Similarly, we picture the entrepreneurially growing firm in Figure 8.6. The figure shows good timing. Entrepreneurship is taken over by management, and relationship marketing by transactional marketing, before it is too late; entrepreneurship starts a second time even when the firm seems to be growing

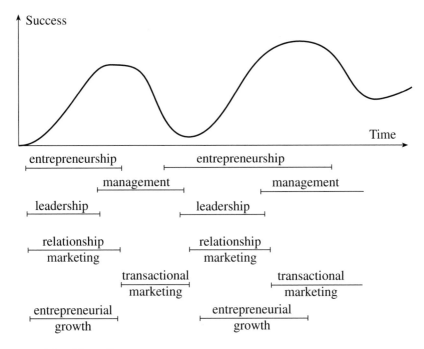

Figure 8.5   The roller-coaster

the most, leadership coincides with entrepreneurship and there are consecutive periods of entrepreneurial and managerial growth.

THE ENTREPRENEURIAL CULTURE, LANGUAGE AND CAPACITY

In Chapter 3, we provided the base model (Figure 3.5) which we reproduce here as Figure 8.7.

In the light of what we have seen in the last chapters, what does this mean in terms of entrepreneurship? As we know, there are two kinds of entrepreneurship, an independent one and an intracorporate one. In both cases, proper and adequate use of language might be the same. This language is provided in Table 6.3 (right-hand column), that is, to use the words 'learning', 'variety', 'actors', and so on – and to act accordingly!

In terms of *culture* (which we defined in Chapter 5 as 'basic behavioural norms, values and assumptions') the situation is a bit more complicated. Language in use will flavour culture, of course (language is mirrored in culture). However:

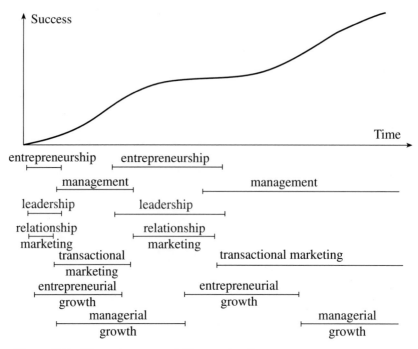

Figure 8.6   The entrepreneurially growing firm

1. The two kinds of entrepreneurship probably take place in the same
    national culture, but the *corporate* culture situation is different in the two
    cases. In the beginning of the life of the focal organization of the firm
    (independent entrepreneurship), there is hardly any *corporate* culture in it
    at all, simply because there has been no time to build one. In the virtual
    organization, on the other hand, culture is crucial from the very start of the
    firm for it to survive. If, within the virtual organization, a proper pro-
    business culture is not created, the firm will not live long.
2. Later, at the intrapreneurial stage, culture within the focal organization of
    the firm (where, probably, as the firm has grown, several people are
    involved) *as well as* in the virtual organization must be active and be the
    right one.

It is very difficult to state in general terms, what should be the proper
content of a 'good' entrepreneurial culture (focal as well as virtual), because
entrepreneurship comes in so many shapes. A few things could be said,
however:

● An entrepreneurial firm is constantly looking for opportunities and

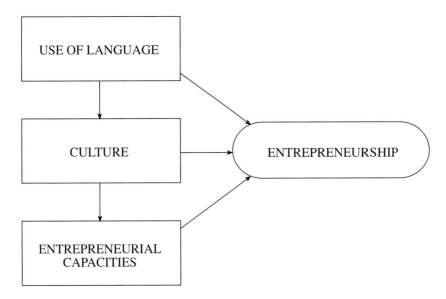

Figure 8.7   Factors generating entrepreneurship

committed to continuous innovation and change, and decision makers in the firm must be committed to the value of innovation and change.

- A proper intrapreneurial culture should probably be simple and transparent for all participants (in the focal as well as in the virtual organization) to understand and participate in. So, simplicity and transparency are important values.
- Intrapreneurial firms have, most likely, some visions for the future, which are to be used as corporate assumptions (and are thereby part of its culture).
- Entrepreneurial firms are definitely action oriented. They believe in action.

As far as *entrepreneurial capacities* are concerned, they are guided by the proper use of language. To go to Table 6.3 again, we can ask that a successful entrepreneur be able to 'learn', to love 'variety', to believe in 'actors' (and be one him- or herself) and so on.

According to Gibb,[15] there are certain core capacities needed to create, design and to lead an entrepreneurial organization, mainly of a focal type:

- creating and reinforcing a strong sense of ownership;
- reinforcing feelings of freedom and autonomy;
- maximizing opportunities for holism;

- tolerating ambiguity;
- developing responsibility to see things through;
- seeking to build commitment over time;
- encouraging building or relevant personal stakeholder networks;
- tying rewards to customer and stakeholder credibility;
- allowing mistakes with support for learning;
- supporting learning from stakeholders;
- facilitating enterprising learning methods;
- avoiding strict demarcation and hierarchical control systems;
- allowing overlap of tasks as a basis for learning and trust;
- encouraging strategic thinking; and
- encouraging personal contact as a basis for building trust.

Hedberg et al.[16] claim that two types of leadership are needed over the life of the virtual organization:

- *Servant leadership*: helping employees and others to learn from change, to innovate, to control, and to develop personally and professionally.
- *Involve leadership*, characterized by:
- generosity with knowledge;
- readiness to allow and admit mistakes;
- courage to accept new challenges;
- assuming responsibility for your own learning; and
- putting the job ahead of short-term self-interest.

Bryman[17] sees the following themes in modern (entrepreneurial) leadership literature:

- vision/mission;
- infusing vision;
- motivating and inspiring;
- creating change and innovation;
- empowerment of others;
- creating commitment;
- stimulating extra efforts;
- interest in others and intuition on the part of the leader; and
- proactive approach to the environment.

According to these three lists, some key capacities of an entrepreneur should be:

- providing and infusing a vision;

- giving a sense of holism, ownership and commitment to everybody;
- providing freedom and accepting ambiguity and mistakes;
- letting everybody participate in building networks;
- encouraging change and proactive learning; and
- breaking all kinds of bureaucratic rules.

Note that these capacities are probably more important in the new than in the old economic era, and also that they are only valid in the Western industrialized world (compare Chapter 5).

A MODEL FOR STUDYING THE ENTREPRENEURIAL MARKETING FIRM

At the end of this chapter, we shall present a model of how to study an entrepreneurial marketing firm. We have found two main parallel patterns for how entrepreneurs interpret and *make sense* of the information from the environment. The first is the traditional analytical and administrative pattern where alternatives are identified and evaluated and decisions are made on explicit criteria and information. This is much in line with traditional normative marketing theory.

The other pattern seems at first glance to be more intuitive and non-rational. However, when analysed more deeply, it is based on the entrepreneur's ability to identify what he or she finds as relevant information and the transformation of this information into a *vision* of customer value. Because of the key position in the (focal as well as virtual) organization, the entrepreneur is able to make up his or her mind quickly about how to *implement* the information into processes for creating and distributing customer value.

We have not, unlike many other scholars, found any indication that either of the two patterns is generally superior to the other concerning success of the venture. However, we have found that entrepreneurs are willing to accept order in many situations without knowing exactly how to process the final value; learning by doing can be the motto. Many entrepreneurs have faith in their own ability and learning during the long voyage to customer satisfaction. This is an important feature in market situations in the new economic era with high uncertainty where it is hard to follow traditional marketing models due to the lack of relevant information.

The ability to create new solutions and use *innovation* to create better and sustainable customer value is another important capacity for many entrepreneurs. One very important aspect in our framework for entrepreneurial marketing is this entrepreneurial capacity, which is driving the other parts in the framework.

Resources are needed for the creation and distribution of value. In contrast to other researchers in entrepreneurship we believe that resources are available for all entrepreneurs with the right capacities. The environment is full of resources. The key is to get access to resources that you do not control in-house. This may be accomplished by partnership in virtual organizations.

It seems almost obvious that the ability to acquire necessary resources is a fundamental condition for growth. But the literature is full of statements about the limited resources available for entrepreneurial small firms. Instead entrepreneurs should understand that they need to use the resources of others and concentrate on mechanisms to accomplish this. Hence, it is important for growth that there is a balance between necessary virtual resources and available focal resources, a *resource balance* is needed to create the best customer value.

Related to this is the continuous monitoring of what capabilities to host in-house and what capabilities to rely on through outsourcing to partners.

From a value-creating perspective the borders of a single, focal company have no particular meaning. Instead it is the totality of resources that can be generated to create customer value for a specific customer offering that is important for the understanding of how customer value is accomplished. The trick is to possess the capability to *structure* a value constellation, to be able to choose the best partners as well as the process of leading and maintaining the value-creating edge and the entrepreneurial spirit among the partners.

Instead of looking only at a focal firm, the whole constellation must be included in the analysis. There are three important levels of actors in the value constellation: the level of the individual (the entrepreneur); the level of the coordinating firm (the constellation captain); and the co-creative level (the network level including all participating partners of the value constellation).

The actors play different roles on each level. One particular role is the role of initiator and prime organizer of the value-creating constellation. This is the only role impossible to outsource and is generally the entrepreneur or the entrepreneurial team at the top of the coordinating organization.

The processes discussed above all take place on the general level. On the operational level we find all the day-to-day processes such as customer service, shipping, e-mailing, contracting, budgeting, meeting with virtual partners, and so on. The list here is indefinite. The same individual actors may play different roles in another value-creating system. In reality there are as many structures as there are spectators. The input is of course resources and information, the outcome is the tangible as well as the intangible aspects of the offering and all actions taken to generate transactions and relationships. In Figure 8.8 the important parts of the model are integrated.

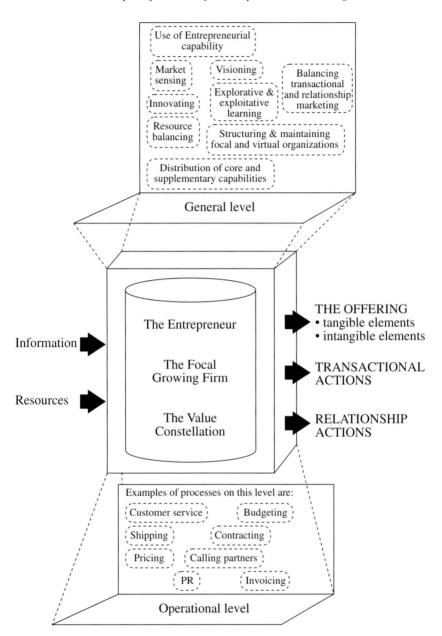

Figure 8.8   Entrepreneurial marketing

NOTES

1. See, for example, Aldrich, H. (1979), *Organizations and Environments*, Englewood Cliffs: Prentice-Hall or Pfeffer, J. and G.R. Salancik (1978), *The External Control of Organizations*, New York: Harper & Row.
2. Birley, S. (1982), 'Corporate strategy and the small firm', *Journal of General Management*, **8** (2), p. 86.
3. Kirzner, I.M. (1973), *Competition and Entrepreneurship*, Chicago: University of Chicago Press.
4. Harrington, H.J. (1991), *Business Process Improvement*, New York: McGraw-Hill; Harrington, H.J., E. Esseling and H. van Nimwegen (1997), *Business Process Improvement Workbook*, New York: McGraw-Hill, p. 1.
5. Keen, Peter, G.W. (1997), *The Process Edge: Creating Value Where It Counts*, Boston, MA: Harvard Press, p. 42.
6. A similar view is held by Normann, R. and R. Ramirez (1994), *Designing Interactive Strategy - From Value Chain to Value Constellation*, Chichester, John Wiley & Sons, pp. 29-30.
7. Benson, J.K. (1975), 'The Interorganizational Network as Political Economy', *Administrative Science Quarterly*, **20** (March), pp. 229-49.
8. Hultman, C. (1993), *Managing Relations in Marketing Channels for Industrial Goods*, Linköping, Sweden: Linköping Studies in Management and Economics No. 25.
9. Minzberg, H. and J.A. Water (1994), 'Of Strategies, Deliberate and Emergent', in Tsoukas, H. (ed.), *New Thinking in Organizational Behaviour*, Oxford: Butterworth-Heinemann, pp. 188-208.
10. See, for example, Webster, F.E. Jr. (1992), 'The Changing Role of Marketing in the Corporation', *Journal of Marketing*, **56** (October), pp. 1-17; Grönroos, C. (1994), 'Quo Vadis, Marketing? Toward a Relationship Marketing Paradigm', *Journal of Marketing Management*, 10, pp. 347-60.
11. Christopher, M., A. Payne and D. Ballantyne (1991), *Relationship Marketing, Bringing Quality, Customer Satisfaction and Marketing Together*, Oxford: Butterworth-Heinemann, p. 9.
12. Hultman, C. (1998), 'Notes on Marketing Actions in the Investigated SMEs', in Hultman, C., C. Gunnarsson and F. Prenkert, *Marketing Behaviour and Capabilities in Some Swedish SMEs - Expanders versus Non-expanders*, Stockholm: FSF 1998:1, pp. 25-44.
13. Mickwitz, G. (1959), *Marketing and Competition*, Helsingfors, Finland: Societas Scientarium Fennica (available for University Microfilms), Ann Arbor, MI, p. 237.
14. Hultman, C., C. Gunnarsson and F. Prenkert (1998), *Marketing Behaviour and Capabilities in Some Swedish SMEs - Expanders versus Non-expanders*, Stockholm: FSF, p. 39.
15. Gibb, Allan (1998), 'Entrepreneurial core capacities, competitiveness and management development in the 21st century', Research Paper: Durham University Business School, p. 14.
16. Hedberg, B., G. Dahlgren, J. Hansson and N.-G. Olve (1997), *Virtual Organizations and Beyond*, Chichester: John Wiley & Sons, pp. 190-92.
17. Bryman, A. (1992), *Charisma and Leadership in Organizations*, London: Sage, p. 111.

9. Some areas of importance for excellent entrepreneurial marketing

INTRODUCTION

Knowledge of entrepreneurial marketing is just in its infancy. We have provided a framework for this area in the previous chapter. To give more substance to this field, we should like to discuss in some depth a few themes of entrepreneurial marketing that we think are important. We shall concentrate on those sectors of the economy, which have entered the new economic era. This chapter is derived from the previous discussion, supplemented with new perspectives on areas of importance for excellent entrepreneurial marketing.

In the new economic era, instead of anticipating the future, the growing entrepreneurial firms should create it through entrepreneurship and innovation. Instead of the rational planning theory, we prefer to use aspects such as resource-based theory, process statesmanship, and entrepreneurship in what can be labelled 'entrepreneurial marketing leadership and management'.

SEVEN THEMES

We suggest a focus on seven areas of marketing excellence in entrepreneurial organizations. These are:

- mastering important value-creating processes;
- finding the best relevant resources available and structuring the value constellation;
- using a complex model for implementing the value-creating vision and an early-warning feedback system;
- changing the rules of the market game through entrepreneurship;
- leading as well as managing – both at the right time;
- exceeding the customers' expectations in the right dimensions; and
- balancing transactional and relationship marketing as well as balancing tangible and intangible aspects in the market offerings into a composite of marketing actions, that is, a complex marketing strategy.

As mentioned several times before, our aim is to be supplementary, not to claim that what we say is mutually exclusive of other marketing models.

Mastering Important Processes

The future seems to turn out less and less as anticipated. In the new economic era with turbulent environments, where factors are related interactively, forecasting will indeed be uncertain.

Further, markets with short lead times require that a growing firm will need to take action almost instantly. Entrepreneurs with power to implement their visions and ideas are able to act in such environments. They both learn and find new solutions during their journey; not even their goal may be clear in advance. The vision of what to accomplish but not exactly how to accomplish it may be the only thing given in advance.

In the economy of the 1960s the big corporations dominated the markets and buyers simply chose from what was offered. Decisions could be made with long-range accuracy. In a market situation characterized by oversupply, heavy competition and dynamic preferences, the situation is radically different. Things may happen so rapidly that firms just have to adapt instantaneously. This fits well with the entrepreneurial marketing model.

The process view allows those in business to focus on the crucial value-creating processes and make adjustments before any damage appears in the market. All the crucial and important value-creating processes in the value constellation need to be identified. Those processes need to be continuously monitored and adjusted when necessary, not forecast in detail in advance.

A process view enables the firm to control actions with flexibility but without the restrictions of a plan as long as there is a clear vision with which to navigate. Budgets and follow-ups on budgets may be too slow. Further, many entrepreneurial organizations do not use sophisticated budget systems. Instead, follow-ups on the outcomes of the performance drivers, as discussed in further detail later, may act as *early-warning indicators* guiding the entrepreneur long before the malfunctioning of a business process becomes fatal.

Processes need to be created or identified and maintained carefully. There are no simple rules or checklists that can be formulated to guide those in command, because there is an almost infinite number of routes along which these processes may develop. However, we need first to identify and second to understand how the relevant value-creating processes are to be directed and conducted towards growth. Hence, the successful business leader must possess the capacities required both to identify and to master the critical customer value-creating processes. Furthermore, growing companies must create and maintain the entrepreneurial spirit that drives the other processes. This is one important key to successful entrepreneurial marketing.

Using the Best Available Resources

Another important area for successful entrepreneurial marketing is the intentional use of the best combination of external and internal resources to optimize the value-creating processes. In a growing entrepreneurial firm most of the resources necessary for value creation are external. We regard this as a positive factor, increasing the potential flexibility and adaptability to changing conditions. The senior staff in a growing entrepreneurial firm must give this area special attention for two main reasons: first because resources must be made available for the value creation and second because the competitive edge is partly derived from the quality of the resources.

In their study of growing software companies in Italy, Capaldo et al.[1] discuss resources and the innovation process. They classify critical resources into the following groups:

- *Entrepreneurial resources* The entrepreneur plays a fundamental role in determining a firm's organizational structure and development; this cluster contains a set of indicators describing the structure and the competencies of the entrepreneurial group.
- *Human resources* Information regarding people working in knowledge-based firms contains fundamental indicators for the description of the organizational pattern; this cluster includes indicators related to the overall composition, the competencies and the development of the human resources of a given firm.
- *Resources linked to external environment* A firm's know-how is strongly influenced by the firm's ability to exploit environmental resources. In this group it is possible to find indicators measuring a firm's ability in setting up and developing contacts and collaboration with other firms and R&D centres or in acquiring new technology.

Some indicators of the resources in each category are shown in Table 9.1. The main resources and capabilities of the firm are all linked to human capacity, knowledge and skills. The rest can be acquired externally. At the end of the day it is the total set of available resources that counts. The appropriateness of the total set of resources and the balance between the external and the internal resources determine the value constellation's structure.

Fundamental questions related to entrepreneurial marketing are:

- What capabilities do we need for the intended value creation?
- For what purpose will those capabilities be used?
- What human knowledge and capacities are to be hosted in-house and

Table 9.1   Classification of a firm's resources influencing the degree of technological innovation

Variables influencing the degree of market innovation	Variables influencing the degree of technological innovation
C1 Entrepreneurial resources	C1 Entrepreneurial resources
C1.1: Number of persons forming the entrepreneurial group	C1.1: Number of persons forming the entrepreneurial group
C1.2: Entrepreneurs' know-how	C1.2: Entrepreneurs' know-how
C1.2.2: Percentage of entrepreneurs with market knowledge	C1.2.1: Percentage of entrepreneurs with technical knowledge
C1.3: Percentage of entrepreneurs with business and management experience	C1.4: Involvement of entrepreneurs in technological design and development
C1.4: Involvement of entrepreneurs in technological design and development	C1.5: Intensity of group relationships with R&D centres, other similar firms
C2 Resources linked to human resources	C2 Resources linked to human resources
C2.1: Total number of employees	C2.1: Total number of employees
C2.2: Percentage of technological developers	C2.2: Percentage of software developers
C2.5: Training	C2.3: Percentage of internal developers having a graduate degree
C2.5.1: Marketing and management training	C2.4: Job rotation
C2.6: Marketing aspects	C2.5: Technical training
C2.6.1: Percentage of entrepreneurs involved in marketing activities	C2.5.2: Technical training
C2.6.2: Percentage of internal persons involved in marketing activities	
C2.6.3: Percentage of external persons involved in marketing activities	
C3 Resources linked to external environment	C3 Resources linked to external environment
C3.3: Intensity of commercial collaboration with other firms	C3: Use of non-proprietary tool or external methodology of technological development
	C3.2: Intensity of technical collaboration with other firms

Source: Adapted from Capaldo et al. (2000), p. 8 (see note 1).

what are to be acquired through partnership?
- How will the whole pattern change, develop or erode over time?

Quinn[2] argues that the knowledge-based service activities are the most important ones to host in-house, no matter whether the offering contains mostly intangible service components or just the tangible components.

Regardless of the answer for each firm, another crucial challenge directly linked to the firm's ability to create competitive customer value is the ability to design and structure the resources in the value constellation and to balance the internal capabilities and resources to the external ones.

Implementing the Vision of Value Creation and Using Early-Warning Feedback Models

A critical process for the entrepreneurial firm is to implement the entrepreneurial vision of what value to create and how to achieve this. This must be done primarily in the entrepreneur's own focal firm, but also in the important parts of the value constellation. Only the relevant parts of the vision need to be implemented. What is relevant is a sharing of intentions, values and knowledge.

If used with care, and at the same time keeping its limitations in mind, we believe that the application of a multidimensional method like the 'Balanced Scorecard',[3] would allow both implementation and follow-up on intra- as well as interorganizational behaviour.

First, the organization needs to decide what perspectives to use in the implementation process. In most commercial organizations the important stakeholders are the *owners*, the *customers* and the *employees*. What takes place in the organization will lead to consequences for those categories of stakeholders. Consequently, the vision needs to be clearly understood, implemented and evaluated with these stakeholders in mind – the perspectives chosen.

Furthermore, it is the *business processes* taken together that create values to the customers, return on investments for the investors as well as salaries and the well-being of employees and managers. This leads to four different perspectives in order to understand, implement and evaluate the vision:

- financial;
- customer;
- human development (inter- and intraorganizational); and
- process (inter- and intraorganizational).

The financial perspective mirrors how well the organization generates money and gives dividends to the invested financial resources. The customer perspective reflects how the customer values the business offerings and other actions taken. The human development perspective reflects how well the firm takes care of and develops its human capital. Finally the process perspective puts the business processes in focus.

The vision may then be broken down into *strategic images* for each of the chosen perspectives, images possible to communicate to the stakeholders, employees as well as the partners in the value constellation. The strategic images tell the stories of what the company wants to look like in, say, one, two or five years' time in the four perspectives, respectively. In this context the images will reflect *what* value is to be created as well as *how* this value is to be created. The strategic images are in a way synonymous with strategic goals, however with the additional condition that these strategic goals must be possible to communicate to everybody in the value constellation in the form of images and/or metaphors.

To quote Kaplan and Norton:[4]

> A strategy is a set of hypotheses about causes and effect. Cause-and-effect relationship can be expressed by a sequence of *if-then* statements. For example, the organization can establish a link between improved sales training of employees to higher profits through the following sequence of hypotheses:
>
> *If* we increase employee training about products *then* they will become more knowledgeable about the full range of products they can sell.
> *If* employees are more knowledgeable about products, *then* their sales effectiveness will improve.
> *If* their sales effectiveness improves, *then* the average margins of the products they sell will increase.
>
> A properly constructed Scorecard should tell the story of the business unit's strategy. The measurement system should make the relationships (hypotheses) among objectives (and measures) in the various perspectives explicit so that they can be managed and validated.
>   The chain of cause and effect should pervade ball four perspectives of a Balanced Scorecard. ...
>   The process continues by asking what internal processes must the company excel at to achieve exceptional on-time delivery. To achieve improved OTD, the business may need to achieve short cycle time in operating processes and high-quality internal processes, both factors that could be Scorecard measures in the internal perspective. And how do organizations improve the quality and reduce the cycle times on their internal processes? By training and improving the skills of their operating employees, an objective that would be a candidate for the learning and growth perspective. We can now see how an entire chain of cause-and-effect relationship can be established as a vertical vector through the four Balanced Scorecard perspectives:

Financial	ROCE (Return capital employed)
Customer	Customer Loyalty On-time Delivery
Internal	Process Quality, Process Cycle Time
Learning and Growth	Employee Skills

Traditionally various output measures such as market share, sales, costs, profit or return on investment are identified and used as goals, few of which reflect the customers' perspective, or that of the employees or partners. Further, when the results of the outcome variables are negative, the information is already too late for the decision maker. The damage has already been done and the firm has lost tempo and/or position in the marketplace. Instead, information is needed that makes it possible to change the relevant processes in time – before there is any negative impact on the value creation. The answer is to identify and continuously monitor the important factors related to the business processes that have a major impact on the firm's ability to create value to customers, profit to investors and development of its human capital.

To be able to reach the situation in the chosen perspectives reflected by the strategic images, there are a number of areas in which the firm must succeed. These areas, or 'performance drivers' as Kaplan and Norton call them, reflect the strategy as well as the context of an entrepreneurial firm and are what cause the outcome. We shall search for:

- what drives profitability;
- what reflects competitive edge in the market segments in which the company chooses to compete;
- what value propositions are delivered to customers in the targeted market segments; and
- the particular internal processes as well as the learning and growth capabilities that enable the financial objectives and outstanding customer value to be achieved.

A good scorecard has a mix of core outcome measures and the performance drivers of these outcomes. If there are no explicit performance drivers there is no communication of the means to achieve the outcomes. As Kaplan and Norton state:[5]

> Our experience is that the best Balanced Scorecards are much more than collections of critical indicators or key success factors organized onto several different

perspectives. The multiple measures on a properly constructed Balanced Scorecard should consist of linked series of objectives and measures that are both consistent and mutually reinforcing. The metaphor should be a flight simulator, not a dashboard of instrument dials. Like a simulator, the scorecard should incorporate the complex set of cause-and-effect relationship among the critical variables, including leads, lags, and feedback loops that describe the trajectory, the flight plan of the strategy.

Besides the multidimensional perspective in implementing the entrepreneurial vision throughout the value constellation, the Balanced Scorecard may allow early-warning follow-ups.

When the market share or profit decreases it is too late to make corrections. A proactive entrepreneurial philosophy of continuously seeking to offer better customer value, in combination with close attention fulfilment of the performance drivers, leads the firm to a high degree of adaptivity to changing conditions. Using combinations of a flexible set of resources in the value constellation, the entrepreneurial firms may have what it takes to continue on a successful path to growth.

Changing the Rules of the Game through Entrepreneurship

In all existing sectors of the economy there are 'rules' – what to expect from a seller at a certain price; the business logic of a particular industry. Entrepreneurship can change these rules! There are several examples among the big multinationals that have grown from small firms because of an innovation: Rank-Xerox (revolutionary new method for instant copying of documents), Tetra-Pac (revolutionary packages of liquids) and IKEA (revolutionary new methods for distribution of furniture).

We have talked to many successful entrepreneurs and they had one thing in common: they were able to develop a company by creating better customer value than was previously offered in the market. In carrying out the research behind this book we met a number of extremely successful entrepreneurs. Few had any idea of the marketing-mix concept[6] and their success was not satisfactorily explained as an ability to make unique combinations of the Ps in the marketing mix.

Better customer value means better performance in terms of what the buyers really need, and that is not enough – often these new benefits are combined with lower prices than before. Better and cheaper is the rule! For the competitors this will be a completely new situation to deal with; it is hard to compete with a player that creates fundamentally better customer value under those circumstances. As Montgomery and Webster state:[7] 'Doing "more of the same better" is seldom the answer to competing with a new player who has changed the rules of the game'.

A firm may grow just by surfing on a big wave of increased customer demand. Traditionally, sales growth is achieved by increasing the market share or by enlarging the markets; attracting more buyers or making present customers buy more. This often requires a substantial amount of different resources, normally open only to the big companies. However, if the ambition is to grow more than the competitors or to grow in what previously was regarded as a mature market, the only true solution is to perform better than the other players, to create outstanding customer value and change the rules of the game!

Hence, an important part of the marketing success in growing entrepreneurial firms is the entrepreneurs' ability to change the rules of the game in the market. Innovations and new combinations of all kinds may create new rules of the ratio between benefits and costs for the customers. If an entrepreneur has access to a formula (new technology, new methods for production or an invention) that radically changes the ratio between value and price, then the entrepreneur has managed to change the rules of the game in the market.

Entrepreneurship, leading to capacity to create new rules by revolutionary customer value, is equivalent to creating a new market, regardless of the historical success of older products. A new player may take advantage of a more 'monopolistic' market situation and grow, without the extensive resources needed in a battle over market shares. It is important to note that the opportunity to change the rules of the game, to create better solutions and outstanding customer value, is open to everybody with the *intellectual capacity* to take the rectified actions.

When a firm grows in the old as well as in the new economic era, it is because there is a customer preference for what is offered in its markets. New technology, methods, ideas and so on, create better solutions to the buyer's needs. This is the entrepreneurs' contribution to the economy, to be innovative and find new and better solutions to offer the market.[8]

Customer value may be improved by different means and at different magnitude. In a theoretical sense increased customer value may be measured on a continuous scale, but from the buyer's perspective it is the major steps compared to what previously was known that create the difference.

At least three different levels of increased customer value can be identified. At the lowest level we find modifications, minor improvements of existing goods or services. The base or origins of the developments is easy to detect as well as the level of the improvements. On this level we also find more value by adding some extra features to the existing ones.

Second, we find new goods or services, new but not in any respect changing the game in the market. When Volvo introduces a new model it is new, it may be better and more modern than the previous one, but essentially it is the same value for the buyer's money.

However, suppose that an auto manufacturer instead had solved the pollution problem and was able to produce a car with almost zero effect on the environment. If so, they managed to change the whole concept of what to expect from a car. It is on this highest level that we find firms able to create superior customer value from a new innovation and entrepreneurial activities.

Such firms create a customer value that deviates radically from what it had been possible to offer previously. Examples are the Xerox copying machine; IKEA's kit of home assembled but cheap furniture; the first cellular-phone system; the first electronic calculator; the first auto-focus camera; and so on. Many of these examples, well known to the public, originate from bigger corporations. There are, however, many unknown examples of smaller, fast-growing companies that manage to change the market rules radically, see for example among Europe's 500.[9]

The conceptual difference between the third and the second category is based on two aspects. There are differences between added value and *improved* value. Added value means that extra value-adding components are added to what the customer expects to get. Fundamentally improved value is created by something that is radically new: videoconferences over the Internet compared to traditional phone conferences; new copying techniques; digital photos allowing costless duplications and new possibilities of distribution over the Net compared to conventional photocopying; and so on. On this level we find innovations that in important aspects change the buyer's expectations. The old products, regardless of previous market share, rapidly become obsolete.

For the seller to exploit the full potential of the offering, requires that buyers have information and knowledge enough to be able to evaluate the superiority of this particular offering! Hence, the perceived value dictates the buyers' actions. Although the value is in the eyes of the beholder, the full value of an offering needs to be communicated with marketing actions taken by the seller.

Normann and Ramirez[10] throw light on this process. To leverage the customer value the focus has to be on the customers' own value creation. The seller needs to be proactive and find the solution before the customers perceive the need. The key to this is to learn to gain understanding of the customers' own value-creation process as well as the value-creation process of the customers' customer, that is, the context in which the customers do business.

Closeness to customers is the standard marketing recipe to secure fruitful conditions for learning about customers. Here, entrepreneurial behaviour is advantageous compared to managerial planning behaviour, because entrepreneurs often live with the business around the clock and continuously try to improve the delivered customer value. In essence, the entrepreneurial firm can grow as illustrated in Figure 9.1.

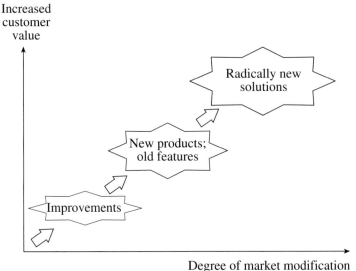

Figure 9.1   Three levels of increased customer value

Leading as well as Managing

During the twentieth century, in particular during the second half of it, management became not only a highly recognized profession but also an academic field of major significance. In many business schools, studying business was often equivalent to studying management, either on its own or as a specialized business function like financial management, marketing management or strategic management.

To many scholars, management became an all-embracing concept that could, if applied properly, solve all kinds of business problems. It all went along with the growth of big, and bigger, business. The idea was to plan, organize and control a larger and larger share of a given way of doing business. Then, at the end of the last century, things started to change. Circumstances for being a good manager changed. A new economic era emerged.

Management, or rather good management, was based on a few principles:

- there was a clear industry structure or, at least, a stable environment;
- changes were not too many and if they did occur, they were predictable;
- there was a hierarchy of people, where planning goes downwards and control goes upwards;
- business was periodical.

These are just a few of those necessary principles on which the possibilities of good management were based.

In the new economic era, all the above principles are gone. The future is not given, it does not wait to come true, it is there to be created right now! In the creation of a new business venture, particularly in its initial entrepreneurial phase, management should be replaced by leadership. This means being a leader in constructing virtual networks and other kinds of alliances and, if there are any employees in the firm, to be a visionary leader for them.

However, leadership cannot go on for ever, not even for an entrepreneur. Therefore, as the venture matures and becomes more settled, management takes over. It is important to remember that neither leadership nor management should be absent at any time of growth. It is the balance and timing when prioritizing any of the two that is important. So, in the early stages of the new independent entrepreneurial venture when starting, or, for the same venture, later in an intrapreneurial process, the first priority is to initiate the venture by playing the role of a leader, and not until later, when the business venture has settled down, to turn to more managerial matters – but, and this is one important message of this book, *not* before.

There should not be too much planning before there is anything to plan, not too much formal organizing before there is an organization for it (focally as well as virtually), and not too much control before there is anything to control. There is a place for a new business venture to try to grow managerially (a term we use in this book), that is, a time for planning, for organizing, for controlling – that is when management takes over; but not before!

Exceeding the Customers' Expectations in the Right Dimensions: Sales Drivers and Sales Requirements

The intense competition in modern markets quickly eliminates actors with inferior offerings to customers. In most markets the surviving firms make offerings to customers of acceptable or even high quality. The quality level of the tangible elements of the competing offerings is often relatively similar, or at least all exceed a certain standard. Nevertheless, some firms sell better than others and grow more than others.

In the traditional marketing perspective this is to be explained by a better combination of marketing activities. The idea that marketing activities are related to demand seems to have emerged among several researchers about the same time in the 1950s. In economic theory, the classic demand curve was based on the assumption that price was the sole instrument that affected demand. But looking at buyers' real behaviour, it was obvious that, for example, product characteristics and advertising were equally or even more important than price. Demand was a function of price as well as of the product and the companies' advertising (promotion). Rasmussen[11] and Mickwitz[12] in Scandinavia and Borden[13] in the United States were among the pioneers to pursue this.

It was a very elegant way of expanding economic theory to include the marketing activities of a firm's behaviour. From a theoretical point of view, these empirical findings only added a few parameters to a well-established theory.

Years later, this theory explaining demand became normative and transformed into the tools of marketing in all business schools. Business people to be were told to find an optimal mix of these tools for each company. The elegant theory of explaining demand had become a normative theory for business behaviour!

Each 'P' of the '4–7 Ps' is aggregated and consists of several elements that constitute the concept. For example, place requires scheduled production, assembly, transportation and so on. In researching this book we found the non-controversial fact that all the Ps and their elements were not equally influential on demand. However, more important is that there were a few very crucial elements, the elements that really created sales. Examples are sometimes a low price or certain elements in the offer such as very high quality in combination with certain features. However, more often *intangible aspects*, such as a good brand or a reputation as a reliable supplier, triggered sales. Most of the other elements in the value offered to the market were necessary up to a certain level – the level required by the buyers to consider the firm as a potential supplier, in other words, to allow the firm to participate as a player in the market game.

Hence, we suggest two conceptual categories of the elements of the value and the other actions taken to influence the market:

- *sales drivers*, elements that really create the sales; and
- *sales requirements* and elements that just have to be at a certain level to allow the firm to participate in the game in the market.

Hill[14] has made similar observations and distinguishes between qualifying and order-winning criteria. Qualifiers are 'those criteria which are necessary even to be considered by a customer as a possible supplier' and order winners are 'those criteria which win the order'. One example of qualifying criteria is the need to be accredited as an ISO 9000 supplier, when it is often necessary in order to be chosen as a supplier to bigger firms. Examples of order winners may be design and reliability.

From a theoretical point of view, the conceptual difference between the categories is their elasticity in impact on the demand curve as illustrated in

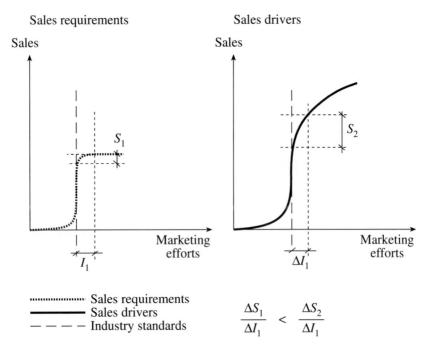

Figure 9.2   Sales requirements and sales drivers

Figure 9.2. Sales requirements must reach a certain level, but there is no reason to overinvest in such elements because these do not represent improved customer value when exceeding a certain level. On the other hand, if these elements do not reach the level expected by the customer the firm's sales would stay low or decrease as illustrated in the left-hand model in Figure 9.2. The efforts should instead be allocated to the sales drivers. Such elements are directly related to improved customer value, the right-hand model in the figure. Investments in such elements influence sales positively.

   For business people it is important to understand the conditions in each market in order to set the best priorities of value creation.

Balancing a Complex Marketing Strategy

The output from the value-creating processes as defined in the model for analysing an entrepreneurial marketing firm in Chapter 8, is the offering and all other actions to create transactions and relationships to the chosen target market. In reality this is a composite of several actions serving different purposes, to create sales and satisfaction. In business terminology the decisions behind all these outputs are called the 'marketing strategy'.

We have previously discussed a balance of the two perspectives in marketing - transactional marketing and relationship marketing as well as a balance of the content of tangible and intangible elements in the market offering and advocated a complex perspective including parts of all. Here this balanced complexity is elaborated into a scheme. The meaning of balance is relative to the context. The idea is to balance the actions in relation to the purpose and the situation.

We find no controversy in stating that almost all of the market offerings contain both elements of goods and elements of service. Further, the tendency that more and more service components are loaded into the offering, as discussed in Chapters 7 and 8, makes this mixture crucial. The balance between tangible and intangible components in the offering to the market is the first part or dimension in the marketing balance sheet.

Besides loading the offering with value, all other actions taken to attract potential and actual customers are important. In traditional marketing, all these actions (as well as the offering) are contained within the concept of the various Ps in the marketing mix.

The view of business actions within relationship marketing is less distinct. Important concepts are, for example, trust,[15] promise/fulfilment,[16] win–win relationships for the participants, and personal sentiments.[17]

Grönroos[18] developed an early framework for marketing in service firms including both marketing-mix and other aspects. Besides the traditional marketing function (marketing mix) there is an interactive marketing function, as a consequence of the nature of services often with a high level of interaction between sellers and buyers in all stages of both the buying and the consumption process.

Further in the 'marketing strategy continuum', reproduced in Figure 9.3, Grönroos[19] advocates that in deciding which consumers to build relationships with, organizations should identify the types of products that they purchase. He argues that as products lie along a continuum from consumer packaged goods at one extreme to services at the other, organizations can select from marketing strategies ranging from transactional to relationship. Specifically he argues that when consumer packaged goods are purchased, a transactional approach should be selected. In contrast, where customers purchase a service, he recommends that a relationship approach is appropriate.

Having identified that certain buyers are better suited to a transaction approach and others to a relationship approach, he concluded that organizations adopting different approaches would invest in different activities. For organizations adopting a relationship approach, it was suggested that combining sophisticated database techniques with direct marketing, big organizations have been able to personalize and tailor the marketing communications that they make with the thousands of individual consumers

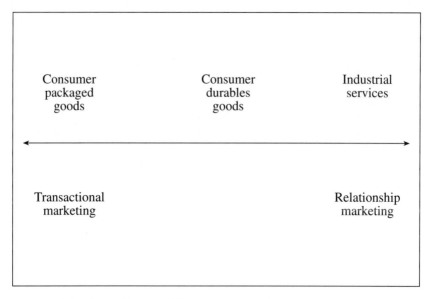

Source: Adapted from Grönroos (1994), p. 11 (see note 19).

Figure 9.3 Marketing strategy continuum

comprising an anonymous mass market. For firms adopting a transactional approach other activities are identified as possible; in particular, manipulation of the marketing mix has been proposed as an appropriate tool.

We do not agree with the 'either–or' idea of marketing implicit here. A firm may take both standpoints, at two different points of time, to different customers or to the same customers – as a mix of two categories of action. Hence, a focus on long-term relationship orientation in marketing must not necessarily be seen as something opposite to a transaction orientation.

There are two strategies to deal with this problem of balance. One path is that firms try to establish and maintain long-term relationships with the important customers. The rationale is that it is more profitable to retain the present customers than to find new ones. The concept here is *customer-relationship profitability.*[20] Sellers should seek to establish and maintain relationships specifically with such customers that offer potential high lifetime profitability. The second road is to purposely regard the situation as two different segments that can be dealt with simultaneously, partially with different marketing methods.

In both cases we found that a complex strategy orientation towards actions to create individual transactions *and* actions to create and maintain long-term customer relationships are important for growth.[21] The opposite of this balanced marketing behaviour, is when the firm focuses only on transactions or long-term customer relationships.

This use of complex strategies is indeed in accordance with other contemporary findings. As discussed in chapter 2, Brodie et al.[22] found that the majority of organizations practised more than one type of marketing approach, if not all types to varying degrees. Some combinations were more common: 'There appears to be a movement towards increased customer orientation (at the very least), if not full efforts to improve customer understanding, and develop synergistic relationship and partnership'.

Chaston[23] took a similar approach and regards duration of the customer relation as one parameter and traditional *vis-à-vis* entrepreneurial marketing approach as another (focusing on the innovative aspect of entrepreneurship). Based on these two variables a hybrid model of SME marketing styles was suggested. Firms could apply any of the following marketing styles:

- *conservative-transactional marketing* (in markets where the customer seeks standard-specification goods or services at a competitive price and has little interest in building close relationships with suppliers);
- *conservative-relationship marketing* (in markets where the customer seeks standard-specification goods or services but is willing to work closely with suppliers to optimize quality and/or obtain mutual benefits from creating an effective purchase and delivery system;
- *entrepreneurial-transactional marketing* (in markets where customers seek innovative goods or services which can be procured without forming a close relationship with suppliers); and
- *entrepreneurial-relationship marketing* (in markets where customers cooperate in partnership with suppliers to develop innovative new goods or services).

Let us integrate the two parts of the previous discussion in a diagram to illustrate what to balance. The balance between tangible and intangible elements in the offering to the market is on the y-axis. The intangible elements are on the upper y-axis and the tangible are on the lower y-axis from the origin. The two types of marketing, transactional marketing and relationship marketing, are regarded as other variables to position the output of the value-creating processes, in Figure 9.4 on the two x-axes from the origin of coordinates: the relationship actions are on the left-hand side of the x-axis and the transactional aspects on the right-hand side.

The extreme positions that it is possible to take are illustrated in Figures 9.5–9.8. Figure 9.5 shows the classic service-marketing situation where the

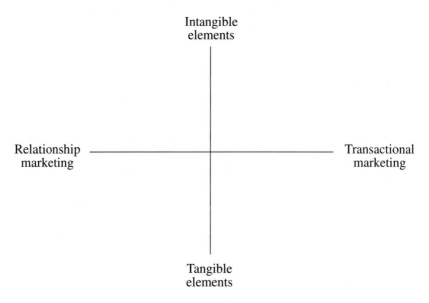

Figure 9.4   Scheme for balanced marketing

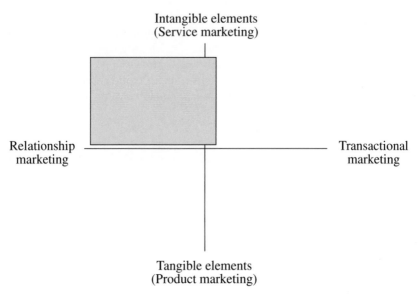

Figure 9.5   Traditional service marketing

market is offered intangible elements by the seller and also uses intense interactions with the clients.

The traditional transactional strategy with pure commodities or goods sold in bulk without any service components, for example, such consumer convenience goods or industrial supplies as screws and bolts is shown in Figure 9.6. In this type of marketing the offerings to the market are not loaded with anything else but the tangible items – what you see is what you get – and the marketing actions are focused on one specific goal, to create as many transactions as possible. As consumers we find this type of marketing a part of daily life as we shop in the local convenience store. However, it is a myth that all successful companies take a lot of marketing actions.

The 'lean marketing' situation is shown in Figure 9.7. Here, hardly any marketing actions are taken. The demand is already there or the offer in itself is regarded as creating enough demand. This illustrates a monopolistic situation, which shows the mature stage of the life cycle where no costs are spent or just the marketing strategy in a very product-oriented company.

An extreme balanced strategy containing almost all elements of marketing is the opposite situation, as illustrated in Figure 9.8. Here we find a situation with intense marketing actions of all kinds with both transactional and relationship intentions. To master the balance of tangible and intangible

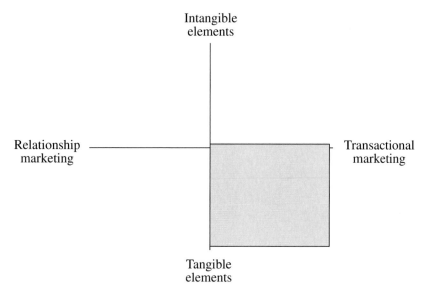

Figure 9.6   Traditional simple product marketing

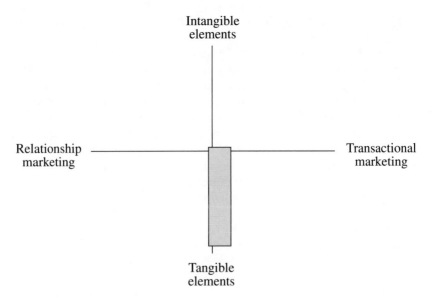

Figure 9.7   Lean marketing

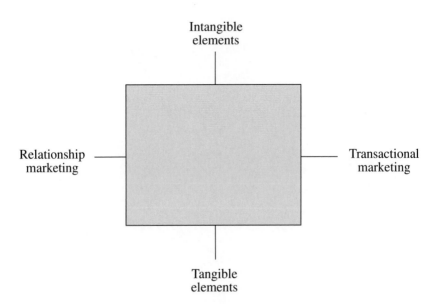

Figure 9.8   Complex, balanced marketing strategy

elements in the value-carrying offering as well as to balance transactional and relationship marketing in the marketing actions are important parts of the output for a growing entrepreneurial company. In essence, balanced marketing is the intentional balance of these dimensions adapted to the context in which the firm operates.

We have suggested in this book a balanced strategy containing all elements of marketing. However, what focus in terms of intangible/tangible elements and relationship/transactional marketing should be used changes over the time of a firm (especially from its start and onwards). One such possibility is illustrated in Figure 9.9, where at time 1 there is a concentration of relationship marketing and intangible elements, and where later, at time 2, there is a concentration of transactional marketing. Many other movements over time than the one illustrated in Figure 9.9 are possible.

The leadership and management challenge is to identify the suitable complex strategy and balance it according to the context. Unfortunately there are no general rules to guide leaders and managers in growing entrepreneurial firms. In principal anything goes! The analytical tool is the scheme and the framework in this book. The artistic part, the creation of a suitable complex strategy is up to the performer!

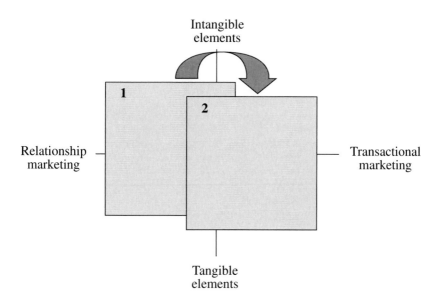

Figure 9.9   A dynamic balanced marketing strategy

SUMMARY

In summary, the entrepreneurial marketing leader and manager must:

- create a value constellation with the relevant resources and balance these resources;
- lead and manage the partnership value constellation, create the glue that keeps the network in the constellation together;
- lead and manage the joint value creation in value constellation, that is, monitoring the processes in the day-to-day activities;
- lead and manage the processes at the general level, such as the distribution of core and complementary capabilities;
- identify and implement, through entrepreneurship and formal and informal market sensing, better solutions to customer needs;
- create superior customer value of tangible and intangible customer utility, as perceived by the customers themselves; and
- create a balance of transactional marketing and relationship marketing.

EPILOGUE

The more we learn about marketing, the harder it is to tell what it is. To use a metaphor quoted from Brown:[24]

> The state of contemporary marketing scholarship, however, could just as easily be compared to a multi-screen cinema. After all, it can legitimately be argued that marketing research has been transformed in recent years from a drab, down-to-heel, monolithic 'picture palace', with only one theoretical programme – positivism/ empiricism – on show, to a fashionable, glittering multiplex offering a wide choice of innovative research programmes. These programmes vary considerably in their content and certification, with some aimed at mainstream audiences, others reliant on art-house appeal, and yet others – mentioning no names – only suitable for the delinquent, institutionalised or suitably restrained. What is more, as many of the programmes are (arguably) incommensurable, they cannot be viewed simultaneously, though they are at least showing under the same roof, *which we call marketing*.

Is this surprising? We find marketing too complex to be understood by looking at only a single screen – to use the metaphor above. Nor are we surprised about the incommensurability between existing perspectives. Different glasses create different images for the spectator.

However, we also believe that even with the same glasses we can expect marketing behaviour to vary with the context in which it is performed. Marketing tasks vary widely. In some cases the marketing task is to secure fast cash for an expanding company in desperate need of money, that is, a strong focus on transactional marketing. A few days later the focus may be to establish relationships with a research group in a foreign university to discuss the latest technology, and in parallel discuss with a customer how to jointly develop the solution to the customer's problem.

A big multinational corporation selling consumer goods may have a different marketing task altogether. Here the main marketing activity may be intense distributor penetration and even physical handling of goods by missionary salespeople – all backed up with heavy mass advertising in television, newspapers and magazines. In the first case a combination of transactional and relationship marketing can be found. In the latter case the prime focus is to create as many transactions in the supermarkets as possible. Furthermore, the resources to implement the tasks may differ widely between the two examples.

The environments of business firms are often fragmented, diffuse, dynamic and uncertain. Hence, it is striking that much of the established marketing knowledge is still based on a perspective that the environment is clear and distinct; a customer is a customer, a supplier is a supplier, a competitor is a competitor and a cooperator is a cooperator. In the modern business world one company may hold all these roles in relation to a focal selling organization![25] Today nobody questions the fact that some firms can have a substantial impact on its environment based on the resources available; others may just have to adapt to the changes they are able to perceive.

Not only do the internal and external task environment differ between firms. The *business culture environment* at large is not the same in all parts of the world.[26] The macro environment can be expected to have an impact on firms' marketing behaviour. The context, both the external and the internal one, varies between firms. Here we can learn from research in leadership and management.

Within the contingency approach in business, no organization structure is superior to all others, nor are all structures equally efficient.[27] A similar statement can be formulated about marketing: no marketing behaviour is superior to all others, nor are all marketing behaviours equally efficient!

In the contingency approach within business, many contingency variables are identified, for example:[28]

- external environment (complexity and dynamism);
- technology;
- firm size; and
- strategy.

We can expect these to be valid for marketing aspects as well. Hence, a multilevel perspective and a contingency approach are the proper approaches if we want to understand the specific aspects of marketing in growing entrepreneurial firms.

Contingency approaches are positioned within business as mid-range theories between the two extreme views, which state that either universal marketing principles exist and are applicable to different sizes of firms or each small firm is unique and each situation should be analysed separately. Adopting this approach allows researchers to focus upon exploring mid-range relationships that hold with a particular context or for classes of settings, rather than to search for a grand theory of strategy that is appropriate across all possible settings.[29]

The basic rationale is that a number of factors influence how marketing is implemented as well as the outcome of the marketing process. The strategy/performance relationship can vary across different environments and different sizes of firms.[30] Many of the processes may be the same, just different in purpose and in content, morphology and outcome.

The marketing processes are determined in the context of specific business environments. The idea of a contingency approach is shared with others. For example, within marketing a contingency approach was suggested by Ferrell and Gresham.[31]

To be able to understand marketing in modern, growing entrepreneurial firms, in all its complexity, we indeed need better glasses than the existing ones given to us through present marketing theories. And we need glasses that are not only bifocal but multifocal, allowing us to view – and understand – many of the parallel programmes on the multiscreen simultaneously.

NOTES

1. Capaldo, G., L. Iandoli, M. Raffa and G. Zollo (2000), 'The evolution of market and technological innovation capabilities in small firms' life', paper presented at the international symposium on Research in the Entrepreneurship Interface in Chicago, p. 8.
2. Quinn, J.B. (1992), *Intelligent Enterprise*, New York: Free Press.
3. Kaplan, R. and D.P. Norton (1996a), *The Balanced Scorecard; Translating Strategy into Action*, Boston, MA: Harvard Business School Press; Kaplan, R. and D.P. Norton (2001), 'Transforming the balanced scorecard from performance measurement to strategic management: Part I', *Accounting Horizons*, **15** (1), pp. 87–104; Kaplan, R. and D.P. Norton (2001), 'Transforming the balanced scorecard from performance measurement to strategic management: Part II', *Accounting Horizons*, **15** (1), pp. 147–60.
4. Kaplan, R. and D.P. Norton (1996b), 'Linking the Balanced Scorecard to Strategy', *California Management Review*, **39** (1) (Fall), pp. 53–79: 65.
5. Ibid., pp. 64–5.
6. Hills, G. and C. Hultman (1998), 'Is University Marketing Education Relevant to Growth Oriented SMEs?', in *Employment - The Great Challenge; Small Business - The Great Solution*, Proceedings to 25th International Small Business Congress, São Paulo, Brazil.
7. Montgomery, D. and Webster, F. Jr. (1997), 'Marketing's Inter-Functional Interfaces: The MSI Workshop on Management of Corporate Fault Zones', *Journal of Market-Focused*

Management, **2** (1), pp. 7-26: 9.

8. Schumpeter, J. (1961), *The Theory of Economic Development*, New York: Oxford University Press.
9. Europe's 500 is an annually presented list of some of the fastest growing companies in Europe.
10. Normann, R. and R. Ramirez (1994), *Designing Interactive Strategy - From Value Chain to Value Constellation*, Chichester: John Wiley & Sons.
11. Rasmussen, A. (1955), *Pristeori Eller Parameterteori: Studier Kring Virksomhedens Afsaetning* [Price Theory or Parameter Theory: Studies of the Sales of the Firm], Copenhagen: Nyt Nordisk Forlag.
12. Mickwitz, G. (1959), *Marketing and Competition*, Helsinki, Finland: societas scientarium Fennica (available for University microfilms, Ann Arbour, MI).
13. Borden, N.H. (1964), 'The Concept of the Marketing Mix', *Journal of Advertising Research*, June, pp. 2-7.
14. Hill, T. (1993) *Manufacturing Strategy - The Strategic Management of the Function*, London: Open University Set Book, p. 59 ff.
15. Luhman, N. (1979), *Trust and Power*, Avon: John Wiley & Sons; Perrow, C. (1986), *Complex Organisations, A Critical Essay*, New York: McGraw-Hill.
16. Calonius, H. (1987), *The Promise Concept*, Helsinki: Swedish School of Economics.
17. See, for example, Håkansson, H. (ed.) (1982), *International Marketing and Purchasing of Industrial Goods - An Interactive Approach*, Chichester: John Wiley & Sons.
18. See, for example, Grönroos, C. (1980), *Marknadsföring av industriella tjänster* [Marketing of industrial services], Lund: Studentlitteratur.
19. Grönroos, C. (1994), 'From Marketing Mix to Relationship Marketing: Towards a Paradigm Shift in Marketing', *Management Decision*, **32** (2), pp. 4-26: 11.
20. Storbacka, K. (1994), 'The Nature of Customer Relationship Profitability, Analysis of Relationships and Customer Basis', in *Retail Banking*, Dissertation at Helsinki School of Economics; Helsinki, Finland.
21. Hultman, C. and L. Sanner (1999), *Implementation of Marketing in Some Swedish SMEs*, Stockholm: FSF 99:1.
22. Brodie, R.J., N. Coviello, R.W. Brookes and Victoria Little (1997), 'Towards a paradigm shift in Marketing? An examination of current marketing practices', *Journal of Marketing Management*, **13** (6), pp. 383-406: 402.
23. Chaston, I. (1997), 'Relationship and entrepreneurial marketing: interaction and determining influence on organisational competencies', paper presented at AMA/UIC Special Interest Symposium in Dublin, Ireland, 9-10 January.
24. Brown, S. (1995), *Postmodern Marketing*, London: Routledge, pp. 177-8.
25. In this respect the Nordic school of marketing is also an innovator, for instance Håkansson, H. and J. Johansson (1992), 'A Model of Industrial Networks', in Axelsson, B. and G. Easton (eds), *Industrial Networks. A New View of Reality*, London: Routledge, or Håkansson, H. and I. Snehota (eds) (1995), *Developing Relationships in Business Networks*, London: Routledge.
26. See, for instance, Bjerke, Björn (1999), *Culture and Business Leadership*, Cheltenham, UK and Northampton, MA, USA: Edward Elgar; Hofstede, Geert (1984), *Culture's Consequences*, Beverly Hills, CA: Sage; Hofstede, Geert and Michael Harris Bond (1988), 'The Confucius Connection. From Cultural Roots to Economic Growth', *Organization Dynamics*, Spring, as well as Chapter 5 in this book.
27. Galbraith, J.K. (1997), *Designing Complex Organizations*, Reading, MA: Addison-Wesley.
28. Otley, D. (1980), 'The contingency theory of management accounting: Achievement and prognosis', *Accounting, Organizations and Society*, **5** (4), pp. 413-28; Pfeffer, J. (1982), *Organizations and Organization Theory*, Marshfield, MA: Pitman; Donaldson, L. (1994), 'The Normal Science of Structural Contingency Theory', in Clegg, S.R., C. Hardy and R.W. Nord (eds), *Handbook of Organization Studies*, London: Sage, pp. 57-76.
29. Siu, Wai-sum and D. Kirby (1998), 'Approaches to small firm marketing', *European Journal of Marketing*, **32** (1/2), p. 53.
30. Lee, M., I. Lee, and F.M. Ulgado (1993), 'Marketing strategies for mature products in a

rapidly developing country: A contingency approach', *International Marketing Review*, **10** (5), pp. 56-72.

31. Ferrell, O.C. and L.G. Gresham (1985), 'A Contingency Framework for Understanding Ethical Decision Making in Marketing', *Journal of Marketing*, **49** (Summer), pp. 158–61.

10. Entrepreneurial marketing: leading and managing in the new economic era

INTRODUCTION

This chapter is a summary of the book. This is done by providing a number of statements which are given in the order in which the book was written. At the same time, we derive advice to the practitioner, trying to grow with a small firm in the new economic era.

STATEMENTS AND ADVICE

Statements and advice are given as they first appear in the book, even if a more detailed discussion came later.

Chapter 1

There are many signs – and evidence – that in the economy of today, the winner is the small firm.

Statement 1: A new business logic is clearly evident, a logic where it is no longer natural that 'big is better'.
Advice A: As owner of a business, remember that any size of your firm can provide advantages, no matter how small it is.

We may or we may not have a new economy, but there are definitely aspects of the business life of today, which are different enough from yesteryear for many firms to consider. The sum of these changes may, for some firms, be summarized under the label of 'a new economic era'.

Statement 2: Enough is happening today, at least in some business sectors of the society, to justify the name 'a new economic era'.
Statement 3: Some business sectors are barely touched by the new

economic era at all; some other sectors feel that some aspects in the business environment are drastically new; still other sectors have to live with the full impact of the new economic era.

This new economic era does not rest. It seems to be moving into more and more business sectors.

Statement 4: The new economic era seems to be like a wave, which is rolling over more and more business sectors - like the wave of a new industrial era.

There are some definite signs of this new economic era, for example, continuous change.

Statement 5: When a firm feels that it is operating in the new economic era, it is forced, among other things, to live with progressively more rapid change, under uncertainty, to compete with knowledge in an industry, the borders of which are disappearing, and with a heavy technological influence.

Therefore, what is needed above all in the new economic era is change agents, which we may call 'entrepreneurs'.

Statement 6: A firm influenced by the new economic era needs, above all, change agents, that is, entrepreneurs. This is the single most important competitive factor in this era.
Advice B: Before deciding on steps to take for your firm, it is necessary to find out whether the firm is influenced by the new economic era or not, and to what extent this is the case.
Advice C: If you believe that your firm is (partly or wholly) in the new economic era, you should, above all, foster the entrepreneurial spirit in your firm.

In the new economic era, small firms seem to thrive better than firms of any other size. There are several reasons for this.

Statement 7: In the new economic era, we are increasingly moving in the direction of favouring small firms.
Statement 8: Reasons favouring small firms in the new economic era include erased entry barriers, fewer natural economies of scale in most business activities, flexibility, advancing computer and telecommunications technology, and customization.

In fact, in all nations most firms *are* small.

Statement 9: In all nations, a majority of business firms are small.

Today, even big firms try to learn why small firms are doing so well, crushing all old business logic in the process.

Advice D: If you are a small firm, act on the advantages of being small. If you are a big firm (in the new economic era), act as if you are small.

There are many attempts to try to define the meaning of a small firm and what types of small firms there are.

Statement 10: Small firms are commonly understood as small in terms of number of employees and in terms of limited other resources; however, this may not prevent a firm from being either successful, or at the forefront of its type of business.
Statement 11: Common classifications of small firms are marginal firms, lifestyle firms and high-potential firms.

One area within business, where the small firm seems to have a special advantage, is in marketing.

Statement 12: There are several potential marketing advantages of small firms, including close customer interface, flexibility, speed and ability to find a market niche.
Advice E: Ensure that the potential marketing advantages from being a small firm are exploited.

Every nation needs all sorts of entrepreneurship, if it wants to progress and prosper. There are many reasons for this.

Statement 13: The role of entrepreneurship in economic development is to include and institute change in business and society.
Statement 14: Small firms produce more innovation than do big firms.
Statement 15: Every country today needs new independent entrepreneurship, entrepreneurship within existing firms, and to organize for entrepreneurship and innovation.
Statement 16: In a modern economy, small and medium-sized firms typically make up around 98 per cent of the total number of enterprises, and contribute over 50 per cent of employment, about 50 per cent of GDP, and over 30 per cent of exports.

Entrepreneurship and small business are not the same thing, and small firms, in particular, need entrepreneurship in order to grow, especially in the new economic era.

Statement 17: Entrepreneurship and a small firm are not the same thing. A small firm does not have to be entrepreneurial, and a firm of any size can be entrepreneurial.
Advice F: Remember that a small firm is unlikely to grow and prosper without being entrepreneurial, especially in the new economic era.

This book attempts to describe how to grow in the new economic era – and what role marketing must play in such growth.

Statement 18: This book is about the role played by marketing in the growth of small firms in the new economic era.

There are similarities, but above all, important differences in marketing of small and of big firms.

Statement 19: Marketing of small firms is not, and should not be, a mini-version of marketing of big firms.

Firms can grow without being entrepreneurial. We could call this 'managerial growth'.

Statement 20: There are two types of growth in a small firm, that is, entrepreneurial growth (growing by doing new things) and managerial growth (growing by doing more of the same thing).
Advice G: When the aim of your firm is to grow, clarify beforehand whether it is a matter of entrepreneurial growth or managerial growth.

The meaning of management and leadership seems to differ substantially today. But, above all, in the new economic era, entrepreneurship seems to be in a sovereign position of its own.

Statement 21: Management is basically a task, business leadership a role, but entrepreneurship, in the new economic era, often seems more like a lifestyle. This is particularly so for growing small firms in the new economic era.

To understand entrepreneurship – and, in particular, to understand market-ing of entrepreneurial ventures – is a serious matter today.

Statement 22: The economic future may well be to understand and develop abilities in entrepreneurial efforts – and marketing of such efforts is a critical skill.

Chapter 2

Marketing theory was developed in big business in the US during the last century, when the old economic era prevailed unchallenged.

Statement 23: Mainstream marketing theory (and much of its praxis) was developed in and fits the old economic era.
Statement 24: Most marketing is influenced by US business practice, research and writing.
Statement 25: Marketing, as it is known today, is a fairly recent invention: it is a twentieth-century phenomenon.
Statement 26: Much of modern marketing originates from big business enterprises.

Marketing theory started by trying to understand (often separately) what products there were, and who was involved and what they did.

Statement 27: Early marketing theory followed the commodity stream, the institutional stream, or the functional stream. The last of these three was the most important one for later development of marketing.

Many marketing schools have been established since that time.

Statement 28: Mainstream marketing can be looked at as a structure of subschools. Some of these are: macromarketing, consumer behaviour, managerial marketing, marketing channels and distribution, international marketing and industrial marketing.

The rules of modern marketing emphasize: always try to look at it through the eyes of the buyers, and be a good marketing manager at all times.

Statement 29: The focus of buyers and their needs is one of the most fundamental aspects of modern marketing.
Statement 30: The managerial paradigm has become the dominant view in marketing.

The managerial marketing paradigm has led to many widely accepted concepts – and they are all based on rationality.

Statement 31: Well-known marketing terms from the managerial school are marketing concept, market myopia, marketing mix, marketing planning, segmentation, product life cycle, market positioning, and market orientation.

Statement 32: Marketing management thinking is based on a rational view of humans, including managers and consumers.

The managerial marketing school has been criticized.

Statement 33: A major criticism of the managerial marketing paradigm is that it is of less relevance outside standardized consumer goods.

There have been many attempts to be more specific about what various types of marketing stand for – and what they do not stand for. One is to try to draw up differences between marketing of goods and marketing of services. This distinction, however, is of less relevance today.

Statement 34: A separation between marketing of goods and marketing of services is of less relevance today as every product is more or less service dominated.

Another discussion was about how much of a firm is – and should be – about marketing.

Statement 35: There is a discussion in managerial marketing theory whether marketing should be seen as a specialist function or as a philosophy which should involve everybody in the firm.

Whatever marketing is all about, there is a general agreement that today every firm should be market oriented.

Statement 36: A common distinction in modern marketing is whether a firm is market oriented or product oriented. Market orientation is commonly regarded as a necessity for long-term success and performance.

An interesting and important discussion in marketing today, especially in the light of what we try to achieve in this book, is whether marketing is all about transactions or all about relationships. We do not favour this 'all'. In this book, we claim that firms in the modern economic era need both marketing orientations.

Statement 37: One fundamental theoretical argumentation in marketing today is whether the concept of transactions (of products) or relationships (to customers and others) are the core of what marketing is all about.

Statement 38: We claim in this book that both transactional and relationship marketing are needed to understand marketing behaviour.

In general, modern marketing is too complex to be understood using only a one-dimensional approach.

Statement 39: It is difficult to fully understand marketing if only one school or paradigm is used. Hence, a multilevel perspective and a contingency approach is often proper in marketing.

Whatever we say about marketing, it is not to be forgotten that most of society is not in the new economic era. Mainstream marketing was not only developed during the time when society did not change much – at least not in the modern way of change – but it also still fits well those sectors of the economy that are (still) not in this new economic era.

Statement 40: The dominant view of marketing fits the old economic era well.
Advice H: If you are affected by the new economic era be very critical and selective when applying the dominant view of marketing.

Chapter 3

The other major area of interest in this book, apart from marketing, is entrepreneurship. From an academic point of view, it is even older than marketing, but its content and meaning are far less precise than marketing today.

Statement 41: In spite of the fact that entrepreneurship has been researched for several centuries, what it means today is far from settled or generally accepted.

Nevertheless, entrepreneurship is a very popular subject today. One reason is the revival of small firms, but there are others.

Statement 42: Factors behind the present popularity of entrepreneurship include the revival of small business, hope that it will provide the new jobs wanted today, and the realization that constant change and innovation are needed in modern times.

In general, economists have lost their interest in entrepreneurship and business scholars have taken over – with gusto!

Statement 43: Academic research on entrepreneurship has been going on since the mid-eighteenth century, until the mid-twentieth century in economics alone.

Nevertheless, the legacy of economics is still with us when we try to understand what entrepreneurship is all about – too much of it in the new economic era, as we see in this book.

Statement 44: What is still with us from the research by economists on entrepreneurship is its association with the aspects of taking risks, management, innovation and exploiting opportunities. In this book, focusing on the new economic era, we stress mainly the last two of these four aspects.

With increased popularity of entrepreneurship have come attempts to try to find its appearance almost anywhere and at all levels of the society.

Statement 45: Over the years the meaning of who can be an entrepreneur has broadened such that some scholars even claim that entrepreneurs can appear in any profession.
Statement 46: The level of entrepreneurship discussed in this book is the level of business firms, not the level of an industry or the society at large.

Attempts and hopes to try to find personality traits among entrepreneurs, traits that should be different from other people, have, by and large, failed.

Statement 47: Research trying to find those personal traits that distinguish entrepreneurs from other people has, by and large, failed.
Advice I: Expect to find an entrepreneur in many different people – in your firm as well as outside of it.

What complicated the picture is that nobody is an entrepreneur all the time – and no firm is entrepreneurial all the time.

Statement 48: Not only is a person never always and forever an entrepreneur, there are also limits to how long firms can stay entrepreneurial at a time.

One line of entrepreneurial research today is to change from trying to answer the question 'Who is the entrepreneur?' to answering the question 'How does the entrepreneur think?'.

Statement 49: One modern line of entrepreneurship research is through psychology, trying to find cognitive models for how entrepreneurs are thinking.

One of the few generally accepted statements about entrepreneurs today is that they may operate independently, on their own or within a firm where they are already working (as an owner or as an employee).

Statement 50: There are basically two kinds of entrepreneurs, that is, those who start new business ventures for themselves (independent entrepreneurs) and those who start new business ventures in the firm where they already operate (intracorporate entrepreneurs or intrapreneurs).

Some climates are more favourable to entrepreneurship than others. However, there is not much agreement about what the content of such climates should be.

Statement 51: Some corporate climates are more favourable to intrapreneurship than others. Factors commonly mentioned in favourable climates include self-selection, the doers decide, many small attempts at any one time, tolerance of mistakes, and freedom from turfiness.
Advice J: Work hard to promote the intracorporate climate in the firm where you are working.
Advice K: If you intend to start a new business venture and do not fit a model for a suitable entrepreneur that you have found in the literature, there is not necessarily a need for you to worry; no such model is generally valid.

In this book we look at entrepreneurship as a process. One such process of particular interest to us is to look at entrepreneurship by applying the network metaphor.

Statement 52: In this book we favour the view that entrepreneurship should be seen as a process with possible differences in content from one case to another, not as a natural result of specific personal characteristics, or as an outcome of given favourable circumstances.
Statement 53: During the past decades, the number of entrepreneurial studies applying the network metaphor has been increasing. This metaphor is of particular interest in the new economic era.

We have found the idea of entrepreneurship being generated by use of language, culture and entrepreneurial capacities useful in this book.

> *Statement 54*: The base model for entrepreneurship used in this book is to explain it by use of language, culture and entrepreneurial capacities. Use of language, in turn, influences culture, which, in turn, influences entrepreneurial capacities.
> *Advice L*: Get a better explanation of your entrepreneurial venture by making its language world and its culture world more explicit.

Traditionally, successful entrepreneurship has been associated with good management. This connection is no longer obvious in the new economic era.

> *Statement 55*: In the new economic era, entrepreneurship would (at least in the beginning of a new business venture) better be connected with good leadership than, as has traditionally been the case, with good management.
> *Advice M:* Apply good leadership more than good management in the beginning of your business venture. Good management comes later.

There are many ways of defining entrepreneurship. This book uses the simple definition of associating entrepreneurship with being successful in creating new business ventures and renewing old ones. However, 'new' is not to be misunderstood. Most new business ventures are, at best, creative minor modifications of what already exists on the market.

> *Statement 56*: In this book, entrepreneurship is defined by its result when successful, that is, as creating new business ventures and renewing old ones. However, in practice, 'new' rarely means radically new here.

Chapter 4

As this book is about marketing of small business ventures trying to grow successfully, it must be of particular interest to know what differences and similarities there are between marketing of small firms and big firms.

> *Statement 57*: One contextual aspect of special interest in this book is the size of the firm, that is, to find out differences (and similarities) in marketing of small and of big firms.

There are many exceptions, of course. In big firms, marketing is a function among others and, like the rest of the firm, rather structured. This also goes for its contacts with the rest of the world outside the firm.

Statement 58: In general, in big corporations, marketing is one function among others and, like the other functions, formalized in a hierarchy and in planning procedures. A vice-president of marketing is commonly in charge of the marketing department. Marketing is also required to be coordinated with the other business functions.

Statement 59: Big firms, most of the time, offer standardized products to consumers, which are often divided into market segments.

Statement 60: Big firm contacts with customers are often one way – from seller to buyer. Knowledge of customers is also commonly based on formalized marketing research and/or expert knowledge.

Statement 61: Decisions in big firms are often made far from the daily contacts with users.

It is harder and costlier to move a big corporation compared to a small one. However, recent changes, not only in the new economic era, make such moves frequently necessary.

Statement 62: The complex planning processes in big firms make change difficult and costly. Following plans is the primary objective in big firms.

Statement 63: Several recent trends are shaking up big corporations. Two examples are mass customization and flexible manufacturing.

In some industries, for instance, in industrial marketing, there is not much difference between small and big firms. One important difference, however, is the size, shape and complexity of the network of which the firm is a part.

Statement 64: In business-to-business industrial market situations, where the focus is on individual customers and where business networks may be constructed by a firm of any size, there are probably not many differences between big firms and small firms. The differences may be only in the degree of complexity of the network.

Statement 65: One important aspect of business networks is that each participant can get access to resources that do not exist and cannot be generated in-house.

Statement 66: Important knowledge from the behaviour of big firms in networks is developed within research in industrial marketing and purchasing.

Statement 67: One important concept in industrial networking is trust.

Another area where differences between small and big firms disappear is marketing of services.

Statement 68: Another area where differences between firms disappear is marketing of services.

Furthermore, some new technology is open to any firm, no matter what size. This fact, plus the possibilities of measuring up to other firms, is of particular interest to small firms in the new economic era.

Statement 69: The developments in information technology open tremendous opportunities on almost equal terms for all businesses, big and small.
Advice N: Be aware of new business opportunities such as marketing of services and information technology opening up for firms of any size.

Decision making and other business procedures are often less formalized in small firms. This is often no disadvantage, especially in the new economic era.

Statement 70: In small firms, decisions (in marketing as in other areas) are often linked directly to specific personal goals and to the psychology of individuals.
Statement 71: In small firms, one action often leads to another action rather than the latter being the result of formalized long-term oriented strategies.
Statement 72: Formalized marketing research is very rare among small firms.
Statement 73: Small firms lack resources and/or knowledge precluding decision making based on the classic strategic marketing approach. This does not, however, seem to restrict the actions of an entrepreneurial small firm.
Advice O: Do not see the absence of formal decision-making systems and the non-existence of 'scientific' marketing models as a disadvantage.

Rather, informality might even be a strength in the new economic era.

Chapter 5

One aspect of a firm that may restrain or promote informality is its use of language and its corporate culture. These two important aspects of a firm are commonly neglected variables in discussing marketing and entrepreneurship.

Statement 74: The dimensions of culture and use of language are commonly neglected variables in discussing marketing and entrepreneurship.
Advice P: Remember that culture and use of language will influence, most of the time, implicitly and even unconsciously, all kinds of action in business.

Generally, it is obvious that the findings in this book are valid mainly in the Western, industrialized part of the world.

Advice Q: Remember that the findings in this book are valid mainly in the industrialized Western part of the world.

The essence of culture is commonly understood as a set of values in a wide sense. These values are taught and over time, due to habit, have often become subconscious. This fact does not make culture less, but rather more, powerful.

Statement 75: Culture is generally seen as having a core of values, as something people learn, as the intersubjective part of life, as being mirrored in language, and as powerfully influencing the life of its members.

Statement 76: Most of the content of culture is hidden in the subconscious.

Statement 77: We look at culture in this book as basic norms, values and assumptions, which in turn manifest themselves in language, behaviour, various institutions and so on.

Advice R: Try to make the various components of culture (as norms, values and assumptions) more conscious and explicit in order to better understand your own and others' entrepreneurship and marketing behaviour plus other cultural manifestations.

There are major differences between Western and Eastern cultures. However, Eastern cultures are not less entrepreneurial.

Statement 78: Western culture is more individual based, where people trust one another.

Statement 79: Western culture is less afraid of uncertainty and has a more positive attitude to change.

Statement 80: Western culture is relatively short-term oriented and has, most of the time, an exploitative attitude to the environment.

Statement 81: Western culture is less power hungry and uses a more egalitarian leadership style.

Statement 82: Western culture has a more 'scientific' problem-solving style.

Statement 83: Western culture asks more for rational people skills and measures personal success more in terms of individual contributions and self-actualization.

Statement 84: Understanding of management and leadership is more in terms of professionalism and consultation in Western culture.

Statement 85: Type of business approach taken is more about innovation, change, rationality and risk in Western culture.

Statement 86: Meaning of an organization is more calculative and impersonal in Western culture; it is also more in terms of a decision-making mechanism.

Statement 87: Understanding of business success is more in terms of growth and development and constantly competing by bringing out new goods and services to the market in Western culture.

Statement 88: There is not less entrepreneurship in non-Western cultures. However, their content and orientation differ. Also, marketing has quite a different meaning in non-Western cultures.

Chapter 6

An interesting fact learned from studying growth of small firms, is that most small firms do not want to grow.

Statement 89: Most small firms do not want to grow.

Advice S: If you do not want to grow, remember that you are in good company. Most other small firms do not want to grow either.

Growth of firms may be generated by many factors. No matter what these factors are, the effect is that growth of a firm is, at the end, determined by new sales.

Statement 90: One suggestion is that growth of a small firm is generated by three factors, that is, the entrepreneur, the character of the firm, and the strategy of the firm. Of these three factors, the entrepreneur is, in principle, the most important one.

Statement 91: A small firm's growth is determined by new sales. New sales can, in principle, take place by selling more of the same product on the same market, by selling a new product on the same market, by selling the same product on a new market, and by selling a new product on a new market. The first three of these four possibilities may be called 'managerial growth', the other three (more or less), 'entrepreneurial growth'.

Advice T: Remember that there are many ways of growing, but growing never takes place by itself. Also remember, that the primary motor for growth to start is the entrepreneur him- or herself.

Growth means change. However, change may be external to a firm as well as internal.

Statement 92: By definition, when growing, a firm always changes externally (on the market). However, growth does not necessarily mean that a firm changes internally as well. It may grow by 'simply' repeating a successful pattern. The more innovative and the more entrepreneurial growth, the more a firm has to change externally as well as internally.

Growing by doing more of the same, that is, managerial growth, and growing by doing new things, that is, entrepreneurial growth, are two different ways of looking at the world of growth.

Statement 93: Managerial growth and entrepreneurial growth are two different sets of terms, that is, language is used differently in the two cases. *Advice U:* Use different language when growing managerially from when growing entrepreneurially (this is in order to think and to act differently in the two cases).

Statement 94: Managerial growth means more planning, entrepreneurial growth more learning. *Advice V:* You can solve very few growth problems by simply applying more planning.

It has increasingly been recognized that the beginning of a new business venture is very much about building networks. Another term for such networks, a term suitable in the new economic era, is 'virtual organizations'.

Statement 95: Establishing a new business venture is, at least in the beginning, very much about building up and operating a network. *Advice W:* Remember that succeeding in establishing a new business venture stands and falls with its networks.

Statement 96: Increasingly, scholars have acknowledged that an organization's learning and value making are inescapably embedded in various forms of partnerships. In this book the term used for such partnerships is virtual organizations.

Statement 97: Virtual organizations are lacking some structural characteristics of 'real' (in this book referred to as 'focal') enterprises, but nevertheless function like enterprises in the imagination of the observers.

Statement 98: The idea of a virtual organization fits nicely what an entrepreneur with a vivid mind can do in the new economic era.

There are two ways of learning, that is, explorative learning, learning new things, and exploitative learning, learning what you know already but learning it better. Virtual organizations provide excellent opportunities for the former, that is, explorative learning.

Statement 99: There are generally two kinds of experiential learning. One is to create variety in experience, which is called 'exploration'. The other is to create reliability in experience, which is called 'exploitation'.

Statement 100: Exploitation takes place mainly in focal organizations; virtual organizations provide excellent opportunities for exploration.
Advice X: If you want to gain variety in experience, it is necessary to go outside the focal organization into virtual networks, which, in principle, exist only in the eyes of the beholder.

Networking is also necessary for intrapreneurs, that is, entrepreneurs who work in firms that want to grow even further by generating new business ventures and adding them to the portfolio of businesses they already have.

Statement 101: Networking is used by intrapreneurs as well. However, much of it (unlike in the case of the independent entrepreneur) takes place inside the focal firm where the intrapreneur is employed (which is partly different from virtual networks between focal organizations).
Advice Y: Remember that, if you are an intrapreneur, networking is also important. However, much of it (unlike in the case of the independent entrepreneur) takes place inside the firm where you are employed.

The problem, of course, is to know when to do what.

Statement 102: The tricky part when creating a new business venture, particularly when growing, is to know when to emphasize the focal organization, when to emphasize the virtual organization, when to concentrate on exploration, when to concentrate on exploitation, and so on.
Statement 103: We refer to entrepreneurial growth in virtual organizations where explorative learning takes place as 'co-creation'.

Chapter 7

In the new economic era, firms must be very market focused and customer oriented. This will influence the future role of marketing.

Statement 104: Marketing will have to change in the future, especially if a firm is operating in the new economic era. Its role as a separate specialist function in the focal firm will be disintegrated and spread across all other business functions. Customers will ask for no less.
Statement 105: A crucial task in the new economic era is to create outstanding customer value, and this value is to be judged by the customers – first and last.
Advice Z: Remember that creating customer value (the value of which is judged by customers – first and last) in the new economic era is a matter too serious to be handled in a specialist marketing function. It is a task for everybody in your organization.

Customer value is basically created in cooperation between firms and other actors in various kinds of alliances.

Statement 106: Ties, links and relationships between cooperating firms may be anything from ad hoc structures lasting only for a while, to formal long-lasting arrangements.

Statement 107: If we want to understand creation of customer value (in general and especially in growing entrepreneurial firms) the relevant object is not the single, focal firm, but the group of actors or firms, which together co-create such value.

Statement 108: The term 'value constellation' can be used to describe the complex set of firms involved in the process or co-creating customer value. The main difference from the value chain is that a value constellation is not to be seen as sequential.

Advice AA: If you really want to understand creation of value for your customers, go outside your firm into the complex of organizations (the value constellation) cooperating for such value to be created. Also, remember again, that it is up to you to see it as a structure, even if virtual.

Such cooperation means an interaction between three levels, where the entrepreneurially growing firm is at the centre of a virtual reality.

Statement 109: Co-creating customer value means an interaction between the three levels of the entrepreneur, the focal firm, and the value constellation. These three levels play different roles in the co-creative process.

Statement 110: Outstanding customer value in the new economic era starts with entrepreneurial action. The initiator of a new value-creation process is the entrepreneur using his or her capacity to find new economic combinations, thus spotting and exploiting new opportunities.

Statement 111: The entrepreneur, through his or her firm, takes the leading role (acts as constellation captain) in creating customer value.

Advice BB: Remember that there are different roles to play at different levels of creating customer value. One level is yourself, one is your focal firm, and one is the value constellation as a whole. However, you, as an entrepreneur, should take the leading role (act as a constellation captain) in creating customer value.

Marketing as transactions and marketing as relationships are two ways of marketing; however, they are never exclusive of each other.

Statement 112: Marketing as transactions is more a matter of managerial growth, it is a concentration on the focal organization, where learning takes place primarily by exploitation and by adding value to the value chain; marketing as relationships is more a matter of entrepreneurial growth, it is a concentration on the virtual organization, where learning takes place primarily through exploration, often by reconfiguring the value constellation.

Advice CC: Remember that marketing as transactions and marketing as relationships require different priorities.

Growth must be created. Such creation starts with imagining reality; an entrepreneur constantly reinterprets reality in order to find out his or her way to exploit it.

Statement 113: An entrepreneurial strategy includes constantly reinterpreting reality in the light of new information – and to act accordingly.

Advice DD: Remember that you should never stop creating customer value; the way it is done should be changed by new realities, and what those new realities are is up to you as an intrapreneur.

Statement 114: Dynamic and chaotic new situations, as in the new economic era, are better handled with quick feedback loops and a mental capacity and predestination to take new action than by trying to meet such changes with planning, even if plans are flexible.

Statement 115: Apart from a few lucky firms, which happen to be at the right market at the right moment, growth must be created. Processes for growth must be developed and maintained. Again the entrepreneur is the individual that makes things happen.

Capabilities have a different content in the new economic era. The most (only?) meaningful resource in this era is intellectual capability; furthermore, accessing resources is what matters, ownership is of less relevance.

Statement 116: In the new economic era, it is more important to access and to balance the necessary resources than to actually own them. Accessing and balancing are done in virtual networks in a value constellation.

Statement 117: The most important (and most scarce) resource to access in a value constellation is intellectual capability. The only necessary resource to host in-house is the ability to organize the value-creating system, to reconfigure the value constellation if necessary, and to make things happen. Ideally, this internal resource should lead to core competencies.

Advice EE: Remember that there are no limits, except in your own imagination, to what resources can be accessed. Also remember that resources do not need to be owned to be useful, and one resource which is scarce in the new economic era is intellectual capability.

There is a core and there are fringes of a firm; however, without a core of creating customer value, it will not survive in the long term.

Statement 118: In this book, we use the term 'core capability' to describe an organization's ability to create strategically competitive offerings to a market.
Advice FF: Constantly train your capability to organize the value-operating system that you are a part of, and make this capability a core capability of your firm.

However, core in terms of creating customer value does not mean that work must be done inside the focal firm only – rather it means just the opposite.

Statement 119: The differences and similarities between virtual organizations and more visible structures are in the eyes of the beholder, and co-creation becomes a structure in the eyes of the focal coordinating firm, a structure, however, linked together by the coordinator.
Statement 120: Some main structures of virtual organizations identified are the spider web, the interconnected island, united front towards the market, the clockwork and the missing link.

The meaning of a single firm, as single, is disappearing.

Statement 121: In value constellations in virtual organizations, the traditional concepts of upstream and downstream fulfil only an illustrative purpose and less and less a real operating purpose.
Statement 122: What is traditionally conceptualized as processes related to value creation within a focal organization are also less valid when we neglect the borders of the traditional organization and use the whole value constellation as a unit for distribution of tasks for co-creation of customer value.
Statement 123: When we move our interest from a focal organization to a virtual organization, the meaning of who is the customer becomes more complicated.

Any product can carry value to customers. We prefer to call them 'offerings' in this book.

Statement 124: In this book we prefer to talk about offerings rather than talking about goods and/or services. Offerings are seen as value carriers and may be described by their value and understood as perceived value.

Advice GG: Do not care about whether you offer goods or services to the market, just concentrate on your offerings as defined, perceived and assessed by your customers.

Chapter 8

In this book the content of our framework of entrepreneurial marketing is based on a few pillars.

Statement 125: The four pillars in the entrepreneurial marketing framework in this book are entrepreneurship, resources, processes, and actors (entrepreneur, coordinating firm, and network).

Statement 126: The single most important reason why networks are so necessary to the small growing entrepreneurial firm is their potential for accessing more (in the new economic era, especially intellectual) resources.

Advice HH: If you find that some resources necessary for growth are missing in your firm, remember that you might access these resources in a network with other firms and economic actors.

One important part of our view of entrepreneurial marketing is to look at it as processes. However, this leaves a good deal of leeway in terms of what to include in those processes.

Statement 127: A process view of a firm leaves a good deal of leeway as to what to include in the study. It is more the purpose of the analysis and the ingenuity of the analyser than anything else that are the deciding factors.

Statement 128: In this book we look at entrepreneurial marketing as interrelated value-creating processes.

Advice II: When in the new economic era and when trying to apply entrepreneurial marketing, look at your firm and the virtual organization of which it is a part as interrelated value-creating processes. However, it is up to you to decide what to include when trying to understand this situation.

Transactional marketing is one type of marketing, relationship marketing is another. Successful entrepreneurs practise both of these. However, they rarely do both with equal extent and intensity at the same time.

Statement 129: Entrepreneurial growth is associated with leadership and relationship marketing, with concentration on the virtual organization, explorative learning and the value constellation; managerial growth is associated with management and transactional marketing, with concentration on the focal organization, exploitative learning and the value chain.

Advice JJ: If you try to grow entrepreneurially, concentrate on leadership, relationship marketing, the virtual organization, learning exploratively and the value constellation.

Advice KK: If you try to grow managerially, concentrate on management, transactional marketing, the focal organization, learning exploitatively and the value chain.

Sustainable growth is made up of timely concentration on entrepreneurial growth or managerial growth over time.

Statement 130: To grow entrepreneurially does not mean to totally neglect managerial growth, focusing on relationship marketing to totally neglect transactional marketing and so on. It is a matter of priorities. To prioritize is the only way to really succeed in the new economic era.

Advice LL: Do not try to be entrepreneurial for too long, or to be managerial for too long. Find out whether circumstances dictate an entrepreneurial or a managerial pattern and act accordingly. Where circumstances change, change the pattern.

As mentioned already in Chapter 3, entrepreneurship can be explained in terms of use of language, culture and entrepreneurial capacities. The specific content of these three factors varies with circumstances.

Statement 131: The proper use of language for an entrepreneur, unlike a manager, is to use terms like learning (in contrast to planning), variety (in contrast to unity), actors (in contrast to systems), process (in contrast to structure), visions (in contrast to business concepts), we become (in contrast to we are), commitment (in contrast to efficiency), small is beautiful (in contrast to economies of scale), surprises (in contrast to standardization), entrepreneurs (in contrast to financial capital), culture (in contrast to education) and leadership (in contrast to management). The more there is entrepreneurship, the more important it is to live in this language world – and to enact the corresponding business world.

Statement 132: Culture can be discussed at various levels. In nations where modern, industrialized Western culture prevails (which we concentrate on in this book), the adequate, entrepreneurial corporate culture should promote aspects such as innovation, change, commitment, simplicity, transparency and action.

Statement 133: Appropriate entrepreneurial capacities (in the Western world) often mentioned in the literature are to be a visionary, to give a sense of holism, ownership and commitment to employees and allies, to provide freedom and accept ambiguity and mistakes, to let others in on the action, and to encourage change and proactive learning, breaking all kinds of bureaucratic rules.

A study of an entrepreneurial marketing firm should have many foci.

Statement 134: Possible foci when studying an entrepreneurial marketing firm are:

● the entrepreneur, the growing (focal) firm or the (virtual) network;
● processes at a general level or at a more operational level;
● the various components of the offering; and
● transactional or relationship actions.

Chapter 9

The essence of excellent entrepreneurial marketing can be summarized in a limited number of areas.

Statement 135: Seven areas on marketing excellence in entrepreneurial organizations are:

1. mastering important value-creating processes;
2. finding the best relevant resources available and structuring the value constellation;
3. using a complex model for implementing the value-creating vision and an early-warning feedback system;
4. changing the rules of the market game through entrepreneurship;
5. leading as well as managing – both at the right time;
6. exceeding the customers' expectations in the right dimensions; and
7. balancing transactional and relationship marketing as well as balancing tangible and intangible offerings into a composite of marketing actions, that is, a complex marketing strategy.

A FINAL WORD

Very little, if any, wisdom in the human world lasts for ever. This is particularly true in the business world. What was counted as proper and adequate (even excellent) behaviour one decade ago (or only a few years ago, sometimes) may be improper and inadequate, even dangerous, to apply today.

Commentators may have different opinions about how much has changed in the business environment of today compared with, say, 20 years ago, whether advanced countries have entered a new economy or not. We, as authors of this book, are of the opinion that enough has changed during the last 10–20 years in some business sectors to claim that they live in a new economic era.

In the new economic era, business firms need to be entrepreneurial and they need to adopt a special view of marketing. Combine these two areas and there is an exciting possibility of doing even better in this era, that is, by applying entrepreneurial marketing.

Index